D1248856

The Reverend Samuel Davies Abroad

The Reverend Samuel Davies Abroad

The Diary of a Journey to England and Scotland, 1753-55

edited, with an introduction, by

George William Pilcher

University of Illinois Press Urbana · Chicago · London 1967

&s FOR MY PARENTS

George W. Pilcher and Elia Huizinga Pilcher

☙ Contents

◄§ Introduction

For seven years, ever since 1746, the College of New Jersey had been struggling for existence by operating in the homes of its first two presidents, Jonathan Dickinson and Aaron Burr. By 1753, however, it had become obvious to those interested in the success of the institution that a permanent location and structure were needed if the school was to expand its role to meet the increasing need for education in the Middle Colonies. This need had become especially critical with the rapid expansion of New Light Presbyterianism in the area and the resultant demand for a larger number of properly educated ministers to serve the new congregations.

It was relatively easy for the board of trustees of the college to find a suitable location. Prince Town not only offered a financial inducement but was also strategically located midway between New York and Philadelphia—the homes of the competing Presbyterian synods. Money, however, had always been a problem. Funds for the operation of the school had never been more than barely sufficient to meet day-to-day expenses, and to draw upon an inadequate treasury for such a project was out of the question. The only solution was a trans-Atlantic appeal to prosperous friends in the British Isles. Many in England, Ireland, and Scotland were fervent supporters of the college and the religious revival known as the Great Awakening.

There were many among the American supporters of the College of New Jersey who had attained an international reputation either by the circulation of their sermons or by their other activities. Chief among these, and first choice of the trustees, was the Reverend Ebenezer Pemberton of New York, a founder and trustee of the college and one of the leaders of American Presbyterianism. But Pemberton's congregation was in the midst of an internal quarrel and he was forced to refuse. The trustees then asked two other individuals to undertake the mission—Gilbert Tennent and Samuel Davies. Tennent, son of the famous William Tennent, had been one of the early radical preachers of the Great Awakening and was currently pastor of a congregation in Philadelphia. Davies was the young leader of Presbyterianism in Virginia and widely recognized as a force for moderation in the Church. But Davies preferred to remain at home.

Samuel Davies had come to Hanover County, Virginia, in 1748 as a twenty-four-year-old preacher and had immediately become a major figure in the religious life of the colony. He led the Presbyterians in their struggle for toleration, he provided rudimentary education for the Negro slaves in his congregation, and he supported missionary work among the Indians of the frontier. All of these activities had forced him to deal with the officials of the colony and to correspond with several influential dissenters in Great Britain. He was thus known, if only by reputation, to many of the proper civil and clerical authorities in Great Britain.

Although he did not recognize the fact, his activities had made him a logical candidate for the mission.

But the very importance of his position in Virginia made it difficult for Davies to absent himself from the colony for any length of time. What would happen to the dissenters during his absence? Who would challenge the government and the established church on their behalf? Who would carry out his educational and missionary endeavors? What would become of his wife and children while he was gone or if he should perish at sea?

As he contemplated such a trip, as he weighed the disadvantages against the good which might accrue, Davies gradually came to realize that, should he go, he would not only be undertaking a mission for the College of New Jersey but he would be working as well for the Presbyterian cause in Virginia. By the time this assessment was finished there was no choice left. He would go to Great Britain. Fortunately Davies set forth his long personal debate in the opening pages of his diary and unknowingly enabled the modern reader to understand more clearly the events of the next twenty-three months.

Davies disembarked in Great Britain on Christmas day in 1753 and spent the next five months in London before journeying to Edinburgh for the meeting of the General Assembly of the Church of Scotland. He then visited the major cities of Scotland and northeastern England before returning to London in October for another month of fund-raising. He left London early in November for a harsh three-month voyage to Virginia.

Unfortunately for the complete success of the mission, Davies was hampered by two developments in eighteenth-century Presbyterianism. In America this denomination had split in 1741 over the related questions of revivalism and proper ministerial education; the competing synods of New York and Philadelphia were the outcome. Davies, a member of the Synod of New York, found that his cause was damaged by the presence in Great Britain of the Reverend William Smith, who was seeking funds for a school sponsored by the Synod of Philadelphia.

In England, the ranks of the dissenters were also in disarray. During the first half of the eighteenth century English Presbyterianism had split into Unitarian and Evangelical groups. The Unitarians were in the majority but continued to style themselves "Presbyterians" to avoid some of the legal disabilities connected with their new beliefs. The minority Evangelical party tended to be associated formally with the Church of Scotland and informally with the more orthodox Calvinist Baptists and Independents (Congregationalists). This confused state of affairs accounts for the relatively cool treatment accorded Davies by the English Presbyterians and his generally more cordial reception by those of differing denominations.

The pages of the diary indicate that the board of trustees made a wise choice when they insisted upon Davies and that Davies made a wise choice when he finally decided to go. Few American preachers could have moved so easily among the English dissenters, and none could have worked so effectively to resolve the peculiar religious problems existing in Virginia. He was not successful in all he attempted, and he recorded some disappointments. But successes did outnumber failures. He helped obtain more than £3,000 for the construction of a permanent college,[1] received sound advice for the promotion of the dissenting cause in Virginia, although little of an official nature was accomplished,[2] met old correspondents for the first time, and made new friends who could supply him with educational materials for his own work. All this made the separation from his family, the seasickness, and the fatigue of the journey seem bearable.

The mission not only helped to build a college, but it elevated Davies to a position in the first rank of the Anglo-American religious leaders of his day. Of course, he would have been well received in Great Britain if he had merely been the ambassador of American Presbyterianism. But his eloquent and powerful preaching style won him widespread popularity in both England and Scotland and elicited many demands for published editions of his sermons. His enhanced reputation caused him to be more intimately connected with the affairs of the college after his return and eventually led to his selection as president in 1759. Unfortunately he held this position for less than two years before his death at the age of thirty-seven.

Davies set forth the personal record of his trip in two small, bound volumes which have become separated and mutilated over the years. The first of these, covering the period from 2 July 1753 until 28 April 1754, is presently in the library of the Union Theological Seminary of Virginia in Richmond. Little is known of the history of this portion other than that it was once in the possession of John Holt Rice of Richmond, a popular religious writer of the early nineteenth century, who published portions of it in his *Virginia Evangelical and Literary Magazine* in 1819. Following this, the diary was placed in the library of the seminary where it was copied by Professor Philander Camp of the seminary faculty in 1845. This copy was deposited in the library

[1] It would be impossible to make an accurate computation of the amount Davies and Tennent actually raised since contributions continued to arrive until the Revolution. This estimate was made in Charles Augustus Briggs, *American Presbyterianism; Its Origin and Early History, Together with an Appendix of Letters and Documents, Many of Which Have Recently Been Discovered* (New York, 1885), p. 309.

[2] A complete record of Davies' role in the toleration struggle can be found in George William Pilcher, "Samuel Davies and Religious Toleration in Virginia," *The Historian*, XXVIII (1965), 48–71.

of the College of New Jersey. In 1850, William Henry Foote, another popular religious chronicler, published portions of volume I in his *Sketches of Virginia*. All three of these copyists had access to a more complete copy than presently exists and the ravages of time have made it necessary to reassemble this segment bit by bit.

The second volume, covering the period from 7 May 1754 until 12 February 1755, is presently in the Firestone Library of Princeton University where it has been treated more kindly and remains virtually complete. This library also possesses one leaf, comprising pages 177 and 178, of volume I.

In preparing this edition of the diary of Samuel Davies I have faithfully adhered to the writer's spelling and capitalization, although those portions taken from *The Evangelical and Literary Magazine* have been allowed to remain as originally published. Such changes as were made seemed necessary to make the diary readable and to facilitate the transcription of eighteenth-century manuscript peculiarities into twentieth-century typescript; thus for example y^e has been changed to the or thee, &c. to etc., & to and, and certain abbreviations and shorthand characters have been expanded. Davies' excisions have been omitted since he made them illegible in most cases, but alterations in his poetry have been included wherever possible (e.g., p. 141). Duplicate wordings such as "and and" have been corrected and conjectural readings enclosed in brackets. Material omitted by the editor because of obliteration and illegibility has been indicated by ellipses enclosed in brackets (e.g., [. . .]) and material omitted by Davies, possibly for inclusion at a later time, is indicated by the word *blank* enclosed in brackets (e.g., [*blank*]).

Many people have aided me in making this diary more readily available to interested readers, especially the librarians at Princeton University and the Union Theological Seminary of Virginia, who have most graciously given their permission for publication. I am also grateful for the financial support kindly extended by Colonial Williamsburg Inc., the Research Foundation of Oklahoma State University, and the Council on Research and Creative Work of the University of Colorado.

⌇⧕ Abbreviations

The following abbreviations have been used throughout the footnotes.

Burke's Peerage   Peter Townsend, ed., *Burke's Genealogical and Heraldic History of the Peerage, Baronetage, and Knightage.* London, 1963.

DAB   Allen Johnson and Dumas Malone, eds., *Dictionary of American Biography.* 20 vols.; New York, 1928–36.

DNB   Leslie Stephen and Sidney Lee, eds., *Dictionary of National Biography.* 22 vols.; London, 1937–38.

FES   Hew Scot, ed., *Fasti Ecclesiae Scoticanæ; the Succession of Ministers of the Church of Scotland from the Reformation.* 8 vols.; Edinburgh, 1915–50.

Foote, *Sketches*   William Henry Foote, *Sketches of Virginia, Historical and Biographical.* Series 1, Philadelphia, 1850. Series 2, Philadelphia, 1855.

Franklin, *Papers*   Leonard Labaree and Whitfield J. Bell, eds., *The Papers of Benjamin Franklin.* 9 vols. to date; New Haven, 1959—.

Namier and Brooke, *Parliament*   Lewis Namier and John Brooke, *The History of Parliament: The House of Commons, 1754–1798.* 3 vols.; New York, 1964.

"Memoir" [John Holt Rice], "Memoir of the Reverend Samuel Davies," *The Virginia Evangelical and Literary Magazine,* I (1819), 112–119, 186–188, 201–217, 329–335, 353–363, 474–479, 560–567.

Plomer, *Dictionary* Henry Robert Plomer, *et al.,* eds., *A Dictionary of the Printers and Booksellers Who Were at Work in England, Scotland and Ireland from 1726–1775.* London, 1932.

Records William M. Engles, ed., *Records of the Presbyterian Church in the United States of America Embracing the Minutes of the General Presbytery and General Synod 1706–1788 Together with an Index and the Minutes of the General Convention for Religious Liberty.* Philadelphia, 1904.

Sprague, *Annals* William Buell Sprague, comp., *Annals of the American Pulpit; or Commemorative Notices of Distinguished American Clergymen of Various Denominations, from the Early Settlement of the Country to the Close of the Year Eighteen Hundred and Fifty-five.* 9 vols.; New York, 1857–69.

Wilson, *Dissenting Churches* Walter Wilson, *The History and Antiquities of Dissenting Churches and Meeting Houses, in London, Westminster, and Southwark; Including the Lives of Their Ministers, from the Rise of Nonconformity to the Present Time. With an Appendix on the Origin, Progress, and Present State of Christianity in Britain.* 4 vols.; London, 1808.

A Diary begun July 2. 1753.

Gratitude to the God of my Mercies constrains me to own Myself the favourite Child of Divine Providence; and it has generally disposed of me in a Manner different from, and sometimes contrary to [my] Expectation, my Purpose and Desire. Such an unexpected and undesired Event was my Separation from my Brethren and Settlement in Virginia;[1] and yet [I] have since looked upon it as a providential Dispensation for the Recovery of my Health, to harden me against Opposition, to encrease my Popularity, to make me acquainted with the World, as well as [Books], to supply the most necessitous Congregation; and upon the Whole, to enlarge the Sphere of my Usefulness more ex-

[1] After leaving Samuel Blair's academy in 1746, Davies served vacant congregations in Pennsylvania, Delaware, and Virginia. He preached for a month in Hanover in 1747. The Presbyterians of Hanover County had unintentionally aided his education when they pressed a sum of money on an earlier evangelist, William Robinson, who had been Davies' tutor at St. George's, Delaware. Robinson used this fund to finance Davies' studies at Fagg's Manor and when an invitation from Hanover reached Davies in 1748, he felt an obligation to settle there permanently. "Memoir," p. 116.

tensively than so insignificant a Creature had Reason to expect. And now as Divine Providence, quite contrary to my Expectation seems to call me to a very important Embassy for the Church and for the Public; and as it will tend much to my future Satisfaction, to have the Record of my procedure by me for a Review in the Hour of Perplexity; I think it expedient to state the Affair in Writing and to keep [a Diary of] all the remarkable Occurencies I may [meet with in] my Voyage, which I intend to begin about [*blank*] hence, unless Providence lay Something in [my way that] may acquit me from the Obligation which I [seem to lie] under to undertake it. And it is my Prayer to the God of my Life, and the Guide of my Youth that he, who condescends to manage even my mean Affairs, would clear up the Path of Duty before me, and make it as agreeable as obvious, whether it lead me to the Ends of the Earth, or confine [me to] the Exercise of my Ministry at Home.

The College of New-Jersey, erected about 8 years ago with the most ample Privileges, is of the greatest Importance to the Interests of Religion and Learning in 3 Colonies, New-York, the Jerseys and Pennsylvania, and to the Dissenters in Maryland, Virginia and both Carolina's.

There is now about 3000£ in the College Fund; but this will hardly be sufficient for the Erection of proper Buildings; and if it should all be laid out for that End, there will be Nothing left for the Maintainance of the Professors and Tutors, to furnish a College Library, and to support pious Youth for the Ministry, who are unable to maintain themselves at Learning.

Upon Application made to Great Britain, [there] has been Encouragement given to expect some Assistance, especially if some proper Persons were sent over to represent the Affair, and to solicit and receive Contributions.

The Trustees first endeavoured to employ Mr. Pemberton[2] in that Service, who was well qualified and had no Family at the Time, and was willing to undertake the Embassy. But his Congregation most unreasonably refused, tho' Mr. Cumming,[3] his

[2] Ebenezer Pemberton, pastor of the First Presbyterian Church in New York City, was one of the founders of the New Light Synod of New York and a member of the Board of Trustees of the College of New Jersey. *Records*, p. 252.

[3] Alexander Cumming (or Cummins). *Ibid.*, p. 307.

Colleague, was still to continue with them and another Minister would have been appointed to officiate in his Stead.

After this Disappointment (near 2 Years ago) some of the Trustees importuned me to undertake the Affair; but considering my Youth and other Defects I could hardly think them in Earnest. However, I mentioned the personal, domestic and congregational Difficulties in my Way, and urged them with as much Earnestness as was necessary to resist their Importunity.

Last Fall, they renewed their Application and I my Refusal: and I never expected to hear more of it.

But last Winter the Board of Trustees unanimously voted me to undertake the Voyage. When I was informed of it by a Letter from the worthy President Burr, it struck me into a Consternation and Perplexity unknown before. All the tender Passions of the Husband, the Minister, the Father and the Son, (all which Relations center upon me) formed an Insurrection in my Breast against the Proposal; and with these I have struggled ever since. My conjugal Anxieties were increased by the languishing State of my tenderer and better Part,[4] which my Absence for so long a Time might perhaps increase. I was also afraid lest my dear Congregation, whose Hearts are so excessively set upon me, should suffer by my Absence. The Dangers of the Seas likewise appeared terrible: and above all, my just Consciousness of my Want of Qualifications for so important an Embassy, sunk my spirits; and yet my Remonstrances on this head would not be regarded by others.

After all the Deliberation and Consultation that was in my Power, I determined to take no Notice of the Many Difficulties in my Way that were superable, but to insist only on these 2 Things as the Conditions of my Compliance; the one for the Support of my Family, and the other for the Relief of my Congregation; viz. That a proper Person should be sent to supply my Pulpit during my Absence; And that he should be maintained at the Expense of the College, that my Salary might run on for the Support of my Family. These Proposals I sent to the Trustees

[4] Davies' first wife, Sarah Kirkpatrick, had died in childbirth in 1747 less than a year after their marriage. In October, 1748, shortly after his arrival in Virginia, he married Jane Holt, daughter of a former Mayor of Williamsburg. MS page in Davies' Old Testament, Virginia Historical Society, Richmond. Anon., "The Holt Family," *Tyler's Quarterly Magazine of History and Genealogy*, VII (1926), 284–285.

in a Letter per Post; but not trusting to that loitering and uncertain Medium of Correspondence, [I] dispatched a Messenger off to bring me an immediate Answer. Upon his Return, I found the Trustees had readily consented to my Proposals; and therefore expected my Compliance with their Vote.

I was also informed of this important Incident, that Mr. G. Tennent,[5] by the Death of his Wife and Mother, had no domestic Incumbrances to prevent his going; and that the Trustees had applied to him for that Purpose, and he had consented to the Undertaking in Conjunction with me. The Expectation of so accomplished a Partner in the Embassy did in a great Measure remove the Despondencies arising from my Want of Qualifications; and in the mean Time confirmed the Sense I had of this, as I looked upon it as a very intelligible Hint from divine Providence of my unfitness for the Embassy alone. On this and sundry other accounts I was very much animated to the Undertaking by the Prospect of so worthy and agreeable a Companion. But then upon hearing that Mr. Tennent was appointed, and that he had consented, I had a new Set of Scruples about the Necessity of my going; for it was at first proposed that I alone should go; which supposed that one alone might perform the Embassy; and if I, or indeed any Member of the Synod could do it alone, then undoubtedly Mr. Tennent can. But these Scruples were removed by such Considerations as these, suggested by the Trustees—That the Going of two would give an Air of Importance to the Embassy, and additional Weight to our Negotiations—That by this Means the Affair, which requires Expedition, would be transacted much more speedily—That this would render the Voyage more agreeable to both—and that my Refusal might furnish Mr. Tennent and his Congregation with Occasion to refuse too. To these I may add, what has most Weight with me, that the Dissenters in Virginia lie under such intolerable Restraints,[6] that it is necessary to seek a Redress; that now is the only proper Season for it and that none can manage this Affair

[5] Gilbert Tennent (1703–64) was the eldest son of William Tennent, the founder of the Log College. He was currently pastor of a Presbyterian Church in Philadelphia and a trustee of the college. *DAB*, XVIII, 366–369.
[6] Davies was specifically concerned with the unwillingness of the General Court of Virginia to license what he considered a sufficient number of meetinghouses. This was set forth explicitly in a letter from the Synod of New York to a group of London dissenters. *Records*, p. 258.

as well as myself, who am concerned in it, and so well acquainted with it.

Another Consideration that had a great Deal of Weight with me, was this, That my Congregation, my Parents and even my tender-hearted, weeping Spouse, did either consent to the Undertaking, when it was laid before them, or discovered a kind of submissive Reluctance. This Disposition could not but extort my approbation, even when it shocked me as an Omen of my Going; and it endeared the agreeable Companion of my Life so much more to me, that so long an Absence from her will, if possible, be still more painful.

The various Opportunities I may have of personal Improvement and that in Things which a Pedant and a Recluse is most deficient; the various Friendships that may be contracted, which may tend much to the Honour and Security of the Dissenters here, who stand so much in Need of Patronage, are also considerable Excitements.

I observe a strange Concurrence of Events happen to engage me in the Embassy, and at once to hint my Insufficiency for it alone, and clear the Way for Mr. Tennent's going too. Had Providence removed his Wife and Mother a little Earlier, before the Trustees had pitched upon me, they would undoubtedly have applied to him only; as I am convinced Nothing but Necessity could have caused them to make Application to me, at so great a Distance, and so unfit (alas! I feel myself so) for the Business. Had his Wife and Mother died sometime after, it would have been too late for him to go; and I must have gone alone. If I had only written per Post, and not sent a Messenger with my Answer immediately, they would have looked upon my Delay as a Denial, and consequently employed Mr. Tennent alone. These and sundry other Circumstances, I think I may, without a Tincture of Enthusiasm, look upon as providential Dispensations, adjusting Matters so as to order my Going, yet not alone, which I am fully convinced would be injurious to the Affair.

When I consider that there is so much Need to make some Attempts for the Security and Enlargement of the Privileges of the Dissenters in Virginia, and that if I were obliged to undertake a Voyage for that End alone, at the Expense of the Congregation, it would be very burdensome to them and me; I cannot but conclude that it is with a View to this that Providence has directed the Trustees to make application to me; for considering my known Want of Qualifications, and the little Acquaintance the most of the Trustees have with me, their Vote appears to me utterly unaccountable, without supposing such a providential Direction. This is the more remarkable, as this seems on many Accounts the most proper Crisis to do something in behalf of the Dissenters here; as Mr. Tennent's Influence in conjunction with mine, will probably be of great Service in the Affair; and as it will not carry so selfish and irritating an Aspect to be managed, by the Bye, as if it were made the sole Business.

I am also encouraged from the Reflection, that my Congregation will not probably suffer in my Absence; as Mr. Wright, I expect, is well accomplished for the Place; and my Cautious and prudent Brother Mr. Todd, will be so near at Hand to assist in Cases of Difficulty.

The Commissioners for Indian Affairs[7] will be glad of this opportunity for the Propagation of the Religion of Jesus among the poor Savages, and it is likely we shall succeed in raising Contributions for that End. And oh! how transporting the Tho't, that these Barbarians may be cultivated by divine Grace in the use of the proper Means, and polished into genuine Disciples of the Blessed Jesus! For this alone, it would be worth our While to spend and be spent!

On these Accounts I do generally conclude it will be my Duty to undertake the Embassy, unless Providence evidently acquit me of the Obligation, by laying some insuperable Obstruction in my Way.

As to the Temper of my Mind under this Conviction of Duty, I have found frequent Seasons of Resignation to the Divine Pleasure, and a Willingness to follow the Call of Duty to the Ends of the Earth. At other Times, I have been Eager for the Undertaking, and afraid of a Disappointment. At others, I have been extremely intimidated, and shrunk away from the Prospect: the Dangers of Sailing, the Difficulty of the Mission, the Pain of a

[7] The Commission for Indian Affairs had been established by the Synod of New York and the Log College in 1741 to administer a fund sent over by the Scottish Society for the Propagation of Christian Knowledge. Leonard J. Trinterud, *The Forming of an American Tradition: A Reexamination of Colonial Presbyterianism* (Philadelphia, 1949), p. 130.

6

Separation, and the Anxieties of so long an Absence, from my People, my Parents,[8] my Children,[9] and especially my dearest Creature, have sunk my Spirit into the Depth of Despondency, so that my Tho'ts Night and Day were hardly ever fixt upon any-Thing else.

My principal Difficulty at present arises from the languishing state of my dear Wife, which I am afraid has some Tendency towards a consumptive Illness. I think I could break thro' the strongest, complicated Ties of the paternal and filial Relation, and cast my helpless Family upon the Care of Providence: But the tho't that my Wife should pine away in my Absence, without the Satisfaction my Company would afford her; or that by the Anxieties of Separation, her Constitution should be injured; this Tho't seems utterly insupportable, and alarms all my tender and anxious Passions. That which at present appears Duty to me is this, That I should go upon the Mission, with this Liberty re-served, that if I hear of my Wife's being dangerously ill, I may immediately return. O! Thou God of our Life, with all the importunity so languid a Soul is capable of exerting, I implore thy gracious Protection for her, that she may be supported in my Absence, and that we may enjoy a happy Interview again.

My temporal Affairs are much embarrased [sic]; and if I should be removed into the eternal World in this Voyage, I know not how my poor, helpless Family could possibly subsist; and none but such as have felt the Anxieties of the Father, the Son, and the Husband in such a Circumstance, can conjecture what I feel at Times under this timerous Apprehension. But I would check it, as arguing a Diffidence in divine Providence, and not well grounded; for I am Mortal at Home, as well as abroad.

My present Anxieties are collected into one Point, viz. my Wife's Indisposition. She was so languishing, and attended with such threatening Symptoms of a growing Consumption, the Day before Yesterday, that I have been in the utmost Perplexity ever since, 'till to-day that I have sat down to state the Affair, and

[8] Davies' parents, David and Martha Thomas Davis, had accompanied him to Virginia in 1748. *DAB*, V, 102–103.
[9] Samuel and Jane Davies had three children at this time; William (1749), Samuel (1750), and John Rodgers (1752). Their two daughters, Martha (1755) and Margaret (1757), were born after Samuel's return from England. MS page in Davies' Old Testament, Virginia Historical Society, Richmond.

come to the Conclusion before mentioned; To go, with this Liberty reserved, that I may return immediately in Case I hear that my Wife's Disorder is become dangerous.

◄§ *July 11.* Thro' the Indulgence of divine Providence, my tenderer Half, animæ dimidium meæ, has been considerably better for some Days; and my Billy and Johnny, that have been disordered, are recovered: which encourages me to undertake the Voyage. But alas! my Conscience is this Day burdened with Guilt, and I cannot apply to the pacifying Blood of Xt. which alone can purge the Conscience from dead Works, to serve the living God.

◄§ *July 13.* Mr. Wright[10] arrived here by Order of Presbytery to know whether I intended to undertake the Voyage. I was exceedingly glad to see my former Friend and Pupil, invested with the Sacred Character, and advanced to the Honour of an Ambassador for Jesus; but it cast me into considerable Perplexity to find, that it was his Opinion there was no Necessity for my going to Europe in behalf of the College, since Mr. Tennent was going; and that he was very unwilling to stay here any Time to supply my Pulpit, and absolutely refused to stay all the Time of my Absence, as it would deprive vacant Congregations of his Labours, and him of an Opportunity to look out for a Settlement, for a considerable Time. I was at length freed from my Perplexities, and determined to go, by considering—That the Trustees are the best Judges of the Necessity of my going with Mr. Tennent, and they are very eager for it, otherwise they would not continue their Application to me; for my Voyage, all Things considered, will probably cost the College more than Mr. Tennent's—That Mr. Wright's Judgment may be something perverted by his Reluctance to stay here so long—That the Affairs of the Dissenters in Virginia would alone be a sufficient Reason for my going; and possibly, I might be obliged to go soon upon this Account alone, if I should not take this Op-

[10] John Wright received his B.A. from the College of New Jersey in 1752 and served for the next three years as a visiting preacher to vacant congregations in Virginia, Delaware, and Pennsylvania. In 1755 he settled in Cumberland, Virginia. Foote, *Sketches,* series 2, p. 53.

8

portunity—And that Mr. Todd,[11] who I am sure will be uneasy in the Absence of his Friend, and who knows the State of Affairs here, is fully convinced that it is my Duty to go. On these Accounts I resume my former Conclusion, that it will be my Duty to undertake the Embassy; tho' I am perplexed to know how my Congregation can be supplied in my Absence, unless Mr. Wright determine to stay here at least 'till next Spring.

ᴥᴥ§ *Sep. 3. 1753.* This Morning I felt the painful Rupture of the tender relative Ties which bind my Heart to Hanover. I took my leave of some Thousands yesterday in Public: and to-day I parted with some of my select Friends, and my dear, dear Spouse, my honoured Parents, and 3 helpless Children, and left them in a Flood of Tears. To thee, O Lord, I then solemnly committed them and now I renew the Dedication. I know not, if ever I shall see them again; but my Life and theirs is in the Hand of divine Providence; and therefore shall be preserved as long as is fit. My tender Passions were melted into a Flood of Tears at Parting; but now thro' the Goodness of God, they are subsided into a Calm, tho' at Times I am twinged with a sudden Pang of Anxiety. Rode in Company with my kind Friends Mr. Morris, Mr. Brame[12] and Mr. Todd, who is to go along with me to the Synod.

I have been uneasy for some Time to find that sundry in my Congregation were not pleased with Mr. Wright's Preaching, etc. But now, to my unspeakable Satisfaction, I find they are generally engaged to him in a tolerable Degree; and I hope his Ministrations will be of more Service than mine, during the Time of his Continuance here, tho' he has [met] with such Occasional Tho'ts as may occur in Conversation, which may deserve to be recollected—Mr. Finley[13] told me he had lately almost embibed

[11] John Todd had come to Virginia at Davies' request shortly after his graduation from the College of New Jersey in 1749. In 1752 he was officially licensed as Davies' assistant. *Ibid.*, p. 45.

[12] Several members of the Brame and Morris families were active among the Hanover Presbyterians. These were probably Samuel Morris, one of the four Hanover dissenters responsible for bringing Davies to Virginia, and Melchisedeck Brame. The first meetinghouse used by Davies was known as "the Morris Reading House." *Ibid.*, series 1, pp. 121–122, 161.

[13] Samuel Finley (1715–66) was the pastor of the Presbyterian Church in Nottingham, Pennsylvania, where he also conducted a school for boys. In 1751 he became a member of the board of trustees of the college and, in 1761, succeeded Davies as president. *DAB*, VI, 391–392.

a Notion which he formerly rejected, viz. That Compassion proceeds from a selfish Principle—Because, both Persons in the Extremity of Misery—and that know Nothing of Misery—are incapable of it.

Saturday. As the Committee is to meet at Mr. Finley's, next Wednesday, I intend to stay here 'till then. To-day the Hurries of my Journey being over, my Tho'ts can find Leisure to make frequent Excursions to Hanover, and tenderly hover round my dear Wife and Family. Ah! what Pangs of Anxiety I frequently feel! May the Lord Bless all that are dear to me, and favour me with a happy Return to them!

Sunday. Preached at Mr. Finley's on Deut. 10,-13. a Sermon which I preached in Hanover with great Satisfaction and Prospect of Success; but alas! I have lost that Spirit with which it was first delivered: and indeed I can but very rarely retain the Spirit of Preaching in the Hurries of a Journey.

The Materials of the Sermon were very solemn, and Nothing appeared to me a more unnatural Incongruity, than to speak the most solemn thing with a trifling Spirit. Indeed the Incongruity appeared to me so great, that I was obliged to omit sundry Things, tho' written before me in my Notes, for Want of a Heart to express them with suitable Tenderness and Fervour. There appeared some small Solemnity among the Hearers; but oh! how far short of what I have seen in this Place in the Days of the Right Hand of the most High!

Conversed with my ingenious and dear Friend, Mr. Finley, in the Evening; and communicated to him my Sentiments upon the great Influence which the body has to deprave the Soul which I apprehend is much greater than is generally supposed; which appears—from the frequent Use of the Metaphor *Flesh* in the Scriptures to denote moral Depravity; which supposes that the Flesh literally taken has a special Causality in it; otherwise there would be no Ground for the Metaphor, but it would be as proper to denominate Sin by the Term Spirit or Soul—from the different Inclinations of the Soul according to the different States of the Body; and as the Variety of bodily Habits may be the Occasions of a Variety of sinful Inclinations, so the Habit of the

Body may be constantly such, amid all its Changes, that it may perpetually influence the Mind to Sin in general; etc.

§ *Monday. Sep. 10. 1753.* Continued at Mr. Finley's; "Stung with the Tho'ts of Home; the Tho'ts of Home Rush on my Heart" and I can find no Relief from them but either in Tho'tless Levity, or in Devotion. Read some Part of the Appeal in Favour of the Candid Disquisitions;[14] and never was more pleased with the Candour, Impartiality and Moderation of an Author. How becoming, how graceful, how advantagious is such a Spirit to the Cause of Truth and its Advocates! May I deeply embibe it! Alas! I have been perplexed this Day with the vigorous Insurrections of Sin in my Heart; but my Resistance and Humiliation has not been proportioned. Oh wretched Man that I am, etc!

§ *Tuesday.* Mr. Roan[15] and Mr. Smith[16] met in Committee, and Mr. Finley and I in Conjunction with them revised and corrected a Draft, drawn up by Mr. Blair, of a Warning or Testimony of the Presbytery of N. Castle against several Errors and evil Practices of Mr. John Cuthbertson,[17] a Scotch Bigot; ordained by one Mr. McMullan who was deposed by the General Assembly of Scotland, and subscribed the Deposition by his own Hand; and one Mr. Nairn,[18] who was one of the Seceders, and afterwards excommunicated by them. The Errors on which the Presbytery animadvert, are these—That God has made over Xt.

[14] John Jones, *An Appeal to Common Reason and Candor, in Behalf of a Review: Submitted to the Serious Consideration of All Unprejudiced Members of the Church of England. With a Word Concerning Some Late Remarks upon the Free and Candid Disquisitions* (London, 1750).

[15] John Roan (c. 1716–75) had preached briefly in Virginia in 1744 but was expelled for attacking the clergy of the Church of England. At this time he was pastor to the Presbyterian congregations in Paxton, Derry, and Mountjoy, Pennsylvania. Sprague, *Annals,* III, 129–130.

[16] Robert Smith was the Presbyterian minister in Leacock and Pequea, Pennsylvania. *Ibid.,* 172–175.

[17] At this time, John Cuthbertson served three Pennsylvania congregations: the Associated Reformed Church in Bart, the Associated Presbyterian Church in Cumberland, and the Muddy Run Associated Reformed Church in Martie. Frederick Lewis Weis, *The Colonial Churches and the Colonial Clergy of the Middle and Southern Colonies; 1607–1776* (Lancaster, Mass., 1939), pp. 23, 36, 56, 60.

[18] Neither McMullan nor Nairn is listed in *FES.*

and all his Benefits to all that hear the Gospel, by a Deed of Gift (as he affects to speak) so that every Sinner that hears the Gospel-Offer, ought to put in a Claim of Right to him as his Saviour in particular—That Saving Faith consists in a persuasion that Xt. is *mine* and that he died for *me* in *particular*—That Redemption is universal as to purchase—that civil Government both heathen and Xn. is derived from Xt. as Mediator.

୫ *Wednesday*. Continued revising the Testimony against Mr. Cuthbertson. Preached a Sermon on Rev. 1. 7. and acted the Orator: but alas! I had not the Spirit of Preaching.

Enjoyed pleasing Conversation with my Dear Brethren; but ah! I am still stung with the Tho'ts of Home. My dear Wife frequently enters my Mind, and raises a passionate Commotion there.

୫ *Thursday*. In the Forenoon assisted in the Review of the Testimony against Mr. C.

Rode P.M. to Mrs. Blair's[19] in Company with Mr. Smith; and enjoyed much Satisfaction in the free mutual Communication of our Xn. and ministerial Exercises. How happy am I in having so many valuable Friends in various Parts! The Sight of Mrs. Blair and my old Walks about her House in the happy Days of my Education, raised a Variety of tender and solemn Tho'ts in my Mind. When I passed by the Meeting-House, where I so often heard the great Mr. Blair, I could not help crying, "Oh! how dreadful is this Place! This is no other than the House of God, and this is the Gate of Heaven."

୫ *Fryday*. Rode from Mrs. Blair's to Chester. And as I was generally alone, my Spirits were very low, and my Mind anxious about my dear Family, my Congregation and my approaching Voyage. "Lord, I am oppressed; undertake for me."

୫ *Saturday*. Rode into Philadelphia, was kindly received by Mr. Tennent and my Friends there. Visited Capt. Grant and was surprized with a Clause in a Letter from Mr.

---

[19] Mrs. Blair was the widow of Samuel Blair (1712–51), who had kept a school at Fagg's Manor near New Londonderry, Pennsylvania. Both Davies and Smith had been educated there. *DAB*, II, 340–341.

De Berdt[20] of London to him, "That the Principles inculcated in the College of New Jersey are generally looked upon as antiquated and unfashionable by the Dissenters in England." A dismal Omen to our Embassy, and I fear to the Interests of Religion!

⁓§ *Sunday*. Heard Mr. Tennent preach an excellent sermon on—"Deliver us from Evil," or as he justly rendered it "from the evil one" ($\pi o\nu\eta\rho o\hat{v}$); In which he exposed the Wiles and Devices of Satan in a very judicious Manner.

I preached two Sermons, one in the Afternoon, and one by Candle-Light on Rev. 1. 7. In the first, I was cold-hearted, and abashed with the Fear of Man; but in the last, I had some Freedom and Boldness. I esteem the least Degree of Liberty and Solemnity in preaching the Gospel a very great Blessing in the Hurries of a Journey. In Conversation was much pleased with the pious Simplicity of my spiritual Father, Mr. Tennent.

⁓§ *Monday Sep. 17*. Went with Mr. Tennent to wait on the Governour[21] and Secretary;[22] but they were not at Home. Waited on 3 Lutheran Ministers, and Mr. Slauter,[23] a Calvinist; and was not a little pleased with their Candour and Simplicity. How pleasing is it, to see the Religion of Jesus appear undisguised in Foreigners! I am so charmed with it, that I forget all national and religious Differences; and my very Heart is intimately united to them.

[20] Dennys DeBerdt, a leader of the London dissenters, became a close associate of Davies during the latter's visit to Great Britain. In 1758 he published an edition of Davies' famous sermon *The Curse of Cowardice*. His interest in colonial education was continued when he collected contributions for Dartmouth in 1766, the year after he was appointed the resident agent for the colony of Massachusetts. *DAB*, V, 180–181.

[21] James Hamilton (c. 1710–83), the son of Andrew Hamilton, the famous defender of John Peter Zenger, had been a leading figure in Pennsylvania politics since 1734. He served as lieutenant governor of Pennsylvania from 1748 to 1754 and from 1759 to 1763. *DAB*, VIII, 186–187.

[22] Richard Peters (c. 1704–76), a Church of England clergyman favorable to Whitefield and the Great Awakening, served as provincial secretary and member of the Pennsylvania Council between 1749 and 1762. *DAB*, XIV, 508–509.

[23] Probably Michael Schlatter (1716–90), who had been sent to Pennsylvania in 1746 as a missionary of the Dutch Reformed Church and had an active interest in the education of the Dutch and German population of the province. In 1754 he was made the provincial superintendent of schools. *DAB*, XVI, 435–436.

13

≈§ Tuesday. Rode solitary and sad from Philadelphia to Trentown. Spent the Evening with Mr. Cowel [24] an agreeable Gent. of the Synod of Philadelphia; but my Spirits were so exhausted, that I was incapable of lively Conversation, and was ashamed of my Blundering Method of talking.

≈§ Wednesday. Rode on and came to Mr. Spencer's[25] at Elizabeth Town, where I was most kindly received, and my Spirits cheered by his facetious Conversation.

≈§ Thirsday. Came to N. Ark, and was received with much Affection by the worthy President.[26] Was honoured with a Visit and free Conversation with his Excellency the Governour.[27] Was uneasy to find that the Trustees seem to expect I should furnish myself with Cloaths in this Embassy. With what Pleasure would I do it were it in my Power; but alas! it is not; and therefore, notwithstanding all the Pliableness of my Nature, I must insist upon their providing for me in *this* Respect, as one Condition of my Undertaking the Voyage.

≈§ Fryd. Waited on his Excellency, in Company with the President and his Lady. Was kindly received; and the Governour insisted that I should preach for Mr. Spencer next Sunday come se'ennight, that he might have an Opportunity of hearing me. O that I may be enabled to shake off the Fear of Man, and preach with the Simplicity and Boldness of an Am-

[24] David Cowell was the Old Light Presbyterian minister in Trenton, New Jersey, and a member of the board of trustees of the college. *Records,* p. 307.

[25] Elihu Spencer (1721–84) was, at this time, the pastor in Elizabethtown, New Jersey, and a trustee of the college. He had formerly served as an Indian missionary under the supervision of David Brainerd and Jonathan Edwards. *DAB,* XVII, 447–448.

[26] The Reverend Aaron Burr (1715–57) was pastor of the First Presbyterian Church in Newark, New Jersey, where the college met in his home. In 1752 he had married Esther Edwards, the daughter of Jonathan Edwards. *DAB,* III, 313–314.

[27] Jonathan Belcher (1682–1757) was a Harvard-educated Boston merchant who served as governor of Massachusetts from 1730 to 1741 when he became governor of New Jersey. He took a lively interest in the college, which he served as a trustee from 1748 until his death and to which he bequeathed his library. He declined the honor of having the main college building named Belcher Hall. *DAB,* II, 143–144.

bassador of Xt! Conversed with Mr. Ross,[28] who informed me of the Spread of Arminianism among the Ministers in N. England, etc.

◄§ *Saturday.* Was employed in drawing up a Petition from the Synod of New York to the General Assembly of the Church of Scotland in behalf of the College.[29] Conversed with Mr. Hoit,[30] a pious Youth at College. Was much depressed in Spirit at the Prospect of the Voyage, and the tender Tho'ts of Home. May the God of my Life support me!

◄§ *Sunday.* Heard the President preach a valedictory Sermon to the Candidates for a Degree, who are to leave the College this Week. His Subject was, "And now, my Son, the Lord be with thee; and prosper thou." And I was amazed to see how readily good Sense and accurate Language flowed from him extempore. The Sermon was very affecting to me, and might have been so to the Students.

Preached twice in the Afternoon, and in the last Sermon my Heart was very solemn and tender; and there appeared some Signs of Concern among the Hearers. In the Evening had a little Dispute with the President about the Truth of one Proposition, which I principally laboured to prove, "That Persons in this Age may be said virtually to have crucified Xt. because they have the same Temper with the Jews, and because their Conduct towards Xt. is as like to that of the Jews as their Circumstances will allow."

◄§ *Mond. Sep. 24. 1753.* My drooping Spirits were exhilerated by free Conversation with the President. Spent the most of the Day in finishing the Petition from the Synod of

[28] This was probably the Reverend Robert Ross of Stratfield, Connecticut, who is mentioned as being a visitor to the 1753 meeting of the Synod of New York. C. C. Goin, *Revivalism and Separatism in New England, 1740–1800; Strict Congregationalism and Separate Baptists in the Great Awakening* (New Haven, 1962), p. 63.

[29] *Records,* pp. 256–258.

[30] Benjamin Hait graduated from the college in 1755 and held successive pastorates in Amwell, New Jersey, Montgomery, New York, and Connecticut Farms, New Jersey. Weis, *The Colonial Churches and the Colonial Clergy,* pp. 21, 34, 63.

N. York to the General Assembly. Attended in the Evening on a Meeting for Psalmody, and was much charmed with the Power of Harmony.[31] Amid the Variety of new Objects that draw my Attention, my Tho'ts often take a sudden Flight to Hanover, and hover over my Chara, and my other Friends there. O may indulgent Heaven preserve and bless them!

Tuesd. Was confined with a sore Leg, which was a little Hurt by a fall out of my own Door a Day or two before I left home; and tho' then but a slight Wound, and I took little Notice of it for 2 or 3 Weeks, it has been so enflamed and irritated by travelling, preaching, etc. that I think it is now dangerous; and sometimes look upon it as a providential Obstruction in my Way of undertaking the Voyage.

Wednesday. This Day I delivered a Thesis, (Personales Distinctiones in Trinitate sunt æternæ) and vindicated it in a public Dispute against 3 Opponents; and afterward was honoured with the Degree of Master of Arts. Dined with the Governour and Trustees. Heard Mr. Todd preach an honest Sermon in the Evening.

Thirsd. Received £80 proc. from the Treasurer to bear the Expenses of the Voyage. Went to N. York in Company with Mr. Hoit, a promising Youth, and had agreeable Conversation with him upon Original Sin, the Influence of the Flesh upon the Spirit to incline it to sin, etc. Arrived at New York in the Evening; and lodged at my good Friend Mr. Hazard's. Was sorry to find the Presbyterian Congregation there in such Confusion.

Fryd. Was confined to the House by my sore Leg, and took a Physic, etc. I had some dangerous and gloomy Apprehensions of the Consequence. Mr. Pemberton, Mr. Cumming, and Mr. Van Horn[32] paid me a Visit.

In the Evening took the Advice of the Honourable Wm.

[31] Davies was probably the first modern American hymnwriter in the tradition of Isaac Watts. See Louis F. Benson, "President Davies as a Hymn Writer," *Journal of Presbyterian History,* II (1903), 277–286, and "The Hymns of President Davies," *ibid.,* 343–373.

[32] David Van Horn was an elder in Pemberton's church. *Records,* p. 252.

Smith[33] Esq. upon the Affair of the Dissenters in Virginia; His Opinion was that the Reversing of the Order of the County Court for a Meeting-House, by the General Court, would be a sufficient Ground of Complaint in England.

Saturd. Waited on Mr. Cumming: sailed to Eliza. Town with Mr. Woodruff.[34] Was pleased with the Company of my Brethren Mr. Spencer and Mr. James Brown.[35]

Sund. Preached in Elizabeth Town according to his Excellency's order, on Jer. 31.18 etc. but had very little Freedom and Solemnity.

Mond. Octob. 1. Took my Leave of his Excellency. Rode with Mr. S. and Mr. B. to Mr. Richard's,[36] a pious Minister under the deepest Melancholy and Temptation, harassed with perpetual Suggestions to cut his own Throat. I gave him my best Advice, and gave an Account of my own Melancholy some Years ago.

Lodged at Mr. Brainerd's,[37] the good Missionary among the Indians, and was pleased with his Accounts of the Progress of Religion among them tho' now they are scattered by Reason of their Land being fraudulently taken from them.

Tuesday. Took a View of the Indian Town; and was pleased at the Affection of the poor Savages to their Minister and

[33] William Smith (1697–1769) was a prominent member of the New York bar who had served with Andrew Hamilton in the Zenger case. As a leading Presbyterian layman—provincial attorney general (1751–52), councilman (1753–67)—he had served as a member of the board of trustees of the college since 1748. It is generally believed that he wrote the college charter. *DAB*, XVII, 352–353.

[34] This was probably Benjamin Woodruff, who had just graduated from the College of New Jersey. Frederick Lewis Weis, *The Colonial Clergy of the Middle Colonies: New York, New Jersey, and Pennsylvania; 1628–1776* (Worcester, Mass., 1957), p. 348.

[35] James Brown was minister to the Presbyterian congregation in Bridgehampton, Long Island. James Truslow Adams, *History of the Town of Southampton (East of Canoe Place)* (Port Washington, N.Y., 1962), p. 138n.

[36] Probably Aaron Richards, Presbyterian minister in Rahway, New Jersey. Weis, *The Colonial Churches and the Colonial Clergy*, p. 79.

[37] At this time David Brainerd was minister to congregations of Presbyterian Indians in Crossweeksung and Cranbury, New Jersey, and engaged to Jerusha Edwards. His expulsion from Yale in 1743 had actually triggered the founding of the College of New Jersey. *DAB*, II, 591–592.

his Condescention [*sic*] to them. Rode on towards Philadelphia, and spent the Time in pleasing Conversation principally on the Affairs of the Indians, with Messrs. Spencer, Brainerd and Brown.

ᵉ₷ *Wednesday*. Came into Philadelphia. Mr. Treat[38] opened the Synod with a Sermon on these Words, "Who was faithful to him that called him, even as Moses also was faithful in all his House." Saw my dear Friend Mr. Rodgers,[39] and many of my Brethren.

ᵉ₷ *Thirsday*. Attended on the Synod.

ᵉ₷ *Fryday*. Did the same. Heard Mr. Bostwick[40] in the Evening preach an excellent Sermon on Act 2.11. He has, I think, the best style Extempore, of any Man I ever heard.

ᵉ₷ *Saturday*. Was informed that Mr. G. T. had taken some Offence at my Conduct as too forward and assuming; but it was soon removed by a free Conversation. Attended on the Synod, and used my utmost endeavours to obtain some Supplies for my dear People, besides Mr. Wright, and succeeded so far that Messrs. Brainerd, Rodgers, Henry,[41] Bay,[42] Blair[43] and J. Finley were appointed to go there 4 or 6 Weeks each. I hope this will turn to the Benefit of my dear Congregation. O that God may

[38] Richard Treat (1708–78), a Yale graduate, was minister to the Presbyterian congregation in Abington, Pennsylvania. Sprague, *Annals*, III, 100n.

[39] John Rodgers (1727–1811) had been educated at Fagg's Manor and was one of Davies' closest friends and associates. He had accompanied Davies to Virginia but had been refused a license by the General Court. At this time he was settled in St. George's, Delaware, moving from here to New York City in 1765. He later became an outspoken opponent of an American episcopate and, in 1784, vice chancellor of the University of the State of New York. *DAB*, XVI, 74–75.

[40] David Bostwick was pastor of the Presbyterian Church in Jamaica, Long Island. Sprague, *Annals*, III, 131–134.

[41] Hugh Henry was minister to four Presbyterian congregations in Rehoboth, Salisbury, and Princess Anne, Maryland, and Laurel, Delaware. Frederick Lewis Weis, *The Colonial Clergy of Maryland, Delaware and Georgia* (Lancaster, Mass., 1950), p. 77.

[42] Andrew Bay held pulpits in Hopewell and Highland, Pennsylvania. *Ibid.*, p. 33.

[43] John Blair (1720–71) was the brother of Samuel Blair and at this time served as a supply minister for the Presbytery of New Castle. In 1757 he took over the Fagg's Manor Church. Sprague, *Annals*, III, 117–119.

go with his Messengers thither! The Commissioners from New-York made application to the Synod for the Redress of their Grievances; and a Committee was appointed to go there for that Purpose, of which Mr. Rodgers and I (much against my Will) are to be Members.[44] Heard Mr. Bostwick in the Evening on, "Godliness is profitable for all Things, etc." and was not a little charmed with both his Matter and Language.

◄§ *Sund.* Had the Happiness of sitting as a Hearer for one Sab. a Privilege I have often desired and needed, but could seldom enjoy.

Mr. Horton[45] preached in the Morning an honest, judicious Sermon on "Xt. the Wisdom of God, and the Power of God." Mr. Bay in the Afternoon on "Behold the Lamb of God that taketh away the Sins of the World." He was much daunted and confused. Mr. Bostwick in the Evening on "When Xt. who is your Life shall appear, then shall ye also appear with him in Glory." My Pleasure under his Sermon was renewed and even encreased.

◄§ *Mond. Octob. 8.* Preached a Sermon in the Morning from Isai. 66.1,2. and thro' the great Mercy of God, my Heart was passionately affected with the Subject; and what tended not a little to encrease my Affection was my observing the venerable Mr. G. Tennent weeping beside me in the Pulpit. Spiritual Poverty and Humility appeared very amiable and charming to me. Humility is not that gloomy sullen mortifying Thing which it is generally accounted; but a most sweet and pleasing Grace. O it is no small ingredient of the Happiness of a Penitent, and a most congruous Ornament to a mean, degenerate Creature.

Visited the Academy in Company with Sundry of my Brethren; and entertained with a View of what was remarkable in it. Heard some of the little Boys declaim; and tho' I was pleased with their distinct and accurate Pronunciation, I tho't in delivering some of the Orations, especially those of Brutus and

[44] The New York Presbyterian Church was embroiled in a dispute concerning the selection of elders. The minutes of the Synod show that Davies, Samuel Finley, and Charles Beatty were chosen as a committee to solve the matter. *Records*, p. 252.

[45] Azariah Horton was the minister to the Presbyterian congregation in South Hanover (or Bottle Hill), New Jersey. Sprague, *Annals*, III, 183n.

M. Antony, they were extremly languid, and discovered Nothing of the Fire and Pathos of a Roman Soul. Indeed this is one great Defect of modern Oratory; a Defect few seem sensible of, or labour to correct. Rode in the Evening as far as Chester on my Way to the Presbytery. Sat up late, and wrote Letters to my Hanover Friends, particularly to my dear Spouse, full of Anxieties. How strongly does She attract my Heart!

ᴥᦪ *Tuesd.* Rode to the Presbytery at Fogg's [*sic*] Mannor, solitary and pensive. Was refreshed in the Company of my dear Brethren. Lodged at Mrs. Blair's, where every Thing suggested to me the Image of the incomparable Mr. Blair, once my Minister and Tutor, but now in superior Regions.

ᴥᦪ *Wednesd.* Mr. Hog,[46] who has been discouraged by the Presbytery hitherto, lest his Genius should not be fit for the Ministry, was licensed, having given more Satisfaction as to his Abilities than was formerly expected. Voted that Mr. John Brown[47] should be ordained to-morrow; and that I should preside. Alas! I am confounded at the Prospect of such a Solemnity, as I have no Time for proper Preparations, and my Tho'ts are scattered amid so much Hurry.

ᴥᦪ *Thirsd.* Spent 2 or 3 Hours in Study, and went and preached a Sermon on Act. 20:28 with a good Deal of Inaccuracy and Confusion; tho' with some tender Sense of the Subject. Mr. Brown was ordained; and I have hardly ever tho't myself in so solemn a Posture, as when invoking the God of Heaven with my Hand upon the Head of the Candidate. May the Lord be his Support under the Burden of that Office which he has assumed, I doubt not, with very honest and generous Intentions! Parted with my favourite Friend Mr. Todd, not without Tears.

ᴥᦪ *Fryd.* Continued attending on the Presbytery. Messrs. Harris[48] and McAdan were examined, with a View to Trial, and

[46] This was probably John Hoge (or Hogg) who, though licensed at this time, did not find a permanent settlement until 1755. *Ibid.*, 79n.

[47] At this time John Brown was a supply preacher for frontier Presbyterian congregations and had just been offered the pulpit in Timber Ridge, Virginia. Foote, *Sketches*, series 2, p. 94.

[48] John Harris had just graduated from the College of New Jersey. In 1756 he became minister to the Presbyterian congregation in Indian River, Delaware. Weis, *The Colonial Clergy of Maryland, Delaware and Georgia*, p. 76.

acquitted themselves to universal Satisfaction. The Complaints of the many vacant Congregations are so affecting, that the growing Number of promising Candidates is a most pleasing Sight. Rode in the Evening in Company with Mr. Charles Tennent[49] and Mr. Rodgers to White-clay-creek.

༞§ *Saturd.* Was much disordered with a Lax and a wind-Colic, and could do little worth mentioning. In the Evening had a Fit of the Feaver and Ague. When I am not relieved by a humble Dependance on divine Providence, I am shocked at the Tho't of being taken ill abroad.

༞§ *Sund.* Was very much pained with the Colic, and in that Condition preached 2 Sermons in Mr. Tennent's Meeting-House, to a People I formerly lived among, on Deut. 29.10.13. I had a little Freedom considering with how much Pain I spoke, and that last Night I had very little Sleep, but was in a kind of Delirium. Rode in the Evening to my dear Brother's Mr. Rodger's, but found that even the Pleasures of Friendship cannot always support a sinking Spirit.

༞§ *Mond. October 15.* Stayed at Mr. Rodgers; much indisposed.

༞§ *Tuesd.* Was somewhat easier.

༞§ *Wednesd.* Preached a Sermon on Isai. 66. 1,2. but alas! I had but little Freedom or tender Affection. My soul was rejoiced to see my old Friends, and observe the Continuance of their Respect for me.

༞§ *Thirsd.* Stayed in St. George's. Read in Mathe Mahew's Sermon on the Death of K. Ch. I. etc. Thro' divine Goodness, I am much recovered, tho' still out of Order with a Cold. O that my Soul might prosper!

༞§ *Fryd.* Mr. Rodgers and I intended to begin our Journey to New-York to attend on the Committee; but Mrs. Rodgers

[49] Charles Tennent was a younger brother of Gilbert Tennent and pastor of the Presbyterian Church in Whiteclay Creek, Delaware. *DAB*, XVIII, 366.

was unexpectedly taken ill, and this morning delivered of a Daughter, about a Month before the expected Time. I found a Disposition to bless the Lord on her Account. How great is his Goodness! My own Indisposition and Mr. Rodgers's not going along with me, will prevent my going to New-York. Rode in the Evening to New-Castle, and spent some Time with Mr. Bedford; but alas! felt little Disposition to religious Conversation. I am confounded when I think how I trifle away my Time.

Saturday. Rode to Philadelphia. In Solitude my Tho'ts were trifling, or distressed me with anxieties about my dear Friends in Hanover and in Company with a Parcel of Gent. I perceived myself too much a Coward in the good Cause of God. Lodged at Mr. Hazard's.[50]

Sund. Preached in Philadelphia first on Jer. 31. 18, 19, 20. Then on v. 33. ("I will be their God, and they shall be my People.") and in the 2 last Sermons I had a little Freedom and Solemnity. Was refreshed with an Information from my dear and valuable Friend Capt. Grant, of a Person that was awakened by my Sermon on Isai. 66. 1,2. Oh! it is an unspeakable Mercy, that such a Creature is not wholly thrown by as useless. Had much Satisfaction in a free and affectionate Conference with Capt. Grant upon experimental Religion, etc. Lodged at his House.

Mond. October 22. Visited Mrs. Johnston in Sickness and had some free Conversation with her about her State. I was secretly afraid of her Piety, and yet I could find no sufficient Evidence to disprove it. Mrs. Rodgers unbosomed herself to me, and gave me an account of some affecting, over-whelming Views of the Wisdom of God in the Works of Redemption, which she had lately had, that were really astonishing. How good is God to his poor Children even in this melancholy World! In some happy Hours they rejoice with Joy unspeakable and full of Glory. Dined at Mr. Macky's, with Capt. Bourn. Spent an Hour

[50] Samuel Hazard was a prominent Philadelphia merchant and a trustee of the college. Thomas Jefferson Wertenbaker, *Princeton, 1746–1896* (Princeton, 1946), p. 398.

at Mr. Bradford's.[51] Saw my Translation of Cleanthes's Hymn to the Creator, published in the Virginia-Gazette.[52]

❧ *Thirsday November 8.* I have been so extremely hurried for about 15 Days that I have not had Leisure nor Composure to keep a regular Diary. I must therefore content myself with a general Review.

Mr. Tennent treats me with the utmost Condescension, and the unbounded Freedoms of Friendship; and my Anxieties at the Prospect of the Voyage are much mitigated by the Pleasure of his Conversation.

I have been treated with uncommon Kindness during my Stay in Philadelphia by Many and have contracted sundry new Friendships, from which I hope to receive Happiness hereafter, and especially to enjoy the Benefit of many Prayers.

I have preached about 20 Sermons in Philadelphia; and tho' my being so long delayed was extremely disagreeable as well as unexpected to me; yet if Providence intended my Stay for the Good of but one Soul, I desire to be content.

In sundry Sermons, the Lord departed from me, and I know not when I have preached so often with so much Languor. But in my 6 last Sermons, I had more Freedom, and my Popularity encreased, so that the Assemblies were very large. Last Sab. Evening in particular, I was solemnized in preaching on that dreadful Text Heb. 6. 7. and tho' I was afraid it would shock many of the Auditory, that they would not hear me again; to my pleasing Surprize, I found them much more eager to attend afterwards than before. At the final Judgment it will be known what was the Effect. Mr. Kinersly[53] and Mr. Jones,[54] Gent. of very good Sense, and of the Anabaptist Persuasion, attended upon my Ministry constantly, and shewed me much Respect.

[51] William Bradford was a prominent Philadephia printer, bookseller, and publisher of *The Weekly Advertiser, or Pennsylvania Journal. DAB*, II, 564–566.
[52] Apparently this issue of the *Virginia Gazette* is no longer extant.
[53] Ebenezer Kinnersley (1711–78) was an ordained Baptist minister, though he never held a pulpit, and chief master of the College of Philadelphia. He was associated with Benjamin Franklin in many experiments. *DAB*, X, 416–417.
[54] Probably Jenkin Jones, a prominent Baptist minister of Philadelphia. Franklin, *Papers*, II, 259–260.

There is a Number of Antinomians in Town, who have been long finding Fault with Mr. Tennent. They generally attended, and approved, except one Sermon: and I cannot but think it somewhat remarkable, that tho' my Sermons were studied 300 Miles distant and long ago, yet they are generally as directly adapted to oppose the small Antinomian Notions, as if they were designed for that End.

To-day I left the City conducted by 7 or 8 of my Friends, Messrs. Hazard, Spafford, Hall, Beaty, Chambers, Bedford, Chief, Man; and came to Chester.

Alas! I find the Insurrection of Sin violent in my Heart; and my Anxieties about Home are sometimes extremely severe, especially when I forebode a long Absence.

I find my Heart at once so exceeding sinful, and insensible of its own Depravity, that I am really shocked at myself; and the Prospect of Death, or the Dangers of the Sea, in my present Temper, strikes me with a shuddering Horror. It is Sin alas! that intimidates me; and this removed, I could face Death in its most tremendous Forms with Calmness and Intrepidity. To be miserable and to be a Sinner is the Same Thing, and I feel that I can never be happy, 'till I am more holy.

Fryd. Nov. 9. Was unexpectedly detained in Chester by bad Weather. Spent the Day in pensive Sadness, "Stung with the Tho'ts of Home;" etc. and distressed with my own Corruptions. "Behold I am vile." Enjoyed Mr. Rothwell's Company.

> Sin haunts my Steps, where e'er I fly,
> In every Place is ever nigh
> As Streams from Mountain-Springs attend
> The Trav'llers still as they desend;
> So Sin, the Source of all my Woe,
> Still bubbles up where e'er I go.
> Sin spreads a dark, tremendous Cloud
> Of Horrors o'er my Solitude;
> Presents a thousand Forms of Death
> To shock my Soul from Duty's Path:
> Wraps present Time in dreadful Gloom,
> And damps my Hope of Time to come
> Intimidates my Soul ashore,
> And makes old Ocean louder roar;

Gives darker Horrors to the Storm,
And Danger a more shocking Form.
Companion dire by Land or Sea!
No Bliss, no Calm, 'till freed from thee,
And Change of Place is change of Misery.

✥ *Saturday. Nov. 10.* Rode from Chester to my Dear Friend Mr. Rodgers, tho'tless alas! of the exceeding Depravity of my Heart. Fell into Company with Mr. Ross,[55] an episcopal Minister, who asked me what Objections I had against being episcopally ordained, and when I mentioned some of my Objections in the most calm Manner, fell into an unreasonable Passion.

✥ *Sund. Nov. 11.* Heard Mr. Rodgers preach a very good Sermon on this Text, "Herein is Love, not that we loved God, etc." and my Mind was deeply impressed with such Tho'ts as these, "We have heard a great deal of the extreme Sufferings of one Jesus; and what Effect has the pathetic Representation upon the Hearers? Why, the Generality hear it with dispassionate Negligence and Stupidity, tho' a few here and there drop a Tear at the Relation. Thus it is when the Agonies of the Redeemer are represented; but were we informed that a dear Friend or Relative was seized by a Company of Ruffians, and put to the most extreme Tortures; what Horror would strike us? What tender Passions rise in every Breast? Why then are we no more affected with the Sufferings of this Jesus? Who is he? is he some worthless Being that we are no way concerned with? Or is [he] a Criminal that deserved all the Agonies he suffered?" If this were the Case, our Stupidity would not be so strange. But how strange must it appear, when we are told that this Jesus is the Man that is God's Fellow! the Saviour of Sinners! crucified for our Sins!

Received the Lord's Supper with some Degree of dispassionate Solemnity and Calmness of Mind; and counted it my Happiness to have an Opportunity of joining in so Solemn an Ordinance with my Dear Mr. Rodgers.

Preached in the Evening on Joh. 6. 37. in an unstudied con-

[55] This was no doubt George Ross (c. 1679–c. 1753) a missionary of the Society for the Propagation of the Gospel in Newcastle, Delaware. Sprague, *Annals*, V, 24n.

fused Manner; yet some seemed encouraged by it to go to the Redeemer.

✑ *Mond. Nov. 12.* Went to see my Relations in the Tract;[56] and when I past by the Places where I had formerly lived, or walked, it gave a solemn Turn to my Mind. Ah! how much have I sinned, wherever I have been! and what solemn Transactions have been between God and my Soul in these my old Walks! Visited two Grave-Yards in my Way, to Solemnize my Mind among the Mansions of the Dead. O how solemn Eternity appeared! how frail and dying the Race of Mortals! and how near my own Dissolution! Returned to Mr. Rodgers's, and unbosomed ourselves to each other with all the Freedom of Xn. Friendship.

✑ *Tuesd. Nov. 13.* Went to Mr. Stuart's[57] at Reedy-Island in Company with my dear Mr. Rodgers, to wait for the Ship coming down. Had a free Conversation with him about my religious Exercises.

My worthy Friend Mrs. Dushane[58] desired me to write an Epitaph for the Tomb-Stone of her Sister, lately deceased; and tho' I had neither Leisure, nor Composure, I wrote 3, leaving it to the Friends of the Deceased to make their Choice.

> Does Beauty spread her Charms? Does Wealth o'er-
> flow?
> Does Health bloom fresh, or youthful Vigour glow?
> Are all Earth's Blessings in Profusion pour'd?
> And all these Sweets with no Affliction sour'd?
> Ah! trust not these, to guard from early Death,
> All these adorn'd the precious Dust beneath.

[56] The Welsh Tract was an area in New Castle County, Delaware, settled mostly by early eighteenth-century emigrants from Wales. Davies' father and uncle, Shionn, had moved into this area from Pennsylvania in 1717.

[57] Probably David Stewart of Port Penn, Delaware, who, with Isaac Dushane, had subsidized the publication of Samuel Finley's sermon *The Approved Minister of God* . . . (Philadelphia, 1749). Roger Paltrell Bristol, *Index of Printers, and Booksellers Indicated by Charles Evans in His American Bibliography* (Charlottesville, 1961), pp. 47, 145.

[58] Probably Elizabeth Dushane, wife of Isaac Dushane, of St. George's, Delaware. Delaware Historical Society, *A Calendar of Delaware Wills, New Castle County 1682–1800; Abstracted and Compiled by the Historical Research Committee of the Colonial Dames of Delaware* (New York, 1911), p. 125.

Or

Ye that in Beauty, or in Youth confide,
Come view this Monument, to blast your Pride;
The Charms of Beauty, Youth in flowery Bloom,
Wither'd at Morn, lie mould'ring in this Tomb,
And you may meet the same surprizing Doom.

Or

This Monument proclaims this solemn Truth;
Beauty is fading, frail the Bloom of Youth;
Life short, a Span, a Dream, an empty Shew,
And all is fleeting Vanity below.
Careless Spectator! learn from hence to die;
Prepare, prepare for Immortality.

✎§ *Wednesd. Nov. 14.* Continued waiting for the Ship, and the Delay made me uneasy; as I have been now about 10 Weeks from home, and yet my Embassy is as much undone, as when I left home. I find the Enterprize to which Providence seems to call me more and more difficult; for my Anxieties about my dear Family, and about my Life as necessary to their comfortable Subsistence are hard to be borne. May the God of Heaven support me and them! Communicated to Mr. Rodgers some new Tho'ts of mine about the divine Government as adapted to the Nature of Man, and about the divine Procedure towards men and Angels; with which he was pleased.

✎§ *Thirsd. Nov. 15.* The Ship is not yet come down, and the Wind is contrary; which affords me some Uneasiness; tho', blessed be God, I feel myself habitually resigned to his Providence. O that I might with chearful Fortitude endure the painful Rupture of the tenderest Bonds of Affection for his Sake, and encounter Danger and Death undaunted in his Cause!

✎§ *Fryd. Nov. 16.* Mr. G. Tennent is come down here to wait for the Ship; and my Spirit was revived with his facetious, and in the mean Time spiritual Conversation.

✎§ *Saturd. Nov. 17.* On Board the London. 12 o'Clock A.M. The Ship came down and we went on Board: and as I went along, endeavoured to commit myself to God, and to implore his Blessing and Protection in this Voyage. Perhaps I may never set my Foot on Shore more, 'till I land in the eternal World: Solemn Tho't! Father, into thy Hands I commend my Spirit. I now seem to enter upon a new State of Existence, when I leave my native Land, and venture upon the dangerous Element of Water. May I live to God, while tossing upon it! May the sickness of the Sea, which I expect, be sanctified to me! and may our Conversation and Preaching be useful to the Company!

► *Sund. Nov. 18.* 5.o'Clock A.M. The Wind blew up fair, and we set sail. The Novelty of my Situation and the Noise on Deck hindered my sleeping, so that I am heavy and indisposed. I bid farewell to my native Shore with a Kind of pleasing Horror; pleased that Providence has given us an Opportunity of sailing after so long a Delay, and shocked with the Tho't that I may never see my dear Friends, and particularly my other Self any more.

I cannot but be deeply sensible of the Kindness of Heaven in ordering my Father and Friend Mr. Tennent to be my Companion in the Embassy, not only for the right Management of it, but for my social Comfort.

O that I may retain a Consciousness of Integrity in the Cause of God, and universal Devotedness to him! 'Tis this, I find can best support me amid the Dangers of Sea and Land.

> When the Storm thickens, and the Ocean rolls,
> When Nature trembles to the frighted Poles,
> The pious Mind nor Doubts nor Fears assail,
> Tempests are Zephyrs, or a gentler Gale.

Wrote some Letters, particularly one of Friendship to Mr. Rodgers. I never parted with any one in a more solemn and affectionate Manner than I did yesterday with him. We retired, and each of us prayed in the tenderest and most pathetic Manner, giving Thanks to God for that peculiar Friendship which has subsisted between us, and committing each other to the Care of Heaven for the future.

The Hurries of Preparation for the Ocean deprived Mr. Tennent of an Opportunity of praying, and speaking to the Company; and I was incapable of it by Reason of Sea-Sickness.

About 3 o'Clock p.m. the Pilot left us, and we entered the vast Atlantic.

*§ *Mond., Nov. 19.* We are now out of Sight of Land— Cœlum undig; et undig Pontus. It would be particularly pleasing to me to survey the Wonders of the Majestic Ocean; but have been confined to Bed most of the Day, and am so much out of my Element that I am neither fit for Conversation, nor curious Observation. However, I feel calm within, and resigned to the divine Will—O Lord, bless my dear Family.

*§ *Tuesd.* Continued in the same Condition as Yesterday —Fair Weather. In the Evening was very low-spirited, and had most solemn Tho'ts of my own State, and the eternal World. Alas! how shocking a Companion is a Sense of Guilt.

*§ *Wednesd. Nov. 21.* The Wind is contrary, and the Waves run high. My Sea-Sickness continues; and I am a very heavy Companion to Mr. Tennent, which is particularly afflictive to me; but thro' the Goodness of God, he is cheerful and courageous.

*§ *Mond. Nov. 26.* I have been so extremely sick and low-Spirited; and the Sea so boisterous, that I have been unable to keep a Diary for these 4 Days; but now, thro' the great Goodness of God, I am somewhat recovered, and the Violence of the Winds and Waves is somewhat abated.

Tho' my bodily Disorder has not been very painful, it has utterly indisposed my whole Frame; and in all my Life I never felt such a Degree of Lowness of Spirits, proceeding not from any gloomy Imaginations, but entirely from the Disorder of animal Nature. I affected Solitude, had no relish for Conversation, no tender Passions, no lively Anxieties about any Thing, but seemed dead to all Things in the Compass of Tho't. I had no Appetite, and the little I eat, I vomited up immediately; and the *Smell* of the Ship, whenever I entered into the Cabin was nauseous beyond Expression. Now and then I forced a little Cheerfulness, but it was wholly unnatural. The perpetual Motion of the Ship which vastly exceeds all the Ideas I could form of it upon Land, kept me in a constant Confusion, and I could neither walk or stand or even sit with Safety, nor lie in Bed composed.

Last Fryday the Wind blew hard, and the Sea run very high, and frequently dashed over the Ship; but on Saturday the Violence was greatly encreased. We sailed about 8 or 9 Knots an Hour, over watry Vallies and Mountains, that seemed unsurmountable. This vast ship so deeply laden is tossed about like a little-Cork, and the Passengers reeled like drunken Men.

This Morning we had no Wind, tho' the Waves swelled high; but about 10 o'Clock it blew fresh and fair.

My Spirits are more lively, and my Appetite is something better, tho' I am still universally disordered.

There is one Thing that I have Reason to bless God for, in a particular Manner viz. That tho' the Ocean was extremely turbulent, and Dangers threatened on every Hand, and tho' my Spirits were sunk to such an unusual Degree of Dejection yet I was hardly at all terrified with Danger, but calm, and resigned.

Yesterday, Mr. Tennent sung and prayed, and made a pertinent, plain Address to the Sailors; and they seemed attentive.

Yesterday and to-day we prayed together alternately in our Room; and I felt some Tenderness and Importunity in so doing. O that we may in this inactive Season be laying up proper Furniture for active Life upon Shore!

It is a most majestic Survey, to see how the Waves rise in Ridges of Mountains, pursue each other, and dash in angry Conflict: and it is most amazing how we can possibly live upon so turbulent an Element. To form and rule such an Ocean is a Work becoming a God.

꿏 *Tuesd. Nov. 27.* Since Yesterday in the Afternoon, I have had a tolerable Flow of Spirits, and been pretty well, except a ling'ring Feaver. The Time begins to pass away agreeably in Conversation with dear Mr. Tennent, and the Capt. who is a very pleasant Companion.

The Wind not very hard, and we have a little Respite from the intolerable Perturbations of the angry Deep.

Prayed in our Room together in the Morning and Afternoon with some Freedom.

꿏 *Wednesd. Nov. 28.* Was more refreshed with Sleep last Night, than since I have been on Board; and find myself to-day more free from my Feaver than Yesterday. Blessed be the God of my Mercies.

'Tis almost quite calm, and the little Wind that blows is not fair. We are now, and have been [. . .].

⋙ [*Frid. Nov. 30.* To-day, so much distress]ed with a Sense [of Guilt that, I] have no Turn [for reading or religious] Conversation; n[or am I any Thing, but] Burden to myself.

This Evening the Wind [is very fresh] and fair; but we have had some [very] dangerous Squalls. We now sail about [*blank*] Knots an Hour.

Read an Account of the Shipwreck [and the] amazing Deliverance of Joseph Bailey[59] and Company; and was more sensible of the Goodness of God in our Preservation.

⋙ *Saturd. December 1st.* I am in better Health than since I have been on Board. Slept comfortably last Night. We have sailed before a fair Wind for about 36 Hours, and have made good Way.

[Read a Sermon of Mr. Ta]ylor's to young [Men against the Errors] that some Antino[mians maintain], and Mr. Dickinson's [able Defe]nce of his Sermon against Con[. . .] Answer to Mr. Beach.[60]

⋙ *Sund. December 2.* This Day has passed by very unprofitably, as we had no Opportunity of carrying on any Thing like public Worship, 'till about 7 o'Clock in the Evening, when I sung a Psalm, gave an Exhortation to the Company, and prayed. Had some Sense of divine Things, and a Desire to affect the Hearers, but no Freedom of Speech in Proportion.

[59] Joseph Bailey, *God's Wonders in the Great Deep: Or, a Narrative of the Shipwreck of the Brigantine Alida and Catharine, Joseph Bailey, Master, on the 27th of December, 1749, Bound from New-York for Antigua. Wherein, the Wonderful Mercy of the Divine Providence is displayed, in the Preservation of the Said Master, with All his Men, from the Time of the Said Vessels Over-Setting, to the Time of their Being Taken up by a Vessel Bound from Boston for Surranam, on the 3rd of January Following; All Which Time, Being Seven Nights, They Were in the Most Imminent Danger and Distress. Written by the Master Himself* (New York, 1750).

[60] Jonathan Dickinson, *A Defense of a Sermon Preached at Newark, June 2, 1736, Entitled the Vanity of Human Institutions in the Worship of God, Against the Exceptions of Mr. John Beach, in a Letter to Him* . . . (New York, [1737]). John Beach, *A Vindication of the Worship of God According to the Church of England* (New York, 1736).

Read a Ch. in the greek Text in the Night Tho'ts,[61] and Mr. Dickinson's second Vindication of Sovereign Grace.[62]

To-day I have been much discouraged with a View of my unqualifiedness for the important Business I am going upon. Had sundry Intervals of tender Tho'ts about my dear Family. O that my painfull Absence from them may be of Service to the Public! This would be more than a sufficient Compensation.

To-day the Wind is squally, but drives us on our Course 7 or 8 Knots an Hour. Last Night was very turbulent; and I could sleep but very little, which made me indisposed today.

Mond. December 3. Was out of Order. The Wind turbulent, and the Seas run high. Alas! how unprofitably my Life glides by in this State of Inactivity!

Tues. December 4. Had very little rest last Night by Reason of the violent Tossing of the Ship. I laboured under a Sense of Guilt, which made me very fearful of the Dangers of the Sea. God pity me of little Faith.

Read Mr. Dickinson's Vindication of Sovereign Grace, etc.

Since I noticed it last, Mr. Tennent and I have prayed each of us twice in our Room, and one of us alternately in the Cabin in the Evening.

The Tossing of the Vessel is utterly inconceivable to one that never felt it.

Wednesday. Dec. 4. The Wind favourable; and my Habit of Body better than usual.

[61] Edward Young (1683–1765) was rector of the Church of England parish of Wellwyn in Hertfordshire. His *The Complaint; or Night Thoughts on Life, Death, and Immortality* (London, 1742) was extremely popular and went through many editions. *DNB,* XXI, 1203–08.

[62] Jonathan Dickinson, *A Second Vindication of God's Sovereign Free Grace. Against the Exceptions Made to a Former Vindication, by Mr. John Beach in His Discourse, Intitled God's Sovereignty and His Universal Love to the Sons of Men, Reconciled. In a Letter to That Gentleman. By Jonathan Dickinson, A.M. Late Minister of the Gospel at Elizabeth-Town, and President of the College of New-Jersey. With Some Brief Reflections on Dr. Samuel Johnson's Defence of Aristocles Letter to Authades, Concerning the Sovereignty and Promises of God. Begun in a Letter to the Author, from the Said Mr. Dickinson. Left Unfinish'd and on Occasion of his Decease, Continued in a Letter to the Dr. from Moses Dickinson, A.M. Pastor of the First Church in Norwalk* (Boston, 1748).

It undoubtedly rains more upon Sea than Land; for there has not been one Day (that I remember) since we left the Capes, but we have had some Rain.

I am very pensive about my dear Family and Congregation. May the God of Heaven bless them!

❧ *Thirsd. Decemb. 5.* Last Night I was so pained with the Tooth-Ache, that I was but about an Hour in Bed, and then had no Sleep; and all this Day I have been in perpetual Pain. But in the Evening I sweat my Head, and thro' Mercy found immediate Relief. It has pleased the Lord to afflict me many Ways in this Voyage. May it be a Preparative for Usefulness, when I enter upon the Stage of Activity on the British Coast! And may I be purged in the Furnace of Affliction!

It is very squally, and the Seas run Mountain-high. It is astonishing we are not swallowed up in this boisterous Deep.

❧ *Fryd. December 6.* The Wind is contrary, and the Seas run very high. We are obliged to lie by, and make no Progress in our Way.

❧ *Sat. December 7.* Was indisposed and low-spirited, unfit for Reading or Society, and affected a Sullen Retirement. Alas! how my Days pass by in a State of Inactivity! Unless I gain more Life upon my Arrival, I shall be but a Cypher, or an Encumbrance to Mr. Tennent in our Embassy. May I be enabled to shew my Resignation to the divine Will in my present State by chearfull passive Obedience! and may it be a Preparative for active Obedience, when my Circumstances admit of it!

Read Mr. Prince's excellent Sermon upon the Agency of God in Droughts and Rains,[63] which suggested to me a Variety of new Tho'ts theological and philosophical. It is the best Discourse upon such a Subject that I ever saw. Read some in Harris's Collection of Voyages.[64]

[63] Thomas Prince, *The Natural and Moral Government and Agency of God in Causing Droughts and Rains. A Sermon at the South Church in Boston, Thursday, Aug. 24. 1749. Being the Day of the General Thanksgiving in the Province of the Massachusetts, for the Extraordinary Reviving Rains, After the Most Distressing Drought Which Have Been Known Among us in the Memory of Any Living* . . . (Boston, 1749; 1750).

[64] John Harris, *Navigantium atque Itinerantium Bibliotheca: Or, a Compleat Collection of Voyages and Travels, Consisting of Above Four Hundred of the Most Authentick Writers* (2 vols.; London, 1705; 1744-48).

About 10 o'Clock at Night my Spirits were somewhat exhilirated in Conversation with my worthy Companion. Found more Freedom than usual in Intercession for my dear absent Friends, particularly for Mr. Rodgers, and my Chara, whom I promised particularly to remember on Saturday Evenings. How my Heart longs and pines after my dearest Creature, and the little Pledges of our mutual Love! Oh! When shall I see them again!

It is much warmer on Sea than Land; for we have not needed Fire above 2 or 3 Days since we have been on Board.

There is a great Plenty of Birds to be seen all over this Ocean.

ᴀᴈ *Sund. December 8.* Have made but little or no Proficiency in Knowledge, or Holiness, or any valuable Acquisition, this Day, by Reason of Indisposition and Lowness of Spirits. Alas! of how little Importance or Usefullness am I in the World! My Soul is mortified to reflect upon my own Insignificancy. Read some of my old Notes, particularly on Ps. 90. 11. and Luk. 13.3. and was both pleased and surprized to find that ever any Sentiments of Importance had proceeded from a Mind now so barren. Read a Sermon of Mr. Kennedy's of Belfast on the Conclusion of the last Peace, on the Words of Hezekiah, "Good is the Will of the Lord since Peace and Truth shall be in my Days." [65]

It is our Unhappiness on Board that we cannot get Opportunity of preaching to the Crew twice on Sunday. However, in the Evening Mr. Tennent preached on Joh. 3. 5. and the Discourse was judicious, plain, pungent and searching, and well adapted to do good. O that the Power of God may attend it to the Consciences of the Company! I would bless the Lord that while I am useless, he enables my dear Partner to do something for him.

At Night Mr. Tennent prudently gave the Conversation a religious Turn, and I endeavoured to keep it up. But alas how ungrateful are such Subjects! and with what Dexterity will men avoid them, or divert the Discourse from them!

Rainy Weather, Wind S.E. and a high Sea for the most Part of the Day.

My dear Chara has often recurred to my Tho'ts, and frequently I imagine myself talking with her. It is a Mercy that

[65] Gilbert Kennedy, *The Great Blessing of Peace and Truth in Our Days: A Sermon Preached at Belfast . . . April 25, 1749, Being the Day of . . . Thanksgiving for the Peace* (Belfast and Dublin, 1749).

God has made any of my fellow Creatures of Importance to my Happiness, but my Absence from them affords me additional Uneasiness. Thus the Sweets of Life have their Stings.

☙ *Mond. Decem. 9.* Spent the Day chiefly in reviewing and improving my Notes; but the violent Motion of the Ship, and my Indisposition rendered me incapable of doing any Thing to Purpose.

In the Evening the Seas run very high, and broke over the Decks with prodigious Violence. While we were at Evening Worship, we shipped a sea which was like to wash the Carpenter overboard. It is really an Instance of the vigilant Care of Providence that we are not swallowed up in these turbulent waters.

☙ *Tuesd. Decemb. 10.* Was employed as Yesterday. The Wind moderate; but not from a favourable Quarter. Read in Harris's Collection of Voyages, concerning the Dutch Settlements in the East-Indies, which are very large and flourishing.

☙ *Wednesd. December 11.* I have Nothing new or remarkable to take Notice of with regard to myself. The wind fresh and fair S.W.

☙ *Thirsd. December 12.* My Mind has been in a very uneasy, timorous Situation all this Day especially in the Evening. Every Shock the Ship received from the dashing Waves gave an equal Shock to my Spirit. Guilt made me afraid of sinking in these boisterous Waters. How timorous a Thing is Guilt! It trembles at imaginary Dangers, and fears where no Fear is.

We have sailed 7, 8, 9 or 10 Knots an Hour for about 40 Hours past, and it is expected we are not above 100 Leagues from the British Coast.

☙ *Fryd. December 13.* Much disordered and low-spirited. I am quite dispirited, when I reflect upon my own Insignificancy, and am afraid I shall be of little or no Service in our Embassy.

Wind fresh and fair, and we have sailed about 350 miles these last 48 Hours. Sounded at 4 o'Clock P.M. and found Ground at 90 Fathom. Sounded at 12 o'Clock at Night, and found Bottom at 70 Fathom. Read in Harris's Collection of Voyages the shocking Account of the Barbarities the Dutch exercised upon the English at Amboyna in the East-Indies. Quid non mortalia Pectora cogis Auri sacra Fames!

⧼§ *Sat. December 14.* Much indisposed in Body, but peaceful and calm in Mind.

Sounded frequently and found Ground from 64 to 45 Fathom. It continues cloudy and we can make no Observation; so that we know not where we are, tho' the Capt. conjectures we are in the British Channel. There is great Danger of running aground, or upon Rocks; but the Lord reigneth; and we are in his Hands.

⧼§ *Sund. Decem. 15.* We find to-day that we have run up the Channel and gone past the Sylly, and as far as the Start Point, before we knew where we were. Thus Providence has been our Pilot, and we have run our Course as directly, and free from Danger, as if we could have made Observation of the Latitude, which we have not been able to do for sundry Days.

Saw sundry Ships, and spoke with one of them, a Danish Vessel, which told us where we were, viz about 20 Miles S.W. of the Start.

Was much indisposed, desponding and inactive in the Forenoon; but in the Evening was something revived in discoursing to the Ship's Company from Luk. 13.3. I had more Freedom and Solemnity than I expected, and the Company seemed seriously attentive. I am often afraid I have done, and shall do no Service to these precious Immortals on Board; and I am yet uncertain what will be the Event. I have this Evening made a feeble but sincere Attempt; and I leave it in the Hand of God, not expecting ever to speak to them More.

Weather moderate, tho' cloudy, and the Wind fair.

⧼§ *Mond. December 16.* Found in the Morning we had passed by the Isle of Wight in the Night, we soon saw Land at Beachy-Head, and went on towards the Downs, etc.

⧼§ *Tuesd. December 17.* We entered the Downs in the Morning, where lay about 33 Ships. Heard that one Capt. Davies from Philadelphia was cast away about 6 weeks ago a little before us in the Channel.[66] We came up with Capt. Mesnard,[67] who sailed from Philadelphia 8 Days before us. I looked upon it as a favourable Providence that we did not take our Passage with him, as it would have been longer. This is the more remarkable, as his Ship was famed for sailing fast, which ours was not. Sundry Boats came to us; and I was shocked to hear the infernal Language of the Boatmen. Alas! the whole World lieth in Wickedness.

Was entertained in taking a View of the Coast, as we sailed along. Saw Dover Castle and Town, and a Seat of the Duke of Dorset's. It is a pretty large Town; and so is Dale, which we saw a little after, where there is a Castle, and at Walmer. Passed by Margate, a considerable Town; but did not come near enough to take a particular View of it. How pleasing does the Land appear after so long a Confinement upon the Ocean! Especially as the landscape is beautifully variegated with Towns, Churches, Windmills, Forests, green corn Fields, etc. We past the N. Foreland and cast Anchor to lie all Night; and the Winds being contrary, the Days very [short and the Darkness hinderi]ng us, it is expected [that it will take us some] Time going from hence [to London, a Distance of] about 70 Miles by wa[ter and] [blank] [by] Land; which is very disa[greeable. But I] am heartily sick of the [Sea].

[It is just 4] Weeks and 4 Days since I left the [Amer]ican Shore; and tho' I have hardly ever [had a] more melancholy Time, yet I have [great] Reason to take Notice of the [Good]ness of Providence to me in my Voyage, [both] as to its Shortness, Safety, Plenty, and [inde]ed the Moderateness of the Weather, Consider[ing] the Season. Alas! That I find myself so [little] disposed to make grateful Returns. I am really shocked at myself, as a Monster of Ingratitude.

Tho' I am now above 3000 Miles from Home, and have been near 4 Months absent, My tho'ts are often wafted thither upon eager Wings, and hover round the dear Objects of my Love.

[66] Captain George Davis of the *Britannia* sailed from Gravesend on 7 November 1753, but foundered on a sandbar the next day with the loss of thirteen lives including his own. *Pennsylvania Gazette*, 23 January 1754.

[67] Probably Captain Stephen Mesnard, whom Franklin used to carry books and papers to and from England. On 27 October 1753, Franklin mentions him as sailing for London "in a week or two." Franklin to William Strahan, Franklin, *Papers*, V, 83.

Whether I shall be again conducted over this spacious Ocean; and [see my Friends is wholly un]known to me; [but I forbear—for I can] hardly bear the [Anxiety of Seperation and the Tho't] of never enjoying [an other Interview With] them especially my other dearer [Half].

We are about 20 Souls on Board; Passengers Mr. Tennent, Mr. Matt. Clarkson, Miss Shirley, John Crosby, and a little Girl in the Cabin; and 2 in the Steerage.

This Morning the Pilot came on Board, one Grovenor, who was Capt. of a little Privateer in the late War, and behaved very gallantly.

At Night when all were gone to Bed, enjoyed an Hour of most pleasant and friendly Conversation with dear Mr. Tennent [upon the arduous Duties] of the ministerial [office.]

[I relate Thi]ngs just as they occur to a [careless] Mind, without any Order; and tho' my [princi]pal Design is to make religious [Rem]arks, yet, for my future Amusement or [Imp]rovement I shall take Notice of the Curiosities [of] Nature and Art.

The English Oysters differ from those in America. They are almost round, flat, and not clustered. There is a Species of Fish here called the Whiting, which is very delicate. The Banks along the Shore from Beachy-Head to this Place are Chalk.

 ʙ *Wednes. Dec. 18.* Lay at Anchor, the Wind and Tide being against us. Would willingly have gone to London by Land, but Mr. T. did not chuse it. Nothing remarkable occurred to-day.

 ʙ *Thursd. December 20.* We [weighed Anchor and Endea]voured to pass thro' the [Narrows, setting up a] Becon, and 2 Buoys to p[ush the Ship along; but,] the Wind and Tide being against [us, we were obliged to] cast Anchor again, and ly by. [The Church of Re]culviers is opposite to us. It has [blank] [Steeples.]

Read the Memoirs of the fortunate [Country] Maid;[68] a Ro-

---

[68] Davies probably had a pirated 1741 translation of *La Paysanne Parvenue* written by Charles de Fieux, Chevalier de Mouhy, in 1735. This edition, by Eliza Haywood, was titled *The Fortunate Country Maid; Being the Entertaining Memoirs of the Present Celebrated Marchioness of L-V- Who from a Cottage Became a Lady of the First Quality in the Court of Francis; Wherein Are Display'd the Various and Vile Artifices Employ'd by Men of Intrigue for Seducing Young Women, with Suitable Reflections.* See James R. Foster, *History of the Pre-romantic Novel in England* (New York, 1949), pp. 38–39.

mance that has a better [Tendency] than most that are so much in Vogue. [I] think it an Evidence of the chimerical [Taste] of the present Age, that it runs mad after these romantic Pieces. Read a Part [of] Roxana,[69] the Hystory of an abandoned Prostitute, pretendedly penitent.

Was shocked at the Wickedness of some [of] the Ship's Crew; and sorry our Endeavours had so little Effect upon them.

✑ *Fryd. December 21.* In the Morning weighed Anchor, and passed thro' the Narrows with Safety. The Passage is but a few Yards wide; and tho' it be something of an Obstruction to the English Trade, as it is attended with Danger, [to pass it; yet this] is more than comp[ensated by its good] natural Fortification against [foreign Invasion].

There [is such] a Number of Vessels in Sight that we seem to form a Kind of Town upon Sea and live in good Neighbourhood.

About 11. The Tide failed us, and we were obliged to cast Anchor, having passed by a Sand Bank, called the Spaniard, where there is a Buoy. We now lie off Shippy-Island; the Land appears high and hilly.

By Calculating our Expenses hither we find that they have amounted to more than £125, which will be very burdensome to the College, unless our Applications in Great Britain be successful.

In the Evening, the Tide favouring, tho' the Wind was contrary, we weighed Anchor, and sailed by the Noure, where there is a Vessel instead of a Light-House, with Lights fixed to her Masts, as it appeared to me at a Distance. The Noure [is about] [*blank*] [Miles above the] Mouth of the River [Thames. At] 11 o'Clock we cast [Anchor].

✑ *Saturd. Decemb. 22.* We [weighed] Anchor about 7 o'Clock in the Morning, and sailed up within about 4 Miles of Gravesend, and the Tide failing, we were obliged to cast Anchor.

[69] Daniel Defoe published this anonymously in London in 1724 and 1741 under the title *The Fortunate Mistress; or a History of the Life and Vast Variety of Fortunes of Mademoiselle de Beleau, Afterwards Call'd the Countess of Wintelsheim, in Germany, Being the Person Known by the Name of the Lady Roxana, in the Time of King Charles II.*

We now see the Land on each Side of the River, and the Landscape is beautifully variegated with green Fields, Forests, Houses, etc. We passed by the little Town of Lee.

Read in The Spirit of Laws,[70] an ingenious Performance, with many new and valuable Sentiments.

In the Evening my Heart spontaneously dictated the following Lines,

> While Objects various, strange and new,
> In numerous Prospects rush to view,
> The [Tho'ts of Friends,] the Tho'ts of Home
> Eng[ross my Heart] and still find Room.
> Ch[ara with] what strange, Magic Art,
> Dost thou [so] distant, charm my Heart?
> ~~Where spacious Seas between us roll,~~
> Not Seas can quench, nor Distance cool
> The Flame of Love that fires my Soul.
> Not Works of Nature or of Art
> Can raze thine Image from my Heart.
> I shrink to view those Days to come,
> While cruel Absence is my Doom.
> Indulgent Heaven! contract those Days,
> And give my anxious Bosom Ease.

᪥ *Sund. Decem. 23.* We weighed Anchor in the Morning, and past by Gravesend, a little Town that has an agreeable Appearance; opposite to which is a Fort, I think called Tilberry. We also passed by Northfleet and Greys, 2 small Villages. Saw a Gibbet, and the Remains of a Malefactor ha[nging] in it. A shocking Sight! Pirates, etc. that com[mit great Cri]mes on Sea are executed nea[r this Place that Se]amen may see them.

The Churches on both Sides [of the] River are very numerous. They seem old Gothic Structures, with square Steeples without Spires. The Custom-House-Officers came on Board, and the Hurries and Impieties on Board rendered the Sanctification of this holy Day extremely difficult. The Lord help me!

Spoke with a Ship from Virginia, Capt. Whiting; prepared a

[70] Charles Louis de Secondat, Baron de Montesquieu, *The Spirit of Laws. Translated . . . with Corrections and Additions Communicated by the Author* (2 vols.; London, 1750). This was the first English edition.

short Letter for my Dear; hired a Boat, and overtook the Ship below Gravesend. As we returned, the Boatman had Occasion to go ashore at Gravesend, where an odd Affair happened, fit to be numbered among the Adventures of a Knight-Errant. We staid in an Ordinary a few Minutes; but as I had but one Penny of Money about me, I could call for Nothing. When we went down to take Boat again, behold, the Boat was gone, and the Boatman called and hallowed for her a good while, but had no Answer. I was obliged to return to [the Ordinary where] I sat pensive and confused with a[n empty Pocket]; and was afraid the Ship would go awa[y and le]ave me, and that I should be obliged to go to London by Land, without any Thing to bear my Expenses. After I had sat till about 7 o'Clock, the Boatman, with Joy pictured in his Countenance, came and told Me the acceptable News that he had found the Boat. Some Fellow had Occasion for her, and took her to a Vessel at some Distance, and as it was very dark, it was a Wonder she was found. The poor Boatman, anxious for his Boat, had cried out, "Well, I would give Sixpence to know where my Boat is." Another immediately held him to his Word, and lent him his Boat to go and look for her. As we were going up to the Ship, it was so dark, that we could not see her, and went about a Mile above her. The old Boatman and his Son fell a Scolding about the Place where the Ship lay, and to decide the Difference we called at 2 or 3 Sloops that lay at Anchor; but after bauling sufficiently, we could find no Body; and we were obliged to grope on till at Length we got safely to the Ship. And the Relation of our Adventure afforded no small Entertainment to the Comp[any].

While I was at Gravesend, there [came] in the Room a Company of Sailors bel[ongin]g to the East-India Ships, who cursed and blasphemed in the most infernal Manner that ever I heard in my Life. My Spirit was quite oppressed to hear them. Alas! to what a shocking Degree of Impiety may human Nature arrive!

We have past by 5 or 6 East-India Ships in the River; they are very large, and magnificent; immensely rich, and well-armed.

Mr. T. had no Opportunity of speaking to the Ship's Company, by Reason of their Hurry. Indeed there is Nothing that has the Appearance of a Sabbath among Sailors. Mr. T. naturally remarked upon it, "That where no good is to be done, the Door is not opened."

Mond. December 24. We set Sail in the Morning, and passed by Green-hive, a little Village, near which Lord Concannon has a Seat; we also passed by a Seat that formerly belonged to Lord Baltimore.

Thro' di[vine Goodn]ess, I find my Body recovered to usual Health; and I believe the fresh Provisions, we yesterday received from Shore, were conducive to it.

Passed by Wolwich, a Town on the left Hand, beautifully varied with sundry Kinds of Buildings. Here is the King's Dock Yard, 15 or 20 Men of War lay at it. Here also is an Office of Ordnance, where Cannon etc. for the King's Ships are cast; and we saw a vast Quantity lying on the Wharf.

Passed by Blackwall, a Town on the right Hand; where lay 2 Men of War, and a great Number of East-India Ships in repair. We counted no less than 12 Wind-Mills, which seemed to animate the Air, when they were all in Motion.

Passed by Greenwich, on the left Hand, and took particular Notice of the Hospital There, which is one of the most stately Edifices I believe, in the World. It [consists of] 2 vast Buildings fronting one another, and the Governour's House above, seems to join them.

Here lay 4 of the King's Yachts, one of which is the most beautiful Vessel that Art can form, and in it his Majesty sails for Hanover. Flamstead-House is in Sight, upon a Hill above Greenwich. We saw the Steeple of St. Paul's, below Blackwall.

We cast Anchor at Deptford, along Side of a Man of War. At Deptford there is another of the King's Dock-Yards. From hence sundry of the Passengers went to London; but Mr. T. and I determined to stay till to-morrow. In the Evening we heard that Mr. Dennys De Berdt had been very inquisitive about us, and probably provided a Lodging for us.

Tuesd. Decem. 25. We sailed up the River, and were not a little struck with the prodigious Number [of Ships] in View. Their Masts look like vast Forests. About 10 o'Clock Mr. Neave, one of the owners of the Ship, came on Board, and invited us to dine at Mr. Neate's, his Partner,[71] where we were kindly received. We came up by the Tower in Sight of London-

[71] Richard Neave and William Neate were partners in a London mercantile house with many customers in America. Franklin, *Papers,* IV, 115n.

Bridge, and landed. As it was Christmas-Day, the Bells in all the Churches were ringing, and formed a Concert of the most manly, strong and noble Music to my Ear, that I ever heard. The Steeple of St. Dunstan's in the East is such curious Architecture that when the Bells ring, it rocks, like a Tree shaken with the Wind, tho' it consists of Stone.

After Dinner our Friends Capt. McPherson and Capt. McCulloch, conducted us to Mr. De Berdt's, who is a most amiable pious Gent. and entertained us very kindly, 'till we could provide a Lodging. Mr. Tennent was extremely low-Spirited and silent, which afforded me no small Concern; and I was afraid of conversing freely, while he was silent, lest I should seem to arrogate the Preference.

⊷§ *Wednesd. December 26.* Were visited by Mr. Hall,[72] a venerable old Gent. author of some of the Seine-street Sermons, who seems to be of a true puritannic Spirit, and full of Religion.

Were visited by Mr. Gibbons,[73] my dear Correspondent, who informed us of the general Apostacy of the Dissenters from the Principles of the Reformation. He told me that Dr. Doddridge's[74] Motto under his Picture was, Dum viviamus, vivamus; and that Dr. Young had erected 2 schools, over the Door of one of which he had written, Doctrinæ Filia Virtus; and of the other, Filia Matre pulchrior. Were visited by good Mr. Crutenden,[75] who sent me over £10 Sterl. worth of Books to be distributed among the Poor in Virginia. Mr. Whitefield [76] having sent us an In-

---

[72] This was probably Thomas Hall, minister to the Independent congregation upon the Pavement, Moorfields, an extremely popular lecturer and preacher. Wilson, *Dissenting Churches*, III, 538.

[73] Thomas Gibbons (1720–85) was pastor of the Independent congregation of Haberdasher's Hall and a leading figure among the London dissenters. During his lifetime he published more than fifty theological works including the first collected edition of Davies' sermons. *DNB*, VII, 1144.

[74] Philip Doddridge (1702–51) had been an extremely prominent London Presbyterian minister, hymnwriter, and schoolmaster. He had contacts with all of the important English and American dissenters and had corresponded with Davies before his death. *DNB*, V, 1063–69.

[75] Robert Crutenden (1690–1763) had previously been a successful London preacher but had taken a position as secretary of an organization concerned with the problems of dissenters. Wilson, *Dissenting Churches*, I, 389–390.

[76] George Whitefield had just returned from an extremely successful preaching tour of Scotland. Davies had probably first heard him speak in Pennsylvania in 1739 or 1740. *DNB*, XXI, 90.

vitation last Night to make his House our home during our Stay here, we were perplexed what to do, least we should blast the success of our Mission among the Dissenters, who are generally disaffected to him. We at length concluded with the Advice of our Friends and his, that a public Intercourse with him would be imprudent in our present Situation; and visited him privately this Evening; and the kind Reception he gave us, revived dear Mr. Tennent. He spoke in the most encouraging Manner as to the Success of our Mission, and in all his Conversation, discovered so much Zeal and Candour, that I could not but admire the Man, as the Wonder of the Age. When we returned, Mr. Tennent's Heart was all on Fire, and after we had gone to Bed, he suggested we should watch and pray; and we rose, and prayed together 'till about 3 o'Clock in the Morning.

Thirsd. December 27. Spent the Time chiefly in private. Conversed with Mr. Loyd [77] a serious Man and dear Mr. Gibbons who spent the Evening with us, revising Mr. Pearsal's[78] Meditations for a 2nd. Edition.

Fryd. December 28. Went up the Monument, a vast Pillar, in Memory of the dreadful Fire of 1666. It has a Latin Inscription signifying the Beginning, and Progress of the Conflagration: Another as far as I remember in these Words, Furor papisticus, qui horrenda patravit, nondum restinguitur. And another to the same Import in English. I went up to the Top along a winding Stairs, in the Form of a Screw. From thence I could take a View of this vast overgrown City, and the People in the Streets seemed degenerated into Pigmies. Went to the Virginia-Coffee-House to enquire for Letters from my Dear, etc. but alas! none were arrived.

We took up our Lodgings at Mr. Thomas Cox's in Winchester-Street, a sober religious Family, Blessed be God.

[77] This could well have been Samuel Lloyd (or Loyd), who was closely associated with the revivalist movement and served as John Wesley's legal advisor. Nehemiah Curnock, ed., *The Journal of the Rev. John Wesley* . . . (8 vols.; London, 1938), IV, 489.

[78] Richard Pearsall, *Reliquiæ Sacræ: or, Meditations on Select Passages of Scripture, and Sacred Dialogues Between a Father and His Children* (2 vols.; London, 1765).

꒳ *Saturday.* Continued retired preparing for a public Appearance.

꒳ *Sund. Decem. 30.* Preached in the Morning for Mr. Winter,[79] Assistant to Mr. Hall, on Isai. 66. 1, 2. But alas! I was dull and senseless. Dined with Mr. Salvage,[80] a most valuable Christian, in Company with a pious Youth, one Mr. Elliston, who is at Learning for the Ministry, and was for some time under Dr. Doddridge's Care. In the Afternoon I preached for one Mr. Dews,[81] who was indisposed, in a Baptist Congregation, with some Freedom on Jer. 31. 18, 20. It is grievous to see how small the Congregations are in this vast City. Spent the Evening at one Mr. Edwards's, a Tur[ky] Merchant, who treated me very kindly. He is a member of the Committee for the Management of the civil Affairs of the Dissenters. I find Mr. Stennet,[82] a Baptist Minister has most influence in Court, of any of the dissenting Ministers. Mr. Tennent preached in the Afternoon at Mr. Hall's, and in the Morning went to hear Mr. Chandler.[83] I find it the Custom here for the Clerks to chuse the Psalm.

꒳ *Mond. Dec. 31.* Went according to his Lordship's Appointment to wait upon the Marquis of Lothian;[84] but as we did not know the Distance, we did not come soon enough, and the Marquis was gone out. We went thro' St. James's Park, which is a beautiful Place. Past thro' the King's Palace, where we saw the Foot Guards in Waiting. Went to see the New Bridge of Westminster, which is the most noble Piece of Workmanship of

[79] The Reverend Richard Winter was assistant pastor of the Independent congregation upon the Pavement, Moorfields. Wilson, *Dissenting Churches,* III, 537–542.

[80] Probably Samuel Morton Savage, at this time assistant pastor of the Independent congregation in Duke's Place, Bury Street, St. Mary Axe. In 1757 he became sole pastor of this church. *DNB,* XVII, 838.

[81] Probably Samuel Dews, minister to the Baptist congregation in Great Eastcheap. Wilson, *Dissenting Churches,* I, 460–461.

[82] The Reverend Joseph Stennet was pastor of the Baptist congregation in Little Wild Street. *DNB,* XVIII, 1037.

[83] Samuel Chandler was a popular dissenting preacher and hymnwriter, and minister to the Independent congregation in the Old Jewry. *DNB,* IV, 42–43.

[84] William Kerr, third Marquis of Lothian, was at this time a representative peer and Lord High Commissioner to the General Assembly of the Church of Scotland. *Burke's Peerage,* p. 1367.

the Kind, I suppose, in the World. It consists of Portland Stone, neatly hewn. Went into Westminster Hall, a spacious old Building, where Courts are held. Tho' the Roof is so long, it is supported without one Pillar. The Walls of London are generally demolished, but here and there they remain; and above the Gates are Buildings of Gothic Structure. There is such a vast Number of Beggars here, that one cannot walk the Streets without being pained with their Importunity; for he can not supply them all; and there are so many Imposters among them that it is hard to distinguish real Objects of Charity. Dined at one Mr. Lloyd's, a solid, humerous, religious old Gent. in Southwark, who seems a hearty Friend to our Mission.

There are so many Parties here, that it is very perplexing to us, how to behave so as to avoid Offence, and not to injure the Business of our Embassy. The Independents and Baptists are more generally Calvinists, than the Presbyterians; tho' I fear some of them are tainted with Antinomianism.

1754

᪐ *Tuesd. Jan. 1. 1754.* Went to hear Mr. Chandler in Salter's-Hall, and was pleasingly entertained with a Sermon on the Parable of the unjust Steward. Mr. C. is undoubtedly a most ingenius, accurate Gent. but I did not discern so much of experimental Religion in [t]his Discourse as I could wish.

Went afterwards to the Amsterdam Coffee-House, where the Congregational and Baptist Ministers meet on Tuesdays. Was introduced into the Conversation of the venerable Mr. Price,[85] Dr. Watts's[86] Colleague; and then went, at Mr. Gibbon's Invitation, to dine at Mr. Shuttlewood's in Trinity-House, where the Corporation meets, that has the Care of Light-Houses, etc. for the Direction of Sailors. Was entertained with sundry curiosities, viz. 2 Indian Canoes, one of the Bark of a Tree; 2 very large

[85] Samuel Price was co-pastor, with Samuel Morton Savage, of the Independent congregation in Bury Street, St. Mary Axe. Wilson, *Dissenting Churches*, I, 318–320.

[86] Isaac Watts (1674–1748) was probably the first of the great modern English hymnwriters, his style being copied by Davies and many others. While co-pastor of the Independent congregation in Bury Street, St. Mary Axe, he had resided in the home of Sir Thomas and Lady Abney. *DNB*, XX, 67–70.

Globes, The Pictures of sundry who have been Benefactors to the Society. Went in the Evening to hear Mr. Whitefield in the Tabernacle, a large, spacious Building. The Assembly was very numerous, tho' not equal to what is Common. He preached on the Parable of the barren Fig-Tree, and tho' the Discourse was incoherent, yet it seemed to me better calculated to do good to Mankind than all the accurate, languid Discourses I have heard. After sermon enjoyed his pleasing Conversation at his House.

৵৯ *Wednesd. Jan. 2.* Waited on the Marquis of Lothian, at his House, and were very kindly received. The unaffected Grandeur of the Nobleman, and the Simplicity and Humility of the Xn. cast a mutual Lustre on each other. He gave all the Encouragement in his Power with regard to our Embassy. This was the first Time that I ever appeared before a Nobleman, and I have Reason to be thankfull, that I was not at all dashed with the Fear of Man. My Lord Leven[87] came and dined with us, and we laid before Their Lordships the State of the College. Lord Leven told us that he had delayed an Application in Favour of some Foreigners 'till the ensuing Assembly, and was afraid that if he should be appointed to [be] His Majesty's Commissioner for the ensuing Year, that Affair would interfere with ours. But, upon the Whole, their Lordships gave us Encouragement by intimating that they were sensible of the Importance of the Design, and had it at Heart. We continued with their Lordships 'till about 5 o'Clock, and then took Coach, and went to Mr. Godwin's,[88] a serious, reserved Gent. in Conversation, but very fluent, as I am told, in the Pulpit.

We laid before him our Design, and he seemed sensible of its Importance.

৵৯ *Thirsd. Jan. 3.* Breakfasted with Mr. Chandler, a Presbyterian Minister, of uncommon Sagacity and Readiness.

[87] Alexander Melville, fifth Earl of Leven and fourth Earl of Melville, was a representative peer and had been Lord High Commissioner to the General Assembly of the Church of Scotland from 1741 until 1753 when he was replaced by the Marquis of Lothian. *Burke's Peerage,* p. 1320.

[88] Edward Godwin was the minister to the Presbyterian congregation of Little St. Helen's and a popular London lecturer. Wilson, *Dissenting Churches,* I, 381–385.

He has been formerly suspected of Arminianism and Socinianism; but now he appears to be a moderate Calvinist.

He promised his Influence in Favour of our Design. We afterwards waited upon Dr. Guise,[89] and informed him of our Business, but he seemed to discourage us, on Acct. of the many annual Expenses lying upon the Dissenters in this City, for the Relief of the Poor, for the Support of Ministers in the Country, the Education of Youth, etc.

Spent the Evening very agreeably with Mr. Gibbons, in Company with Mr. Crutenden and Mr. De Berdt. I laid before them our Business; and they candidly gave me their best Advice. We find it is a Disadvantage that we have so few Letters to the Presbyterians here, who are the most numerous and rich. For the Sake of Expedition, we have agreed to go separate at Times, and therefore Mr. Tennent went this Evening to good Mr. Hall's. I have been so pained with the Tooth-Ake, that I had little Sleep these 3 Nights, and I write this about 3 o'Clock in the Morning.

As we enjoyed the Happiness on Board to pray together in our Room twice a Day Mr. Tennent and I determined to observe the same Method in our Lodging, beside the stated Devotion of the Family.

Fryd. Jan. 4. Being much indisposed with the Tooth-Ake, I was obliged to stay at Home. Wrote a Letter to my Dearest, with uncommon Solicitude. O when will these Days of cruel Absence be over! Mr. Tennent went and introduced the Affair of our Mission to Mr. Spilsbury,[90] Mr. Stennet and Mr. Bradbury;[91] and had some Encouragement from them all.

[89] John Guyse, Independent minister in Pinner's Hall, was a member of the influential King's Head Society which had been established to assist young men seeking academic training for the dissenting ministry. *DNB*, VII, 837.

[90] Francis Spilsbury was co-pastor of the Presbyterian congregation which met at Salter's Hall and a popular lecturer. Wilson, *Dissenting Churches*, II, 56–60.

[91] Thomas Bradbury (1677–1759) was minister to the Independent congregation in New Court, Carey Street. An extremely popular lecturer, he had been known to Queen Anne as "bold Bradbury." He was criticized by some dissenters for annually commemorating the death of Queen Anne by a sermon, after which he dined with friends in a tavern and loudly sang a national song known as "The Roast Beef of Old England." *Ibid.*, III, 450–452, 504–535.

꧁ *Sat. Jan. 5.* Mr. T. being indisposed, and fatigued, I visited Mr. Bowles,[92] the famous Print-Seller, in the Morning. He is a Gent. of good Sense, but of uncommon Humour; and I verily tho't, by the Reception he gave the Affair of our Mission, that he would be no Friend to it; but before we parted, he surprized me with a Present of a Map of London, and a Promise of 5 Guineas to the College. Dined at Mr. Jasper Mauduit's,[93] the hearty Friend of the Dissenters in Virginia, one of the Committee that has the Management of the secular Affairs of the Dissenters in Court.[94] He promised me that Something farther, if possible, should be done in their behalf, before my Return. We communicated the Affair of the College, and Mr. Tennent happening to mention repeatedly that the *Calvinists* as the principal Persons concerned in it, it was like to engage us into an unseasonable Dispute with Mr. Mauduit's Brother[95] upon the Calvinistic Principles. We found they were both of latitudinarian, anticalvinistic Principles, and would not countenance the College, unless it were upon a catholic Plan. We shewed them the Charter, and they were satisfied. One of them informed us, that the King has given a considerable Sum for the Support of English School-Masters among the German Protestants in Pennsylvania,[96] and that if we could make it appear that our College might be useful for the Education of such, we might probably have a Share of it for that Purpose. We were also informed that the Society here for propagating Xn. Knowledge[97] would probably give Some-

[92] Thomas Bowles was known to his contemporaries as "the great print seller." He dealt in books, maps, and prints in the Cornhill district of London. Plomer, *Dictionary*, p. 32.

[93] Jasper Mauduit was a London woolen draper and a spokesman for the dissenting interest. *DNB*, XIII, 82–83.

[94] This seems to have been an informal association of leading Presbyterian and Independent clergymen under the direction of Benjamin Avery. Carl Bridenbaugh, *Mitre and Sceptre* (New York, 1962), pp. 39–53.

[95] Israel Mauduit (1708–87), who later served as agent for the colony of Massachusetts, was associated with his brother in the woolen business. At the time of the American Revolution he became a noted pamphleteer for the patriot cause. *DNB*, XIII, 82–83.

[96] In 1753, George II had given a large sum of money to a committee headed by Samuel Chandler. His purpose was to bind the Pennsylvania Germans more closely to the British interest in the coming war with France. Whitfield J. Bell, "Benjamin Franklin and the German Charity Schools," *Proceedings of the American Philosophical Society*, XCIX (1955), 383.

[97] The Society for Propagating Christian Knowledge had been founded in March of 1699 with the purpose of encouraging religion in the colonies

thing out of their Fund, in Case a Number of Indian Youth might be educated in our College. Both these Proposals would have a happy Tendency, could they be carried into Execution. But we are afraid the Philadelphia Academy will interfere with the former.

In the Evening, wrote a Letter of Thanks to the Marquis of Lothian, and another to Lord Leven, enclosing a Copy of our Instructions, which his Lordship had desired.

<&§ *Sund. Jan. 6.* Heard Mr. Newman,[98] a Presbyterian in or near Charter-House Square, on Ps. 116. 16. "Lord, I am thy Servant; I am thy Servant" and tho' I am informed he is an Armenian [*sic*], I was much pleased with his Sermon. It was full of manly, rational and ingenious Sentiments; and more in Mr. Howe's Strain, than any Sermon I ever heard. He is Minister of the Congregation of which good Dr. Wright[99] was Pastor.

Preached in the Evening in Mr. Gibbon's Meeting-House on Luke.2. 34, 35. and had some Freedom and Solemnity. Conversed a little with the great Grandson of Oliver Cromwell;[100] and I remember a few Days ago, I drunk Tea with his great Grand-Daughter, one Mrs. Field. Drunk Tea with 2 grand-Daughters of the famous Sir Henry Ashurt,[101] the Friend of the ejected Ministers. Mr. Tennent preached for Mr. Chandler, and was kindly treated.

I am so hurried, that I have no Time to write my Journal, but about 12 o'Clock at Night. Therefore I am obliged to be very short.

---

through the training and support of missionaries and by establishing libraries. W. K. Lowther Clark, *A History of the S.P.C.K.* (London, 1959), p. 7.

[98] Probably Thomas Newman (1692–1758), who was minister to the Blackfriars Presbyterian congregation in Little Carter Lane, Doctor's Commons. *DNB*, XIV, 351–352.

[99] Samuel Wright (1683–1746) was an extremely popular Presbyterian preacher and first pastor of the congregation in Doctor's Commons. *DNB*, XXI, 1042–43.

[100] William Cromwell, for whom Thomas Gibbons preached a funeral sermon in 1772.

[101] Sir Henry Ashurt (1614–80) had been a wealthy and prominent London philanthropist, Presbyterian, and supporter of the Parliamentary cause. Among his diverse interests were missionary work among the North American Indians and the Society for the Propagation of the Gospel. *DNB*, I, 653.

✎§ *Mond. Jan. 7.* Went to visit Mr. Oswald,[102] and Mr. Buckland,[103] Book-Sellers; but the former was not at Home. In the Evening visited Mr. Winter, a congregational Minister; but his dry Orthodoxy, and severe Reflections upon those that deviated from rigid Calvinism, were disagreeable to me. Heard good Mr. Whitefield in the Evening on "Who hath delivered us from the Power of Darkness, and hath translated us into the Kingdom of his dear Son."

In the Morning Mr. Tennent and I waited on Mr. Newman, and communicated our Business. He is a grave Gent. and treated us kindly. He intimated, that the Academy which the Presbyterians are about to erect, would probably interfere with our Concern, and gave us Ground of Discouragement.

✎§ *Tuesd. Jan. 8.* Dined at Mr. Eleazar Edward's, a Turky Merchant in Devonshire-Square, of the Baptist Persuasion. There we enjoyed Mr. Stennet's Company, and his Son's.[104] He is a judicious, prudent and candid Gent. and has more Influence in Court, than any dissenting Minister in London. Mr. Tennent having visited Mr. Partridge,[105] the Agent of Pennsylvania, was advised to apply to some of the Court, particularly to the Lord Chancellor,[106] Lord Hallifax[107] and Mr. Pelham;[108] and he seemed inclined to do it. But to me it appeared very doubtful. I was afraid that in Case the College should be discountenanced by them they would find some Flaw in the Charter and so overset it; and that a Refusal at Court would have a bad Influence on those that might otherwise contribute towards it. We consulted Mr. Stennet, and he was fully of my Mind. He gave us an Ac-

[102] John Oswald was a bookseller in Chancery Lane specializing in theological works. Plomer, *Dictionary*, pp. 186–187.

[103] James Buckland (1711–90) dealt in theological works in Paternoster Row. *Ibid.*, pp. 37–38.

[104] Samuel Stennet (1728–95) assisted his father, Joseph Stennet, at the Baptist congregation in Little Wild Street. *DNB*, XVIII, 1037.

[105] Richard Partridge (1681–1759) was a non-Quaker who was very influential in Quaker circles. Americans visiting London used him as a clearing house for information. At various times he served as the agent for the colonies of Rhode Island, New York, New Jersey, Pennsylvania, and Connecticut. *DAB*, XIV, 283–284.

[106] Philip Yorke, first Earl of Hardwicke. *DNB*, XXI, 1261–66.

[107] George Montagu Dunk (1716–71), second Earl of Halifax, was head of the Board of Trade. *DNB*, VI, 199–201.

[108] Henry Pelham served as Prime Minister from 1744 until his death in 1754. *DNB*, XV, 689–692.

count of the Affair of the Glebe in N. Eng. in which the episcopal Party was cast, after a Trial of some Hours in the privy Council; He also related a Conference he had with the Duke of N. Castle[109] and Abp. of York[110] about the Mission of Bishops into America which was very entertaining; but I have no Time to relate such Things. In the Evening we visited Mr. Ward,[111] the Book-Seller, who appeared a zealous Friend to the College.

At Night finished a Letter to my Dearest, with such tender Affection as I could hardly bear.

Wednesd. Jan. 9. Waited on Mr. Penn[112] the Proprietor of Pennsylvania. He treated us kindly, but gave us no Encouragement as to our Mission, on Account of the Academy in Philadelphia, which he apprehended himself under peculiar Obligations to promote. Went thence to Kensington to see Mr. Ziegenhagen,[113] his Majesty's German Chaplain, a good old Lutheran Minister. He has much of the Solemnity of a Christian, and a tender Concern for the Church of Xt. in general. Dined at an Inn; but when we called for the Reckoning, we found the generous old Gent. had prevented us, and sent Word that he would pay for all our Expences there. Called at Mr. Pitius's at the Savoy, a Lutheran Minister; but he was not at Home.

Thirsd. Jan. 10. Visited Dr. Jennings,[114] and were kindly received. He appears a sociable, affectionate and pious

[109] Thomas Pelham-Holles (1693–1768), Duke of Newcastle-upon-Tyne and Newcastle-under-Lyme, was the brother of Henry Pelham, whom he succeeded as Prime Minister. Since 1724 he had been interested in the colonies as Secretary of State for the Southern Department. *DNB*, XV, 702–706.

[110] Matthew Hutton (1693–1758), seventy-eighth Archbishop of York, was a close friend of Pelham and Newcastle. *DNB*, X, 1358–59.

[111] John Ward was a bookseller and publisher in the Cornhill section of London. Although he dealt mostly in theological literature he published Governor Cadwallader Colden's *History of the Five Indian Nations* in 1755. Plomer, *Dictionary*, p. 256.

[112] Richard and Thomas Penn were the proprietors of Pennsylvania. Davies probably met Thomas. *DNB*, XV, 752–753.

[113] Friedrich Michael Ziegenhagen (1694–1776) served as Royal Lutheran Chaplain at St. James' Palace from 1722 until his death. He was greatly interested in foreign missions and in assimilating the Pennsylvania Germans into the British Empire. Franklin, *Papers*, III, 468n.

[114] Dr. David Jennings (1691–1762) conducted an academy in the home of Samuel Morton Savage in Wellclose Square. He regularly lectured to the Presbyterian congregation at Little St. Helen's. *DNB*, X, 764–765.

Man. He keeps an Academy of about 20 Students. He seemed to favour our Design: but was apprehensive that the Privileges granted in our Charter were so ample, that he feared, if it were known in Court, they would be curtailed; especially since the Government here would not allow the Colleges in New England the Power of conferring any Degree above A.M. tho' it was granted them by a Law of their own Province. Spent the Evening agreeably at one Mr. Gibson's in Comp. with Mr. and Mrs. De Berdt.

Fryd. Jan. 11. Visited Dr. Earle,[115] an old Presbyterian Minister of a good Character, but of a stern uncomplaisant Behaviour. He received us drily, and would not so much as read, or hear our Recommendations; but after all, cordially promised that he would enquire of Mr. Stennet or Mr. Chandler about the Affair of our Mission, and that if they approved of it, he would concur with them in proper Measures to promote it. Visited Mr. May,[116] a Presbyterian Minister, but he pled that he had no Influence, that his Congregation was much in debt, etc. etc. and absolutely refused to concur. Went to the N. England-Coffee-House; conversed with Mr. Partridge, the Agent for Pennsylvania.

Spent the Evening agreeably at Mr. Ward's, where I had a short Interview with one Mr. Thomson,[117] a young Minister. I forgot to mention, that in the Morning we waited on [*blank*] Belchier Esquire[118] Member of Parliament and gave him a Letter from Gov. Belcher. He treated us kindly and promised his Assistance.

[115] Jabez Earle (c. 1676–1768) was the Presbyterian minister to an Independent congregation in Hanover Street, Long Acre. In the course of his lifetime he had three wives, whom he referred to as "the world, the flesh, and the devil." *DNB*, VI, 319–320.

[116] Probably William May, who died the next year. He was co-pastor of the Presbyterian congregations in Bartholomew-Close and Great Alie Street. Wilson, *Dissenting Churches*, I, 397; III, 384.

[117] Josiah Thomson (1724–1806), an active worker for the dissenting interest, was minister to the Baptist congregation in Unicorn Yard. *Ibid.*, IV, 235–236.

[118] William Belchier of Epsom, Surrey, was a member of the Lombard Street banking firm of Belchier and Ironside. He served as a member of Parliament from Southwark between 1747 and 1761. Namier and Brooke, *Parliament*, II, 80–81.

Saturd. Jan. 12. Went to visit Mr. Streatfield,[119] but he was not at Home. Spent an Hour in agreeable Conversation with Mr. Gibbons, and another with Dr. Guise. Dined at Dr. Belchier's;[120] but was low-spirited, and so unsociable that I was ashamed of myself. There is such a Number of Ministers here, that it is rare for a Stranger to be envited to preach; and we have little Prospect of Usefulness that Way as yet. The Presbyterians particularly, being generally Armenians [*sic*] or Socinians, seem shy of us.

Sund. Jan. 13. Heard Mr. Lawson,[121] in the Morning on Joh. 1. 12. and he seemed to aim honestly at experimental Religion, and delivered himself extempore with Fluency, tho' not with a great Deal of Accuracy. In the Afternoon preached for Mr. Gibbons on these Words, "I will be your God, and ye shall be my People." I had a good Deal of Readiness and Vivacity, tho' alas! but little tender Solemnity. Spent the Evening in pleasing Conversation with dear Mr. Gibbons, who was much affected and pleased with my Sermon, and proposed to me to publish it with a Collection of his, which he intended for the Press. He shewed me a incomparable Elegy of a Minister upon his Daughter who died in her 11 Year, which was commonly ascribed to Mr. Howe; and indeed is worthy of him. He told me that Dr. Trapp composed an Epitaph for himself, in which were these 2 Lines addressed to his People,

"If in my Life I tri'd in vain to save,
Hear me, at last, O hear me from the Grave."

He read me a few Letters of one Mr. Thomas, whose Life[122] he has published; which were as excellent as any Thing I ever heard of the Kind.

[119] Probably George Streatfield, a leader of the Independent congregation meeting in Pinner's Hall. R. Tudor Jones, *Congregationalism in England, 1662–1962* (London, 1962), p. 180.
[120] John Belchier (1706–85) was a noted physician and surgeon of Guy's Hospital in London. *DNB*, II, 144.
[121] Robert Lawson (1721–71) was minister to the Scots Presbyterian congregation meeting in Founder's Hall, Lothbury. Wilson, *Dissenting Churches*, II, 498–503.
[122] No such biography is listed in either Wilson, *Dissenting Churches*, or the *Catalogue of the British Museum*.

Mr. Tennent preached for Mr. Gibbons A.M. and for Mr. Stennet P.M. I find a good Number of People are displeased with his using Notes.

⁓ *Mond. Jan. 14.* Visited Mr. Lawson, the Minister of the Scotch Church, and had a very friendly Reception. Spent an Hour with Mr. Whitefield. He thinks we have not taken the best Method in endeavouring to keep in with all Parties, but should "Come out boldly," as he expressed it; which would secure the Affections of the pious People from whom we might expect the most generous Contributions. Dined and spent the Evening very agreeably with Mr. Cruttenden, who is a most hearty Friend.

⁓ *Tuesd. Jan. 15.* Heard Dr. Guise in Pinner's-Hall preach a judicious, experimental Discourse on these Words,— "And the Peace of God shall keep your Hearts thro' Jesus Xt." It was well adapted to comfort the People of God; but the Languor of his Delivery, and his promiscuous, undistinguising [*sic*] Manner of Address, seem to take away its Energy and Pungency. Dined at Mr. Jones's,[123] a pious, judicious Xn. and spent the Evening there with Mr. Whitefield, Mr. Gibbons, etc. Mr. Tennent's Heart was opened for free religious Conversation, and we spent a few Hours very profitably. In sundry Places here, we hear of Mr. Hudson,[124] a good Minister that was lately here from Carolina and preached with uncommon Acceptance.

⁓ *Wednesd. Jan. 16.* Mr. Tennent went to visit Mr. Oswald, and I visited Mr. Pike[125] in Hoxton Square an independent Minister. He appears sound in Principle, and a great Friend to experimental Religion, and promised to promote the College. He has a penetrating, philosophical Genius, and is

[123] At the end of his diary, Davies kept a list of "Correspondents" for future reference. Among these he listed Edward Jones of Queen Street, Cheapside.
[124] Probably William Hutson, who had been minister to a Presbyterian congregation in Stoney Creek, South Carolina, since 1743. Weis, *The Colonial Churches and the Colonial Clergy*, pp. 31, 94.
[125] Samuel Pike (1717–73) was the Independent minister of the Three-Cranes Meeting House in Fruiterer's Alley, Thomas Street, where he also ran an academy for ministerial students. *DNB*, XV, 1175–76.

properly a Man of Books. He made me a Present of his Philosophia Sacra,[126] and his Sermon on "Charity and zeal united." [127] I spent about 2 Hours in learned and religious Conversation with him. I found his Method of examining any Doctrine is, to read over the whole Bible in the original, and having extracted all the Texts that refer to it, to form a Judgment upon the Whole. I next visited Dr. Lardner, the celebrated Author of "The Credibility of the Gospel-Hystory";[128] and I was really surprized at the Sight of him, as he differed so much from the Ideas which I had formed of so great a Man. He is a little, pert, old Gent. full of sprightly Conversation; but so deaf that he seems to hear Nothing at all. I was obliged to tell him my Mind and answer his Questions, in Writing; and he keeps Pen and Paper always on the Table for that Purpose. He treated me very kindly, and constrained me to dine with him. I next visited Dr. Grosvenor,[129] a venerable, humble and affectionate old Gent. who, under the Infirmities of old Age, has declined the Exercise of his Ministry for 2 or 3 years. I have hardly seen a Man that discovers so much Tenderness and Humility in his very Aspect. He offered me Baxter's or Williams's Works;[130] but I told him

[126] *Philosophia Sacra; or, the Principles of Natural Philosophy, Extracted from Divine Revelation. (The Explanation of the Copper-Plate)* (London, 1753).

[127] *Zeal and Charity United. A Sermon (on Phil. i. 27) Preached . . . Before the Society Concerned in the Education of Godly Young Men for the Ministry . . .* (London, 1753).

[128] Nathaniel Lardner (1684–1768) was a prolific writer and lecturer and the nonordained minister to the Presbyterian congregation in Poor Jewry Lane, Crutched Friars. He is considered to have been one of the founders of the tradition of critical research in early Christian literature. Through his scholarship he became intimate with many members of the high Anglican clergy and with biblical scholars throughout England, Europe, and America. *DNB*, XI, 589–592. There were several London editions of his *The Credibility of the Gospel History, or, The Facts Occasionally Mentioned in the New Testament Confirmed by Passages of Ancient Authors. . . .*

[129] Benjamin Grosvenor (1676–1758) was Presbyterian minister to a congregation meeting in Crosby Square from 1704 to 1748—the largest and richest dissenting congregation in London. In 1748 he retired to devote his time to reading. *DNB*, VIII, 721–723. Among other things, he published *Health, an Essay on Its Nature, Value, Uncertainty, Preservation and Best Improvement* (London, 1716) and *The Mourner: Or, the Afflicted Relieved* (London, 1731).

[130] Probably *The Practical Works of the Late Reverend and Pious Mr. Richard Baxter . . .* (4 vols.; London, 1707) and Daniel Williams, *Practical Discourses on Several Important Subjects . . . To Which Is Prefixed, Some Account of His Life and Character . . .* (5 vols.; London, 1738–50).

I could receive them only for the Use of the College, and in that View they would be very acceptable. He thereupon insisted that I would accept of 2 Pieces of his for my own private Use. viz. "The Mourner," and an Essay on Health. Spent the Evening in writing to my dear Brother Mr. Todd.

✒ *Thirsd. Jan. 17.* It being rainy, we stayed at Home preparing a petition in behalf of the College.

✒ *Fryd. Jan. 18.* We submitted our Petition to Mr. Chandler's Correction. He advised us to represent in it the Use of the College—"to keep a sense of Religion among the German Protestant Emigrants, settled in the British Plantations, to instruct their Children in the Principles of our common Christianity, and to instruct them in the Knowledge of the English Language, that they may be incorporated with the rest of his Majesty's Subjects." Mr. T. approved of the Addition; but I could not help scrupling it, because the College is not immediately intended to teach the English Language. However, I submitted.

✒ *Sat. Jan. 19.* Visited Dr. Avery.[131] He is an amiable Gent. very affable, and of a soft, ready Address; and seems qualified by divine Providence designedly to act for the Dissenters in Court. He said he tho't it his Duty, as he is now in the Confines of another World, to withdraw from the public Management of their Affairs, that they might learn to manage without him, before he go off the Stage. He seemed diffident about our success in our Mission, on account of the prodigious Expenses lying upon the Dissenters on various Accounts.

Went to St. Dunstan's Coffee-House, where we had some friendly Conversation with Mr. Smith,[132] a young Clergyman of

[131] Benjamin Avery (d. 1764) was a prominent London physician of Guy's Hospital who had previously served as pastor of a Presbyterian congregation in Bartholomew Close. He was very active in the dissenting cause and had contributed, along with Simon Brown, Benjamin Grosvenor, Samuel Wright, John Evans, Jabez Earle, Moses Lowman, and Nathaniel Lardner, to the "Bagwell Papers," a collection of essays on political and theological liberalism published between 1716 and 1719. *DNB,* I, 746–747.

[132] William Smith, provost of the Philadelphia Academy, was in London seeking support for a college in New York City. He published *A Poem on Visiting the Academy of Philadelphia, June, 1753* (Philadelphia, 1753). Bridenbaugh, *Mitre and Sceptre,* pp. 152–153.

the established Church, the Author of the Poem upon visiting the Philadelphia Academy. He did not appear so great an Enemy to our Design, as we expected.

At 2 o'Clock we were sent for by a Company of Lords and Gent. who have the Disposal of the Money lately given by the King for the Support of English Schools among the Germans in Pennsylvania. Mr. Chandler, who is the Company's Secretary, introduced our Affair, and our Petition was read. There was no Time to consider it, and it was deferred 'till their next Meeting. For my Part, I have no Hope of Success.

Spent a Part of the Night in great Perplexity, not knowing what to preach on to-morrow.

ᴥᷢ *Sund. Jan. 20.* Preached for Mr. Prior,[133] a Presbyterian Minister on Heb. 12. 14. an innaccurate, blundering Discourse; and alas! I had no sense of my Subject.

Heard Mr. Tennent P.M. preach an honest, plain Sermon; and while I was pleased with its Simplicity, I was uneasy least its Bluntness might be offensive. Dined at Capt. Sibson's with Mr. Prior, etc. Went in the Evening and heard Mr. Prior preach at Salter's-Hall, to a large Auditory (a thing rarely seen here) on "My Yoke is easy, etc." He is by far the best Orator I have heard in London; and excepting a few arminian Sentiments, his Sermon was truly excellent. He is an affable, affectionate Gent. and is the likest Man to Mr. Pemberton both in Conversation and in the Pulpit that I have seen. Returned home melancholy and low-Spirited from a Review of my poor Day's Work, and sought Relief in Conversation with dear Mr. Tennent. I am afraid I shall do little Good in this City. The Congregations are so small, that it is enough to damp one's Zeal in preaching to them.

ᴥᷢ *Mond. Jan. 21.* Spent most of the Day in revising and transcribing a Petition in behalf of the College; and we resolved to soften the Terms in the Clause about the German Protestants. Spent the Evening at Mr. Gibbons's, where Mr. Lluellin[134] and

---

[133] William Prior was pastor of the Presbyterian congregation of Great Alie Street, Goodman's Fields. Wilson, *Dissenting Churches,* II, 5.

[134] Possibly Thomas Llewellin, who was described as "Minister of the Gospel in London" when he was awarded an M.A. by Aberdeen in 1754. Peter John Anderson, ed., *Roll of Alumni in Arts of the University and King's College of Aberdeen, 1596–1860* (Aberdeen, 1900), p. 194.

Mr. Stennet Junior were met for improving Conversation; and I find it is their Method to meet every Monday Night.

⁌ *Tuesd. Jan. 22.* We went to Mr. Chandler's, with a Design to submit our Petition to his Correction. We found Mr. Slaughter[135] and Mr. Smith there. When we introduced the Conversation about the Germans, and observed that our College would be a happy Expedient to unite the Calvinists among them with the English Presbyterians; Mr. Smith replied that an Union would not be desirable; for a Separation would keep up the Ballance of Power. Mr. Tennent answered, that Union in a good Thing is always desirable. Upon which Mr. Chandler says, "I have seen a very extraordinary Sermon against Union," and he immediately reached to Mr. Tennent his Notingham-Sermon.[136] It threw us both into Confusion, and gave such a Damp to my Spirits as bro't me in Mind of my Mortifications in the General-Court in Virginia.[137] Mr. Tennent went about to vindicate himself, and when I had recovered from my Consternation, I put in a Word. But all had no Effect. We found that Sermon and the Examination of Mr. Tennent's Answer to the Protest, had been put into Mr. Chandler's Hands; and he had formed his Judgment so precipitantly from a partial View of the Case, that he told us "He would do Nothing for us." Mr. Smith alleged—that the College was a Party-Design,—that tho' the Charter was catholic, yet so many of the Trustees were Presbyterians, that they would manage Matters with arbitrary Partiality—that the Trustees in New-York City complained that there were not more Trustees of other Denominations, etc. etc.

We went away perplexed, and heard an excellent Sermon in

[135] This was probably the same Michael Schlatter Davies had met in Philadelphia before he sailed. Schlatter was in Europe at this time seeking teachers for the German schools in Pennsylvania. *DAB,* XVI, 435–436.

[136] *The Danger of an Unconverted Ministry, Considered in a Sermon on Mark iv. 34. Preached at Nottingham, in Pennsylvania, March 8. anno. 1739, 40* . . . (Philadelphia, 1740). This sermon had helped to precipitate the Presbyterian schism of 1741, which was healed in 1758. *Records,* pp. 258–262, 285.

[137] Between 1748 and 1753 Davies was forced to make many appearances in court in Williamsburg. He was seeking licenses for new meetinghouses and trying to prevent the revocation of existing licenses. In these cases he was usually opposed by Peyton Randolph. A possibly apochryphal account of these encounters can be found in "Memoir," p. 118.

Pinner's-Hall by Mr. Rawlins[138] on a Subject very seasonable to us, "He will regard the Prayer of the Destitute, etc." Went to the Amsterdam Coffee-House, where the Ministers meet, and afterwards dined at Mr. Ward's. Returned Home, and prayed together for Direction, and consulted what Measures we should take to remove Mr. Chandler's Prejudices. The Lord direct us in this difficult Affair! I am shocked to think of the inveterate Malignity of the Synod of Philad. who have sent their Accusations after Mr. Tennent so far.

෴ *Wednesd. Jan. 23.* Waited on Mr. Chandler to remove his Prejudices. His turning against us seems to have so threatening an Aspect upon our Mission, that it kept me awake part of last Night, and mingled with my anxious Dreams. Mr. Tennent made honest humble Concessions with regard to the Notingham Sermon, as—that it was written in the Heat of his Spirit, when he apprehended a remarkable Work of God was opposed by a Set of Ministers—that Some of the Sentiments were not agreeable to his present Opinion—that he had painted sundry Things in too strong Colours—and he pled—that it was now 13 Years ago and that since he had used all his Influence to promote Union between the Synods; of which he produced his Irenicum,[139] as a Witness—that if the Sermon was faulty, it was but the Fault of one Man, and should not be charged upon the whole Body, etc. We shewed him the Minutes of our Synod, etc. to give him a View of the State of the Debate. As he disapproves of all Subscriptions of Tests of Orthodoxy, he disapproved of our adopting Act. I exerted all my Powers of pathetic Address to give him a moving Representation of the melancholy Case of the Churches under

---

[138] Richard Rawlin (1687–1757) was a London schoolmaster and minister to an Independent congregation in Fetter Lane. *DNB*, XVI, 768.

[139] *Irenicum Ecclesiasticum, or a Humble Impartial Essay upon the Place of Jerusalem, Wherein the Analogy Between Jerusalem and the Visible Church Is in Some Instances Briefly Hinted. The Nature, the Order, the Union, of the Visible Church, Together with Her Terms of Communion, Are Particularly Considered, and Their Excellency Opened. Moreover the Following Important Points Are Largely Explained. 1. What Is to Be Understood by the Peace of Jerusalem. 2. What by Praying for the Peace of Jerusalem. 3. How, and Why We Should Pray for Its Peace and Prosperity. Under the Aforesaid General Heads, the Following Particulars Are Discuss'd, viz. The Nature, Kinds, Hindrances, Means, and Motives of Peace and Union, Together with an Answer to Objections. Also a Prefatory Address to the Synods of New-York and Philadelphia* (Philadelphia, 1749).

our Care—of the dreadful Consequences of a disappointment in our Mission—of the Hardships we had exposed ourselves to, in prosecuting it, etc. Upon the whole, he seemed to be something softened, and promised that he would not use his Influence to blast our Design; but would himself contribute towards it.

He invited me to preach for him next Sund. come Se'ennight; which I did not expect.

Waited upon Dr. Lawrence,[140] a Presbyterian Minister who treated us with great Freedom and Friendship. He advised us to prepare 2 Petitions, one for the Presbyterians, and one for the Independents; for the Animosities among some of them were so strong that the very Sight of the Names of one Party would hinder the other from Subscribing; and the Independents would cry it was a Presbyterian Project, when they saw the Petition recommended by Presbyterians, and vice versa.

Dined with good old Mr. Price, Dr. Watt's former Colleague, in Company with Mr. Savage his Assistant. He is a humble affectionate Gent. and seemed to Have our Mission at Heart; but apprehended we should have little Success here at present, because the Collections for their own Funds are just at Hand. We requested him to recommend our Petition; but he declined it at the Time. From the present View of Things, I think if we can but clear our Expences, we shall be well off.

Went in the Evening to Mr. Bradbury's. He is still sprightly and gay, and sings a Tune now and then, tho' so very aged. He subscribed a Recommendation of the Petition, and seemed peculiarly concerned for its Success.

◄§ *Thirsd. Jan. 24.* Went to Dr. Guyse, Dr. Lardner, Dr. Benson,[141] and Mr. Prior, to get our Petition recommended; and they all complied. Dr. Guyse is a steady, deliberate Gent. and now appears more in our Interest, than upon our first Application. Dr. Benson talked in a sneering Manner of the Account of the Conversions in Northampton N. Eng. published here by Dr. Watts and Dr. Guyse. He is a Gent. of great Abilities, but counted a Socinian. Mr. Prior is a sociable sprightly generous

[140] Samuel Lawrence (1693–1760) was pastor of a Presbyterian congregation in Monkwell Street. Wilson, *Dissenting Churches,* III, 208–209.

[141] George Benson (1699–1762) was co-pastor, with Nathaniel Lardner, of the Presbyterian congregation in Poor Jewry Lane, Crutched Friars. *DNB,* II, 255–257.

Gent. of latitudinarian Principles, but a hearty Friend to every laudable Institution. He unenvited subscribed 10 Guineas to the College. We waited also on Mr. Hall; but he declined subscribing then, to make Way for his Seniors. He is an Israelite, and bitterly laments the Declesion of the Times. In the Evening I wrote to Mr. Wright, etc. but alas! I am so hurried, that I have no Time for Correspondence.

Fryd. Jan 25. Went with much Hesitation to Mr. Chandler's; and he, to our agreeable Surprize, recommended our Petition. This will have a happy Effect, not only as his Name will have Influence with Many, but as it will bind him to Secresy with regard to the Calumnies spread about Mr. Tennent for he cannot with a good Face give injurious Representations of a Design which himself has recommended.

We went next to Mr. Stennet's, and he also subscribed. But Mr. Newman,[142] a Presbyterian Minister chuse to have more Time to consider. Dr. Lawrence, one of the few Calvinistic Presbyterians, did also chearfully subscribe; and so did Mr. Rawlins, a good old Independent Minister, whom we waited upon in the Evening. Dined with Mr. Bradbury, who has been in the Ministry about 57 Years. He read us some Letters which past between Mr. Whitefield and him an. 1741; occasioned by Mr. Wh. reproving him in a Letter for singing a Song in a Tavern in a large Company in Praise of old English Beef. The old Gent. sung it to us, and we found it was partly composed by himself, in the high-flying Days of Q. Anne. He is a man of singular Turn, which would be offensive to the greatest Number of serious People. But for my Part, I could say,

> I knew 'twas his peculiar Whim,
> Nor took it ill—as come from him.

Saturd. Jan. 26. Spent the Morning in writing Letters; and went to Newington to dine with Mr. Bowles,[143] who treated us very kindly, and gave me 5 Guineas for the College.

[142] Thomas Newman was minister to a Presbyterian congregation in Carter Lane, Doctor's Commons. Wilson, *Dissenting Churches*, II, 147–153.

[143] Possibly Thomas Bowles, "the famous print seller," his brother and partner, John Bowles, Jr., or John's son Carrington Bowles, a later partner in the firm. Plomer, *Dictionary*, pp. 31–32, 255–256.

᠎᠎ *Sund. Jan. 27.* Preached for Mr. Price A.M. in Berry-Street; and when I entered the Pulpit, it filled me with Reverence to reflect that I stood in the Place where Mr. Clerkson, Dr. Owen,[144] Dr. Watts, etc. had once officiated. My Subject was Jer. 31. 18, 19, 20. and I was favoured with some Freedom. Blessed, be God, I have not been disturbed with the Fear of Man, since I have been in this City. Dined with good old Mr. Price, who treated me with all the tender Affection of a Father.

Preached P.M. in the Scotch Church in Founder's-Hall, where Mr. Lawson is Minister, on Rev. 1. 7. I was encouraged to see a crowded Auditory, of Persons from various Congregations; and tho' I had not much Solemnity, was enabled to speak gracefully and oratorically. Drunk Tea at Mr. Mauduit's; who is a very candid, serious Man, tho' a Friend and occasional Hearer of Dr. Benson. He gave me some Encouragement that Something would be done in Favour of the poor Dissenters in Virginia. Heard Mr. Furnace[145] in the Even, on the Case of Felix, an ingenius Discourse.

᠎᠎ *Mond. Jan. 28.* Waited on good Mr. Pike, and he readily subscribed our Petition; but had it much at Heart, that only pious Youth should be admitted to Learning for the Ministry; a Method that has been pursued here for some Years, by the Kings-Head Society.[146] He told us, that he believed all that would be given by his Friends must be appropriated for this Purpose; and that they would give upon no other Footing. The venerable Dr. Grosvenor also signed our Petition. Dined at Dr. Lawrence's, an open-hearted, candid Gent. and went thence to Mr. Rawlin's, a judicious, experimental Divine, who also signed, and promised that what could be got among his Friends, he would take the Trouble of collecting himself. He married a good Fortune, but a bad Wife; and now, since her Death, he has a considerable Estate, and keeps his Coach. Mr.

[144] David Clarkson (1622–86) was pastor from 1682 until 1685, John Owen (1616–83) from 1673 until his death. Wilson, *Dissenting Churches*, I, 260–288.
[145] Probably Philip Furneaux (1726–83), minister to an Independent congregation in Clapham. *DNB*, VII, 770–772.
[146] The King's Head Society had been founded in 1730 by William Coward, a prominent London merchant, to strengthen evangelism by sponsoring the education of ministerial candidates. Jones, *Congregationalism in England: 1662–1962,* pp. 140, 176.

Lawson not only subscribed, but gave us 4 Guine[as]. Visited Mr. King,[147] a talkative Minister who am[id] all his pretended Friendship, discouraged us.

&§ *Tuesd. Jan. 29.* Went in the Morning to Dr. Jennings, a courteous, sociable Gent. who keeps an Academy. He signed the Petition, and envited me to preach for him. Went thence to Salters-Hall, and heard Dr. Earle, the old Minister in London, on these Words, "An Inheritance among them that are sanctified thro' Faith in me." He preached extempore, with much Accuracy and Judgment and what he said had a Tendency to do good. I waited on him and Mr. Barker,[148] a celebrated Minister in the Vestry Room; and tho' the old Gent. treated me, as he does every Body else, with his natural Sternness, he and Mr. Barker readily signed the Petition. Went from thence to Hamlin's Coffee-House, where the Presbyterian Ministers meet on Tuesday; and there Dr. Allen[149] and Dr. Benson subscribed. Dr. Benson did it with this Sneer, "That he was no Friend to Subscriptions," meaning of Tests of Orthodoxy. He asked me whether an Arminian, an Arian or Socinian would be admitted into our College. The Reason of his Enquiry was, that the Charter says "that Persons of all *Denominations* shall be admitted to equal Advantages of Education;" and he apprehended that an Arminian, etc. was not said to be of any particular Denomination. Mr. Tennent went among the honest Independents at the Amsterdam Coffee-House; and got sundry Names. Dined at Mr. Holmes's,[150] a courteous Gent. of Mr. Newman's Congregation, in Company with dear Mr. Gibbons, a great Grandson of Oliver Cromwell's, etc. I was much pained with a Wind Cholic. In the Evening went to the Amsterdam Coffee-House, where the Independent Ministers meet for friendly Conversation, and to consult about the Affairs of the Churches;

[147] William King (1701–69) was minister to an Independent congregation in Hare Court. Wilson, *Dissenting Churches*, III, 299–302.
[148] John Barker (1682–1762) was the regular pastor and "Morning Preacher" of the Presbyterian congregation meeting in Salter's Hall. *DNB*, I, 1122–23.
[149] John Allen (1701–74), a practicing physician, was minister to the Presbyterian congregation in New Broad Street, Petty France, and co-pastor of the one in Hanover Street, Long Acre. Wilson, *Dissenting Churches*, II, 225–227.
[150] Probably Thomas Holmes of Newgate Street, a prominent London hosier active among the dissenters, whom Davies listed among his "Correspondents." *Ibid.*, I, 187–188.

for they have no other Associations; as the Presbyterians have no other Presbyteries. Indeed there seems to be no Government exercised jointly among either of them. The English Presbyterians have no Elders, nor Judicatures of any Kind; and seem to me to agree in but a very few Particulars with the Church of Scotland. I find the Calvinistic Presbyterians as well as the Baptists choose to frequent the Independent Coffee-House, rather than associate with their Presbyterian Brethren of Arminian or Socinian Sentiments at Hamlin's. Mr. Halford [151] and Mr. Towle[152] subscribed our Petition; and the rest present, particularly Dr. Guyse, appeared hearty in our Interest.

ᐗᔥ *Wed. Jan. 30.* We waited upon Dr. Gill,[153] the celebrated Baptist Minister. He is a serious, grave little Man, and looks young and hearty, tho' I suppose near 60. He signed our Petition, tho' he modestly pleaded that his Name would be of little Service, and that the Baptists in general were unhappily ignorant of the Importance of Learning. Went thence to Mr. Price, and got his Subscription. At 12 o'Clock, waited on the Committee of which Dr. Avery is Chairman. We laid before them our Credentials, and requested them to recommend our Petition; but they apprehended it would be improper. They cordially gave us their best Advice. They had no time to consider the Case of the oppressed Dissenters in Virginia; but promised it should be done at their next Meeting. There were 14 present. Spent the Evening in writing Letters: and at Night visited Mr. Savage, who is famed for his Liberality to all pious Undertakings. I found the good Man was cooled towards us, because we associated with the Rich and Great, and Persons of all Denominations promiscuously; and did not keep a more public Intercourse with Mr. Whitefield, and employ some House to preach in frequently. He seemed also insensible of the Necessity of Learning in a Minister; and was doubtful whether he would give any Thing towards our College.

[151] John Halford was pastor of the Independent congregation in Back Street, Horslydown. *Ibid.*, IV, 268–269.
[152] Thomas Towle (1724–1806) was minister to an Independent congregation in Rope Maker's Alley. *Ibid.*, II, 547–554.
[153] John Gill (1697–1771), a popular lecturer and writer, served a Baptist congregation in Horslydown, Southwark. *DNB*, VII, 1234.

≈§ Thursd. Jan. 31. Visited Mr. Richardson,[154] an Independent Minister and Mr. Walker, Tutor of the Oriental Languages in Dr. Marriot's Academy,[155] who readily signed our Petition.

Mr. Tennent went to Mr. Denham;[156] but had no Admission. Dined at Mr. Hall's, and was cheared and edified with his facetious and yet heavenly Conversation.

≈§ Fryd. Feb. 1. Took a Walk to Westminster, to get the Names of the Scotch Ministers to our Petition; but could find none at Home, but Mr. Crookshank[157] and Mr. Patrick,[158] who readily signed. The former was indisposed, and I had not much Conversation with him; but he appears an affectionate humble Man. Mr. Patrick appears a serious Man, and deeply lamented the Declension of Religion in London, among the Dissenters; and said that the Revivals of Religion which they had, were chiefly in the Church of Eng. by Means of Mr. Whitefield, etc. In my Return, I took a Walk thro' St. James's Park, and find it contains a vast Quantity of Land.

≈§ Saturd. Feb. 2. Went to Westminster, and got Mr. Kippies[159] and Mr. Oswald [160] to sign the Petition. Mr. Kippies

[154] John Richardson was minister to an Independent congregation in Peach-Alley, Lime Street. Wilson, *Dissenting Churches*, I, 250.

[155] Zephaniah Marryat (1684–1754), supervisor of an academy for the King's Head Society from 1743 until his death, was also pastor of an Independent congregation in Deadman's Place. *Ibid.*, IV, 199–203. John Walker had tutored in the academy since 1735 and would continue to do so when it was moved after Marryat's death. Jones, *Congregationalism in England; 1662–1962*, p. 176.

[156] Possibly John Denham, who was pastor of a Presbyterian congregation meeting in Great Alie Street, Goodman's Fields, about this time. Wilson, *Dissenting Churches*, I, 397.

[157] William Crookshank (c. 1690–1769), minister to a Scottish Presbyterian congregation in Swallow Street, was well known as a historian of the Church of Scotland. *Ibid.*, IV, 46–48.

[158] John Patrick (c. 1706–91) was minister to the Scottish Presbyterian congregation in Lisle Street. *Ibid.*, 35–36.

[159] Andrew Kippie (1725–95) was pastor of a Presbyterian congregation in Princes Street, Westminster. *DNB*, XI, 195–197.

[160] Probably Thomas Oswald (1722–87), pastor of a Scottish Presbyterian congregation in Crown Court. *FES*, VII, 468. But perhaps James Oswald, member of Parliament for Kirkaldy Burghs in Scotland and a member of the Board of Trade. *DNB*, XIV, 1220.

was a Pupil of Dr. Doddridge's, and is a very modest, affectionate Youth. He succeeds the late Dr. Hugh's.[161] Mr. Oswald seems to be a devout, humble Man. He is acquainted with Mr. Erskine,[162] Mr. McLaurin,[163] and sundry good Ministers in Scotland, his native Country. Dined at good Dr. Guyse's, in Company with his Son,[164] who is also a Minister, and a sociable, pleasant Companion. Went thence to Mr. Burrough's,[165] an Arminian Baptist, with whom the late Dr. Foster[166] was Colleague for some Time. Spent the Evening with Mr. Edmund Calamy,[167] the 4th of that Name. He is a sensible, pleasant Gent. but has embibed the modish Divinity. He has declined the Exercise of his Ministry for about 3 years, by Reason of Indisposition.

&§ *Sund. Feb. 3.* Preached A.M. for Mr. Crookshank on Luke. 13. 24. with considerable Freedom, and the Assembly appeared attentive and some of them affected. Preached P.M. in the old Jewry for Mr. Chandler, on Luke. 2. 34. to a very brilliant Assembly. But a Blunder I made in mentioning the Text, threw me into Confusion, which I did not recover thro' the Whole Discourse; and I felt more of the Fear of Man than since I have been in this City. Drunk Tea with Mr. Chandler at one Mr. Adair's; but was so mortified with the Review of my Sermon, that I had no Heart for Conversation; and I returned home exceedingly dejected. I was afraid that my poor Manage-

[161] Obadiah Hughes (1695–1751) had been minister to the Presbyterian congregation in Princes Street from 1743 until his death. *DNB*, X, 185–186.

[162] John Erskine (1721–1803) was one of the leaders of the evangelical movement within the Church of Scotland. He was a friend of George Whitefield and a correspondent of Jonathan Edwards. At this time he was minister in Culross but was called to an Edinburgh church in 1758. *DNB*, VI, 850–851.

[163] John Maclaurin (1693–1754) was pastor of the Northwest parish in Glasgow, active in philanthropic movements among the highlanders, and a founder of the Glasgow Hospital. *DNB*, XII, 642.

[164] William Guyse was assistant to his father at the Independent church in New Broad Street. *DNB*, VIII, 837.

[165] Joseph Burroughs (1685–1761) was an extremely popular Baptist preacher at the Barbican Chapel. *DNB*, III, 447.

[166] James Foster (1697–1753) had been co-pastor at the Barbican Chapel from 1724 until his death and minister to an Independent congregation meeting in Pinner's Hall from 1744 until his death. *DNB*, VII, 494–495.

[167] Edmund Calamy (c. 1697–1755) had retired from the ministry in 1749 but continued active in the dissenting cause. *DNB*, III, 687.

ment would bring Disgrace upon Religion, and the Affair of our Mission. In short, I have not had so melancholy an Evening for a long Time. The Lord help me!

⚓ *Mond. Feb. 4.* Visited Mr. Denham, a Presbyterian Minister but he was so afflicted with the Gout, that he could not give me Audience; but put me off till next Mond. Went thence to Mr. Prior's, and spent an Hour with him in free Conversation. He is an amiable, candid, and generous Gent. He gave me 10 Guineas for the College; and he is a learned ingenious man, I think the Trustees should compliment him with the Degree of A.M. as a Reward to his Merit and Generosity. He made me a Present of 3 Discourses of his, one of which I heard him deliver at Salter's-Hall; and I presented him with one of mine, preached before the Presbytery. Dined with Mr. Muir,[168] a Scotch Minister settled in an Independent Congregation, a very affectionate Man, and he seems to have a serious Sense of Religion. Went to Mr. Mitchel's,[169] who is also a Scotch Minister of an Independent Congregation but not so sociable as the former to me. They both signed the Petition. Spent a social Hour very pleasantly with Dr. Jennings, who, tho' a great Student, and an universal Scholar, has Nothing of the stiff Pedant in his Behaviour. Spent a few Minutes with good Mr. Hitchin,[170] who is famous for a zealous, experimental Preacher, and hearty Friend to Mr. White-field. He chearfully signed the Petition, and promised his In-fluence. Spent the Evening most agreeably at Mr. Towle's, an ingenious young Minister of the Independent Persuasion. We interchanged our Tho'ts on sundry Subjects, and particularly I communicated to him my Tho'ts on the Divine Government as adapted to the Nature of Man, the Beauty of rectoral Justice, and various Methods which God has wisely taken to display it etc. He advised me to digest my Tho'ts upon these Subjects, and publish them because they were new. I find, to my Surprize, that my Poems,[171] and Sermon before the Presbytery[172] are very ac-

---

[168] Probably David Muir, who was minister to a Scottish Presbyterian church in Wapping at this time. *FES*, VII, 501.

[169] No Mitchel is mentioned in either Wilson, *Dissenting Churches*, or in *FES*.

[170] Probably Edward Hitchin, minister to an Independent congregation in White Row, Spitalfields. Wilson, *Dissenting Churches*, III, 454.

[171] *Miscellaneous Poems, Chiefly on Divine Subjects. In Two Books. Pub-*

ceptable to sundry here; and I have been pressed by some to let them pass an Edition here; but I am afraid of every Thing that might be looked upon as ostentatious in my present Circumstances. Mr. Towle proposed to keep a Correspondence with me for the future; a Proposal very acceptable to me.

Tuesd. Feb. 5. Heard good Mr. Rawlins at Pinner's-Hall, on his former Text, "He will regard the Prayer of the destitute etc." and tho' his Delivery is heavy I have heard very few preach so solid, judicious, and experimental a Discourse. Went among the Independent Ministers at the Amsterdam Coffee-House, and obtained 3 Names more to our Petition, viz. Dr. Milner,[173] Mr. Thomson, and Mr. Hayward.[174] Dined at one Mr. Charles Buckston's, with Mr. Gibbons; who treated me very kindly, and gave me 5 Guineas for the College, without Solicitation.

We have now got 60 Names to our Petition; which I think quite sufficient; but Mr. Tennent thinks we should get the Recommendation of the principal Ministers, round about the City, as well as in it. But this, I am afraid will take up so much Time, that we cannot finish our Applications for private Contributions, before we are obliged to set out for Scotland. I think it is a remarkable Smile of Providence, that we have had so much Success in getting the Ministers of the City to recommend our Petition, as it will have Weight not only here, but with the General Assembly. Spent a Part of the Evening at Mr. Mauduit's, who had sent for me to advise us to draw up a more particular Account of the College, and the Sum necessary to carry it to Maturity, that People might regulate their Donations accordingly.

---

lished for the *Religious Entertainment of Christians in General* (Williamsburg, 1752). There was never an English edition.

[172] Prior to this time, Davies had published two of his sermons delivered before the Newcastle Presbytery: *A Sermon on Man's Primitive State; and the First Covenant. Delivered Before the Reverend Presbytery of New-Castle, April 13th 1748* (Philadelphia, 1748), and *A Sermon Preached Before the Reverend Presbytery of New-Castle, October 11. 1752 . . . Published at the Desire of the Presbytery and the Congregation* (Philadelphia, 1753).

[173] John Milner conducted a school in Peckham. Wilson, *Dissenting Churches*, IV, 370.

[174] Samuel Hayward (1718–57) was minister to an Independent congregation in Silver Street. *Ibid.*, III, 106–111.

Wednes. Feb. 6. Went to Mr. Stennet's, who went with us to introduce us to the Duke of Argyle,[175] to deliver Governor Belcher's Letter. We found 8 or 10 Gent. and Noblemen waiting in his Grace's Levee. His Grace took us into his Library; a spacious, elegant Room, about 40 Feet long, and 20 broad; furnished all round with Books, Philosophical Instruments, Curiosities, etc. His Grace told us, after reading the Letter, that as the College related to the Plantations, we ought first to apply to the Lords of Trade and Plantations; and if they approved of it, he would willingly countenance it, both here and in Scotland. He advised up to apply to Lord Halifax, or Lord Duplin;[176] and Mr. Stennet accordingly, went to the latter, (while we staid at a Coffee-House), and shewed him our Instructions from the Trustees, and the Petition we had drawn up. Mr. Stennet told him he applied to his Lordship *in Confidence;* and his Lordship assured him he would do Nothing to injure us. He thereupon told him, we had our Charter only from a Governour; and asked him whether he tho't it would be deemed valid in Court. His Lordship replied that he doubted it; but he would soon satisfie himself, by enquiring into the Extent of the Governour's Commission. And in Case it appeared valid, he would advise us to lay the Matter before the Abp. of Cant.[177] and he himself would go with Mr. Stennet to Mr. Pelham in our Favour, and so introduce the Matter in Court. For my Part, I am afraid of all Applications to that Quarter, lest we lose our Charter, and stir up an Opposition; and it is against my Mind that the Matter has been carried so far. Dined at Mr. Stennet's, who gave us 5 Guineas for the College. Went home anxious about the Fate of an Application to the Lords of Trade, and to the Court.

[175] Archibald Campbell (1682–1761), third Duke of Argyll, was a representative peer, member of the Privy Council, Lord Register and Keeper of the Great Seal of Scotland, and manager of Scottish affairs in the Walpole cabinet. *DNB*, III, 793–794.

[176] Thomas Hay (1710–87), ninth Earl of Kinnoull and Viscount Duplin, was a member of Parliament from the borough of Cambridge, Lord of the Treasury, member of the Board of Trade, and a noted classical scholar. He was closely associated with Walpole, Pelham, and Newcastle. *DNB*, IX, 275–276.

[177] Thomas Herring, eighty-fourth Archbishop of Canterbury, was widely recognized as friendly to the dissenters and often attended their sermons. Sidney L. Ollard, *A Dictionary of English Church History* (London, 1912), p. 95.

~§ *Saturd. Feb. 9.* My Hurries are so uninterrupted, that I cannot every Day keep an Account of my Proceedings. Providence has smiled upon our Undertaking so far, that we have about 80 Guineas promised, 20 of which are from the Reverend Mr. Rawlin, who has a large Estate without Children, and a Heart proportionally generous.

~§ *Sund. Feb. 10.* Preached in a vacant, Baptist Congregation who formerly had one Mr. Bently[178] for their Minister. They have generally, as I am informed, embibed some Antinomian Notions, particularly that no Offers of Grace should be made to the Unconverted, because they are dead in Sin, and incapable to receive them. I preached before and afternoon on Isai. 45. 22. with some Freedom; but as my Sermon was full of Exhortations to Sinners to look to Xt. I suppose it did not well suit the Taste of the People. Dined with good Mr. Savage, who used a very inoffensive Freedom in making Remarks upon my Sermon, which he seemed to think, was not sufficiently evangelical. Preached in the Evening at Shakespeare Walk, to a very crowded Auditory on Zech. 7. 11, 12. and had unusual Freedom, tho' my Body was much exhausted, and my Voice broke by a bad Cough, with which I have been afflicted ever since I left home. My Subject was terrible, and I was afraid it might be offensive; but the uncommon Security of this Place requires an Alarm. The People seemed eagerly attentive; and there appeared a greater Prospect of Success than I have had in this City. This Lecture is attended alternately by the Ministers of the Town; and is intended to support a Charity-School of 30 Children. I addressed myself to the little Creatures, and they seemed very attentive.

~§ *Mond. Feb. 11.* Visited Mr. Mill, and delivered Mr. Donald's Letter. He, and his Partner, Mr. Oswald, advised us to apply to the Lord's of Trade to encourage our Embassy. But I am afraid of the Consequence. Went to Mr. Denham,[179] a Presbyterian Minister and had a long and difficult Dispute with

[178] This was probably the Baptist congregation in Crispin Street, Spitalfields, to which William Bently had formerly ministered. Wilson, *Dissenting Churches*, IV, 408.

[179] Probably John Denham of Great Alie Street. *Ibid.*, I, 397.

him, about the Importance and Necessity of our College, the
Validity of the Charter without the Royal Approbation, etc.
which he managed with great Dexterity. It was my Happiness
to have my Tho'ts ready, and I made such a Defence, as silenced
him. His Name is of great Importance, and I was solicitous to
obtain it to our Petition; but had lost all hope of it, when, to my
agreeable Surprize, he subscribed. Visited Dr. Jennings, who took
me to his Academy, and shewed me all his philosophical Curiosities, Two Orrerys, an Experiment to shew that all the Colours of
the Rainbow blended, form a White, a Mushroom etc. petrified,
2 or 3 Testaments in MS. before the Art of Printing, which were
elegantly written; sundry Stones in the Shape of a quoiled Snake,
Shells, Minerals, Æolus's Harp, a Plica pilonica, etc. etc. He has
a most curious, philosophical Turn, and is very sociable and
communicative. He promised 5 Guineas at least towards the
College. Spent the Evening agreeably with Mr. Savage, Dr.
Watts's Successor, and Sub-Tutor with Dr. Jennings.

  Tuesd. Feb. 12. Went to Salter's Hall, and heard the
great Mr. Barker,[180] on these Words, "Not as tho' I had already
attained etc." His Sermon was very accurate and judicious, and
in the Calvinistic Strain. I find, that tho' real Religion, and the
Principles of the Reformation are better retained among the
Independents, and tho' there be a considerable Number of
learned and judicious Ministers among them, yet the greatest
Number of learned and polite Preachers are among the Presbyterians and sundry of them deserve that Character, who arminian-
ize and socinianize very much.

  Went to the Presbyterian Coffee-House, as it is called, and
got Mr. Furneaux's Name to the Petition. Dined with my serious
Friend Mr. Mauduit, who promised 5 Guineas to the College.
Had a long Conversation with Samuel Dicker Esquire[181] a
notorious Deist.

 [180] John Barker (1682–1762), Presbyterian minister to a congregation in
Mare Street, Hackney, was one of the regular lecturers at Salter's Hall. *DNB*,
I, 1122–23.
 [181] Possibly Samuel Dicker of Walton-on-Thames, member of Parliament
for Plymouth and formerly a prosperous West Indian planter. He was
currently associated with a large Bristol mercantile establishment. Namier
and Brooke, *Parliament*, II, 320.

✌❦ *Wednesd. Feb. 13.* Waited on Mr. Towle, who gave us 5 Guineas; but it rained so much, that we staid at Home P.M.; and I wrote a few Letters to my Friends in Hanover. That dear Place contains all that is dearest to me in the World, my Congregation, my Friends, my Parents, my Children, and especially my dearest Chara. Alas! my Heart breaks, at the Tho't. Heard Mr. Whitefield in the Evening.

✌❦ *Thirsd. Feb. 14.* Waited on Mr. Stennet to hear Lord Duplin's Opinion of the Validity of our Charter; but he was indisposed, and had not waited on his Lordship. Visited Mr. Brine,[182] a Baptist Minister who is reputed a Speculative Antinomian, tho' a good Man. Dined with Mr. Anderson,[183] of the South-Sea-House, a friendly, polite Gent. and a Secretary of the Correspondents here with the Society for propagating Xn. Knowledge in Scotland. I find his Uncle was the Grandfather of the Anderson's in Hanover. Visited Dr. Avery, who treated us with the most unreserved Candour. Spent the Evening with Mr. Thomson Junior an ingenious young Baptist Minister who tho' educated a strict Calvinist, has embibed the modern Latitudinarian Principles. I had an amicable Dispute with him about the Lawfullness and Expediency of Subscribing Tests of Orthodoxy, besides the Scriptures.

✌❦ *Fryd. Feb. 15.* Visited the venerable, stern Dr. Earle, and he gave me 5 Guineas for the College. Went thence to Mr. Spilsbury's, Presbyterian Minister at Salter's Hall. He seemed reluctant to assist, and put me off. Dined with Mr. Bowle's, Junior and had agreeable Conversation with the old Gent. tho' my Spirits were very low, and I had no List for Action. He made some candid Remarks upon my Sermons, and told me that he heard Mr. Chandler and his People were not well pleased with my Sermon there, but tho't it too rigidly orthodox. Spent the Evening most agreeably with my Friend Mr. Cruttenden, who is a very considerable Poet, as I find by some Poems of his he put into my Hands to correct.

[182] John Brine (1703–65) was Baptist minister to a congregation meeting in Currier's Hall, Cripplegate. He has been described as being "Supralapsarian" in theology. *DNB*, II, 1253–54.

[183] Adam Anderson (c. 1692–1765), a clerk in the South Sea House, was a trustee and one of the founders of the colony of Georgia. *DNB*, I, 370–371.

Sat. Feb. 16. We have reason to observe the Goodness of God in the Success we meet with in the Business of our Mission, having already got near £200, which I really tho't at first would be as much as we could get in all. Our obtaining the Attestation of so many Ministers to our Petition (in all 67) appears the best Expedient we could have fallen upon; and as they are of the 3 Denominations of Dissenters, it gives us Access to People of all these Denominations. We have concluded to print 500 Copies of our Petition,[184] to put into the Hands of our Friends, to disperse among such as might contribute to the Design, that the Way may be prepared for our making personal Application to them. This Morning I waited on Dr. Lardner, Mr. Pike, and Mr. Guyse, who gave me about 7 Guineas between them towards the College. Had some Conversation with Mr. Guyse, who is a free sociable Gent. tho' very low spirited to-day. I hardly think there has been one in London these many Years, who has contracted so extensive Acquaintance with the Ministers of this City, as I have, in less than 2 Months. I am sometimes low-Spirited, and bashfull, especially in Company with my Seniors, that I cannot behave so as to recommend myself. However, I hope to settle such a Correspondence as may be for my future Advantage. Dined at Mr. Wright's, Son-in-Law to Mr. Mauduit; and spent the afternoon at Home, preparing for to-morrow, when I am to preach for Dr. Jennings.

I find the Hurries of our Business, the Variety of Company and Objects, and the Want of Time for Tho'tfullness and Retirement have dissipated my Tho'ts, and deadened my Devotion. I am extremely uneasy in my Situation. I long to be at Home in my Study, and with my dear Family; for the Character of a Recluse Student suits me much better than that of a Man of Business. But it is the Providence of God that called me to this Instance of Self-denial, and I must submit; nay I would chearfully acquiesce in it.

[184] *A General Account of the Rise and State of the College, Lately Established in the Province of New-Jersey, in America: and of the End and Design of Its Institution. Originally Published in America, An. 1752, by the Trustees of the Said College; and Now Republished, in Pursuance of Their Order, with Some Alterations and Additions, Adapted to Its Present State; for the Information of the Friends of Learning and Piety in Great Britain; by the Revd Messrs. Gilbert Tennent and Samuel Davies, Agents for the Said Trustees . . .* (London, 1754). Later in the year two editions were published in Edinburgh.

Tho' I take but too superficial Notice of it, yet alas! I feel Sin still strong in me. Cœlum, non Animum mutant, qui trans Mare currunt.

When I seriously think how depraved I am, I hardly know what Conclusion to draw about myself. God pity me, the vilest of his Creatures.

Sund. Feb. 17. Heard Dr. Jennings A.M. on Rom. 8. 7, 8. and he spoke in the Language of the convictive Preachers of the last Age, to my great Satisfaction. Dined with one Mr. Eads, a very serious good Man. Preached P.M. on Ps. 97. 1. with usual Freedom and Clearness, and to the great Satisfaction of the good Dr.

Spent the Evening with him; and he is so free and communicative of Knowledge, that his Company is very entertaining and instructive. I meet with none in London like him in this Respect. He read me a Dissertation of his upon the Tree of Life. A late Writer supposes that the Word rendered Tree, tho' singular, has a plural signification, and meant all the Trees of the Garden, except that of Knowledge. So the Gr. ξυλον, and the Eng. *Wood* has a plural Signification. The Author supposes that all the Trees in Eden might be called a *Wood of Life,* because they were sufficient for the Support of Life without the other Productions of the Earth, which are raised by Labour. The Dr. supposes that there were other Trees of Pleasure and innocent Luxury, but not absolutely necessary for Adam's Subsistence, and that the Tree of Life was a particular Species of Trees, the Fruit of which was the necessary Support of Life, as Bread is now, etc.

Sat. Feb. 23. This Week I have been so hurried, that I could not keep a daily Journal.

Last Tuesday we dispersed our Petitions among the Ministers to give away among their People. We have been diligent in making private Applications; but met with many Disappointments, partly by Gent. being from Home, or indisposed, or unwilling to contribute; and partly by the Prejudices raised in the Minds of some by Mr. Tennent's Notingham Sermon, which is dispersed thro' the Town from Hand to Hand very officiously. Mr. Tennent was so damped with it Yesterday, that his Spirits were quite sunk, and he gave up the Hope of Success, and wished himself in Philadelphia again. But this Morning we had reason to observe the remarkable Interposition of Providence, in raising us up after a Dejection. Mr. Tennent waited on William Belchier Esquire a Church-Man, that seems to have no Sense of Religion; and from whom we expected little or Nothing: but he surprized us by subscribing £50. Blessed be the God of Heaven, who has the Hearts of all Men in his Hand, and rules them as he pleases. I went to Hackney, about 3 miles off; had an Interview with Mr. Hunt,[185] one of the Ministers there, a serious, sociable Man. Waited on Samuel Lesingham Esquire a Gent. in great Repute among the Dissenters; and Stamp Brooksbank and [blank] Sheafe[186] Esquires the latter of which gave me a very cold Reception. Hackney is a very agreeable Place, where there are sundry magnificent Seats and Gardens. This Week I have waited on [blank] Lamb Esquire,[187] Mr. Benj. Bond Senior, Mr. Tim. Hollis, Sir Josh. Van Neck,[188] etc. and spent last Wednesday Night very agreeably with Mr. Stennet Junior an affectionate Baptist Minister. Dined yesterday with Mr. Robert Keen in the Minories, a pious, affectionate young Gent. in Company with good Mr. Cruttenden.

We have been solicited to preach a Charity-Sermon next Wednesday for the dissenting School in Bartholomew-Close; and as Mr. Tennent refused, and cast it upon me, I was obliged to consent; tho' when I considered my Hurries, Want of Preparation, the Number of Ministers that may attend, etc. the Prospect strikes me with Horror. May God prepare me! Dined last Thirsd. at Mr. Brine's, a Baptist Minister and a warm Advocate for the Doctrines of Calvinism, with something of an antinomian Tincture.

---

[185] Among his "Correspondents" Davies listed William Hunt of Hackney. The name also occurs in Wilson, *Dissenting Churches,* II, 42, as minister in Hackney after 1738.

[186] This was probably Samuel Sheaf of Eastcheap, a prominent Presbyterian layman who helped found the Society for Promoting Religious Knowledge Among the Poor, a benevolent organization called upon by all denominations. David Bogue and James Bennett, *A History of the Dissenters from the Revolution in 1688 to the Year 1808* (4 vols.; London, 1808–12), II, 323–324.

[187] Perhaps Matthew Lamb, a London barrister and member of Parliament for Peterborough. Namier and Brooke, *Parliament,* III, 17.

[188] Sir Joshua Van Neck, first Baronet of Heveningham Hall, a Dutchman by birth, was reputedly "one of the richest merchants in Europe." *Ibid.,* 573.

ঌ *Sund. Feb. 24.* Preached the Morning Lecture at Mr. Godwin's Meeting House, in little St. Helen's, at 7 o'Clock, the earliest that ever I preached in my Life. There was a considerable Assembly, considering it was so early. My Subject was, "Yield yourselves unto God," and as I had but one Hour's Time for the whole of public Worship, I could handle it but superficially. Took a Coach, and went to Mr. Oswald's Meeting-House, where I preached both before and afternoon. My Subject A.M. was John. 3. 6 and P.M. Joh. 3. 3. I spoke with some Freedom. But Alas! that Spirit of awful Solemnity, so commanding and impressing to an Audience which has frequently animated my Sermons, seems now to be departed from me: and when I speak on solemn Subjects with the Air of Unconcernedness, or meer natural Vivacity, I feel guilty, and seem to myself to make a very ridiculous Appearance. Such Preaching, alas! has but little Weight with an Auditory. The Congregation in the Afternoon was very full, which encouraged [me].

ঌ *Monday. Feb. 25.*[189] Went to Hackney, but were disappointed of waiting on sundry we intended. Went thence to Newington, and visited Mrs. Abney, daughter of the late Sir Thomas Abney,[190] a courteous humble lady. The steward shewed me Dr. Watts, his study, and some of his manuscripts. I find he wrote but little of his sermons. As his books were taken away, there was nothing that pleased me so much as the pictures of sundry great men, ranged in the order the Dr. has left them. There were two vacancies, in one of which is written with the Drs. own hand,

Est locus pluribus umbris.—Hor.

And in the other,

Quis me Doctorum propria dignabitur umbra.

This is the place the Dr. so tenderly describes in his elegy upon Gunston. I saw the turret, and the venerable oaks and elms, etc.

[189] The entries for February 25 and 26 are taken from *The Virginia Evangelical and Literary Magazine*, II (1819), 334, 353–354.
[190] Elizabeth Abney resided at Abney House in Stoke Newington where Isaac Watts had lived for thirty-six years prior to his death. *DNB*, I, 54–55.

ᵔᵍ Tuesday February 26. Staid at home in the morning, preparing to preach a charity sermon to-morrow; the prospect of which is very terrifying to me. Went P.M. to the house of Lords with the Rev. Mr. Thomson, and was introduced by a Mr. George Baskerville, a Lawyer, whose company I enjoyed on the way, and in the evening. He is the most facetious mortal I ever conversed with; and sometimes he gives such a loose to his wit, that one would think he has no respect to any thing sacred; and yet he gave five guineas to the College, and talked at times very pertinently on divine subjects. The house of Lords is but an ordinary old building; but the assembly is the most brilliant and august that one can conceive. It was opened by a prayer read by the youngest bishop; at which all but members were ordered to go out; but Mr. Thomson and I were conveniently concealed behind a curtain, and were not excluded. The bishops made an odd appearance to me in their dress of black and white! The judges were to give their opinions and the reasons, *seriatim,* upon a case relating to the insurance of a privateer, whose company had mutinied. Five of them spoke, each near an hour, and I was charmed with their clear Reasoning; and one or two of them had a handsome address.

ᵔᵍ Wednesday February 27. Preached a charity Sermon at Mr. King's Meeting-House, on "I will be their God, and they shall be my People." There was a large Auditory; and a considerable Number of Ministers, viz. Dr. Guyse, Mr. King, Mr. Gibbons, Mr. Guyse, Mr. Hickman, Mr. Brine, etc. I have hardly ever preached with greater Disadvantage; partly by Reason of a Fright occasioned by searching my Pockets some Time before I could find my Notes; and partly from my great Hurry; for I found after I had consented to preach, that the Committee that have the Management of the secular Affairs of the Dissenters, were to meet on the same Day; and Mr. Mauduit wrote to me to get Mr. Tennent to preach for me, (which he would by no means do) or conclude exactly at 12 o'Clock. These things cast me into a Perturbation of Mind; and yet I had as much Freedom and Tenderness as I have had in this City; for which I desire to be humbly thankful. The Ministers thanked me heartily for my Sermon, and seemed well pleased with it.

Immediately after Sermon, I took Coach and went to Pinners-Hall to wait on the Committee. They had been consulting the Virginia Laws, and reading the Papers I had sent them; and they told me that they were all heartily engaged in my Interest, but after the best Deliberation, they were apprehensive that the Act of Toleration was not so adopted as to become a proper Law of Virginia, but only one Paragraph was received, which exempts Dissenters from Penalty for exempting themselves from the Established Church. This surprised me, as I still think my Reasons for my former Opinions are unanswerable. They at least advised me to get a Petition drawn up to the King and Council, and subscribed by the Dissenters in the frontier Counties, which they apprehended would be of more Weight than one from Hanover, because they were educated Dissenters, and were a good Barrier against the French and Indians. They appointed some of their Members to assist me in drawing up the Petition; and I intend to wait on them as soon as possible for that End. May the Providence of God smile on the Attempt!

Monday March 4. Had but little Heart for Business. Visited Mr. Waugh[191] the Bookseller, and his Father-in-Law, Mr. Field. Spent the Evening at Mr. Mauduit's in Conversation upon the Case of the Dissenters in Virginia. I find Peyton Randolph[192] Esquire, my old Adversary, is now in London; and will no doubt oppose whatever is done in Favour of the Dissenters in Hanover.

Tuesd. March 5. We determined to publish a larger account of the Rise and present State of the College; as we find some are not fully satisfied with the short Account given in our Petition. This has cost us some Pains, and the more so, as Mr. Tennent's Stile and mine are so different. Went to the Amsterdam Coffee-House, to see the Ministers, and spread our Petitions, about 1 o'Clock.

[191] James Waugh was a bookseller and publisher of devotional literature in Lombard Street. Plomer, *Dictionary*, p. 258.
[192] Peyton Randolph (1721–75) was King's Attorney for the colony of Virginia and a stanch opponent of the expansion of Presbyterianism. In the early 1750's he had objected to the licensing of additional Presbyterian meetinghouses. *DNB*, XV, 367–368.

Wednesd. March 6. Heard Mr. Halford Preach a Charity-Sermon in Mr. Chandler's Meeting-House for the Fund to support the Widow's and Children of dissenting Ministers. His Text was, "Whatsoever thy Hand findeth to do etc." His Matter was tolerably good, but delivered in a most wretched Manner. I met him at the Door, as he was coming into the Meeting-House, and asked him, how he did? he answered, "I am in fear and much trembling;" and when I told him that I hoped the Lord would be with him, the good Man burst into Tears. This gave me Occasion to reflect upon my own Presumption, who preached there with much less Diffidence. Visited Mr. Jackson,[193] who was educated a Church-Man, but is now a Dissenter; who has had the Reading of all our Papers relating to our mission, and would do Nothing implicitly. He said he was afraid our College would fall into Episcopal Hands; and that he was not well-affected to Governour Belchier's Character, for accepting of the place of Gov. of New Eng. and espousing the Interests of the Court, when he was sent over as Agent to oppose them. But to my agreeable surprize he gave me 10 Guineas for the College. Waited in the Evening on Mr. Blackwell,[194] whom, thro' Mistake, I took to be a Dissenter, but found to be a Church-Man, and one of the Contributors to the Society for propagating Xnity in Foreign Parts. He made as wide a Mistake, and took me to be a Moravian, till I undeceived him. He appeared a very candid Gent. and took the Affair under Consideration.

I have been more than usually anxious this Day about my dear Wife. Oh! that I knew how she is! I find that neither Time nor Distance can erase her Image from my Heart.

This Day the Honorable Henry Pelham Esquire Prime Minister died; which has struck the Town into a Consternation. He has left a general good Character behind him; and the Court is puzzled whom to chuse in his Place.

[193] Richard Jackson (1721–81) was a prominent London barrister and widely known as an expert on colonial affairs. He later became a close friend of Benjamin Franklin and Peter Collinson. Namier and Brooke, *Parliament*, II, 669–672.

[194] Possibly Ebenezer Blackwell, a partner in Martin's Lombard Street Bank and an intimate friend of the Wesleys, who made a practice of giving large donations to charitable causes. Nehemiah Curnock, ed., *The Journal of the Rev. John Wesley* (8 vols.; London, 1938), II, 259.

⚡ *Thirsd. March 7.*[195] Went towards Westminster, and called upon Dr. Lobb F.R.S.[196] and many others; the Dr. treated me kindly, and invited me to dine with him next Tuesday; but the rest were either not at Home, or not disposed to give. Spent an Hour very pleasantly with Mr. Patrick, a Scotch Minister, who seems to have a tender Sense of the declining State of Religion. I am frequently very low-spirited, and a thick Gloom covers my Mind. Anxieties about Home, and the Fatigues of our Mission frequently exhaust my Spirits so that I am unfit for Activity. How happy am I in my dear Companion Mr. Tennent, with whom I can use the most unbounded Freedoms, when we retire into our Room!

To-Day the Reverend Mr. Joesph Stennet has been honoured with the Degree of D.D. from the College of St. Andrews, upon the Recommendation of the Duke of Cumberland.[197]

⚡ *Saturday March 16.* My Hurries will not allow me an Hour in a Week to write my Journal; and therefore I must content myself with a general Account.

Last Sund. I preached A.M. for Mr. Gibbons on these Words, "So then neither is he that planteth any Thing etc." and as I was deeply sensible of the With-drawing of divine Influences, and the Inefficaciousness of the Means of Grace without them my tender Passions were frequently moved thro'out the Sermon, and in the Conclusion burst out into a Flood of Tears. Sundry of the Hearers were tenderly affected, particularly Mr. Cromwell great grandson of Oliver; who gave Mr. Gibbons 3 Guineas for the College after Sermon, and thanked me for my Discourse with Tears in his Eyes. He afterwards conducted me to Dr. Stennet's, and talked freely and warmly of experimental Religion. Dined at Mr. Samuel Stennet's, in Company with his Brother who is also a Minister. Preached P.M. for Dr. Stennet, and my Spirits were so exhausted with my forenoon Discourse that I had not

[195] One page, containing the first portion of the entry for 7 March 1754, is missing from the manuscript in the Union Theological Seminary, Richmond. It is now in the Firestone Library of Princeton University.

[196] Theophilus Lobb (1678–1763) had been a minister in Haberdasher's Hall until 1736 when he retired to devote his full time to medicine. A member of the Royal Society and the Royal College of Physicians, he published many popular medical and devotional works. *DNB*, XII, 24–25.

[197] William Augustus (1721–65), third son of George II, was Duke of Cumberland. *DNB*, XXI, 337–348.

much tender Solemnity. Spent the Evening with Mr. Stennet Junior who seems a pious ingenious Youth.

We have determined to publish a larger Account of the College for the Satisfaction of such as have a hystorical Curiosity, or desire to be informed of it as a Matter in which they are concerned as Contributors. And we have been busy this Week in preparing and spreading it thro' the Town.

Spent an Evening very agreeably with Mr. Cruttenden, who read me a ingenious Dissertation of his in Favour of Dr. Watts's Version of the Psalms, and upon my Request, made me a present of it.

Spent another Evening with that heavenly Man Mr. Hall whose Conversation is an agreeable Mixture of Piety and wit.

Had an Interview with Mr. Wm. Hervey, Brother to the celebrated Author of the Meditations.[198] He is a modest, humble Gent. and tho' of the Church of Eng. has a zealous Regard for the exploded Doctrines of Calvinism and experimental Religion.

Heard Mr. Read [199] last Tuesd. at Salter's Hall, on these Words, "Enter not into Judgment with thy Servant etc." But there was such a Legal Spirit diffused thro' the Sermon, that I tho't it rather calculated to promote the Security, than the Conversion of Sinners. I could not help thinking of a Punn I have heard of a Minister's, who preached a Sermon upon these Words, "Salt is good, but if the Salt have lost its Savour, etc.," and when he was desired to publish it, he said "he believed he would and dedicate it to the Preachers at *Salter's*-Hall; for they wanted *Seasoning*."

Yesterday I drew up a Petition for the Dissenters in Virginia, and carried it to Dr. Avery to correct. The Death of Mr. Pelham, the Project of sending a Bishop over to America, the Confusions between the Governour and Assembly in Virginia, and Mr. Randolph, my old Adversary being now in London, are all

[198] James Hervey (1714–58) was rector of the Church of England parish in Weston and a friend of John Wesley. His *Meditations and Contemplations* was first published in two volumes in London in 1748. *DNB*, IX, 733–735.
[199] Henry Read (1686–1774) was minister to a Presbyterian congregation in Southwark. His brother, James Read, was minister to a Presbyterian congregation in New Broad Street. Wilson, *Dissenting Churches*, II, 222–225; IV, 312–314.

great obstructions at present to the Relief of my oppressed People. And the Committee on these Accounts think this a very improper Time to make any Applications in their Favour. As Dr. Stennet has a great deal of Influence in Court, I gave him last Night a particular Account of the Rise and Progress of the Dissenting Interest in Virginia, and the Restraints and Embarrassments the People laboured under from the Government. He was very much moved with the Account and promised me his utmost Influence in their Favour. He had been Yesterday waiting upon the Duke of New-Castle to condole the Death of his Brother, and told me, that it was the most tragical Scene he ever saw.

Dined to-day at Mr. Wm. Stead's in Company with Mr. Cornthwaite[200] his Minister a seven-day-Baptist Socinian.

Had an Interview a few Days ago with Mr. Grant, Minister in Northhamptonshire. He has no Learning, but is a very solid, judicious and pious Man, and I am told, popular and successful in his Ministry.

Sund. March 17. Preached A.M. for Mr. Lawson at Founder's-Hall upon Luk. 13. 24. and the Hearers were attentive, tho' neither they nor myself were very solemn. Preached P.M. at Unicorn Yard for Mr. Thomson, on Psa. 97. 1. and acted the Orator with a tolerable good Grace. Preached an Evening Lecture on Jer. 31. 18–20 for Mr. Mitchel at Mr. Hitkin's Meeting-House; and the Sight of the Auditory, the most crowded I have seen in London, cast me into an agreeable Ferment, and constrained me to pray in the Pulpit for Divine Assistance; and I hope I was answered; for I had more than usual [Freedom and Solemnity].

Tuesday, March 19.[201] . . . Went to the Amsterdam coffee-house among the Baptist and Independent ministers, where I enjoy most satisfaction. Received the thanks of the

---

[200] Probably Robert Cornthwaite, minister to the Mill Yard Baptist congregation, Goodman's Fields, about this time. W. T. White, ed., *Minutes of the General Assembly of the General Baptist Churches in England, with Kindred Records* (2 vols.; London, 1910), II, 49n.

[201] Portions of the entries for 17 and 19 March 1754 are missing from the original. The first paragraph of the entry for 19 March was printed in *The Virginia Evangelical and Literary Magazine*, II (1819), 356.

governours of the charity-school in Bartholomew Close for my sermon there, which were presented to me in a very respectful manner by Dr. Guyse, as their Deputy. Tho' it be hard to repress the workings of vanity even in a creature so unworthy as I, under so much applause; yet I think my heart rises in sincere gratitude to God for advancing me from a mean family and utter obscurity, into some importance in the world, and giving me so many advantages of public usefulness. Indeed I hardly think there is a greater instance of this in the present age. Alas! that I do not better improve my opportunities.

Went to Hamlin's Coffee-House among the Presbyterians, where they are generally very shy and unsociable to me. They have universally, as far as I can learn, rejected all Tests of Orthodoxy, and require their Candidates at their Ordination, only to declare their Belief of the Scriptures. Mr. Prior, with the Appearance of great Uneasiness, told me that he heard we would admit none into the Ministry without subscribing the Westminster Confession; and that this Report would hinder all our Success among the Friends of Liberty. I replied, that we allowed the Candidate to mention his objections against any Article in the Confession, and the Judicature judged whether the Articles objected against were essential to Xnity; and if they judged they were not, they would admit the Candidate, notwithstanding his Objections. He seemed to think that we were such rigid Calvinists, that we would not admit an Armenian [*sic*] into Communion, etc. I proposed to converse with him another Time for his Satisfaction. Alas! for the Laxness that prevails here among the Presbyterians. Quantum o mutati!

Spent Yesterday Evening with Mr. Mauduit, who had been waiting upon the House of Commons to obtain a Repeal of a Clause in a Bill, that might be injurious to the Dissenters, tho' levelled against the Jacobites; and he succeeded; the Members of Parl. especially now before the Elections, being very unwilling to disoblige the Dissenters.

The Court :s all in Confusion about chusing one to fill up Mr. Pelham's Place; and the King is much perplexed.

He says he hoped to spend his old Age in Peace; but all his Peace is buried in Mr. Pelham's Grave.

As I have received no Letters as yet from Hanover, I am extremely anxious about my dearest Creature, my Family and my Congregation. Did they know my Uneasiness, I am sure they would write to me.

✑§ *Sund. Mar. 24.* Preached for 2 Gent. of very different Sentiments, Dr. Guyse and Dr. Benson: at the former's Meeting-House A.M. on Matt. 22. 37, 38. and Rom. 8. 7. and at the Latter's on Ps. 97.1. Dr. Benson's People make a very polite Appearance; but I could see little Signs of Solemnity among them; and alas! I neither had, nor tho't it proper to indulge a passionate Solemnity.

Last Thirsday Evening, I preached a Lecture at Deptford, on Isai. 66. 1, 2. to a Number of poor, honest People; Lodged at Mr. Salway's there. Called in my Return at Peckham, and visited Dr. Milner,[202] who keeps a boarding School of about 20 Boys. He is a Gent of good Powers, and extensive Learning, especially of the Classic Kind. I find he is the Author of the large Grammars of the Latin and Greek, which was so serviceable to me, when at Learning.

Preached Yesterday P.M. for Dr. Stennet in a small Congregation of seven-Day Baptists, who seem very serious People.

✑§ *April 7, 1754.*[203] . . . We have had most surprising success in our mission; which notwithstanding the languor of my nature, I cannot review without passionate emotions. From the best information of our friends, and our own observation upon our arrival here, we could not raise our hopes above £300; but we have already got about £1200. Our friends in America cannot hear the news with the same surprize, as they do not know the difficulties we have had to encounter with; but to me it appears the most signal interposition of providence I ever saw. [Preached last] Sunday A.M. for Dr. Benson, and P.M. for Mr. Gibbons, and Yesterday for Do.

I have sent a Petition to Virginia, at the Direction of the Committee, to be subscribed by the Dissenters there, and transmitted to be presented to the King in Council.

[202] John Milner kept a boarding school in Peckham. Oliver Goldsmith was one of his students. *DNB*, XIII, 465.

[203] The page missing from the original at this point contains entries for the period between 24 March and 7 April 1754. Part of the entry for the latter date appeared in *The Virginia Evangelical and Literary Magazine*, II (1819), 356.

❧ *Sunday April 14.* The same Objects occur and the same Business engages my Attention, with little Variety. Last Sunday, I went to Hackney, and heard my good Friend, Mr. Hunt, on these Words,—"Ye are bro't nigh by the Blood of Xt." with Pleasure. Received the Sacrament administered in a Form I have not yet seen.

Preached in the Afternoon in the Pulpit where Dr. Bates and Mr. Henry[204] once stood, and found some Freedom. (1 Joh. 3. 2.). Lodged at my kind Friend's, Mr. Bowles, and offered a few extempore Tho'ts to the Family, at his request. (Isai. 45. 22.)

Waited upon Lord Leven, Judge Foster, Sir Joseph Hankey, etc. The Business of our Mission goes on with surprizing Success. Spent an Evening with Dr. Benson, and had a friendly Dispute with him about subscribing Articles of Faith. Had an Interview with Mr. Prior, and endeavoured to satisfie him about the Catholicism of our College.

Received a Letter from my dear Brother Mr. Todd, which informed me of the Wellfare of my Spouse and Family. The very Sight of it, threw me into a passionate Ferment, that did not soon subside. O how kind is God to me and mine!

To-day preached for Mr. Towle A.M. (Gen. 19. "Escape etc.") and P.M. for Mr. Kippis, (Matt. 25. ult.).

Had an Interview with Mr. Walker, a Minister lately come from New England, who is no Friend to Mr. Tennent, but has been representing his Character in an injurious Light.

❧ *Sund. April. 21.* Preached at Peckham, (a Village about 3 miles from London) for Dr. Milner, on Ps. 97. 1. and 1 Joh. 3. 3. But I had not much Freedom or Solemnity, tho' I found some of the People were well pleased with the Discourses.

Lodged at Dr. Milner's; but as he was not at Home, I spent the Time in Conversation with his Son,[205] a Dr. of Physic, an ingenius Philosophical Youth.

❧ *Sund. April. 28.* Preached for Dr. Allen, at Dr. Earle's Meeting-House, on 2 Cor. 3. 18. with much oratorical Freedom;

[204] William Bates and John Henry had ministered to a Presbyterian congregation in Parish Street during the 1740's and early 1750's. Wilson, *Dissenting Churches*, IV, 279.

[205] Thomas Milner (1719–97) was a London physician and experimenter with electricity. *DNB*, XIII, 465.

but alas! not with much Xn. Solemnity and Affection. My Address caught the Attention of the Auditory; but I am afraid the Truths had not a proportionable Impression on their Hearts. The old, good stern Dr. Earle was one of my Hearers, and cordially expressed his Approbation; Went immediately to assist Mr. Oswald at his Sacrament and served two Tables, and communicated myself according to the Mode of the Church of Scotland. Preached p.m. on Joh. 12. 32, 33. with some Freedom. But amid my incessant Hurries, I have but little rational solid Concern about my own immortal State.

My Nature is quite fatigued and exhausted with the Labours of my Mission in this vast City; and I am afraid my Constitution will be broke with them.

I was last Week pleasingly entertained with an artificial Aviary. etc.[206]

ᴖᶳ New-Castle upon Tine. May 7. 1754.

The General Assembly of the Church of Scotland drawing near, and the Hurries and Confusions of the Election of Members of Parliament for London rendering the few additional Applications we might otherwise have made, inexpedient at the Time, we set out for Edinburgh in a Post-Chaise, last Fryday. This Method of Travelling is very expeditious; as we have Change of Horses at every 10 or 15 Miles.

We have been under the special Guardianship of Providence both by Sea and Land ever since we left Home: but never more remarkably than in this Journey. We were twice in the most eminent Danger of Death; last Saturday near Caxton by one of the Horses becoming unruly and by his running and kicking and his breaking the Shafts, harnessing etc. all to Pieces: and Yesterday by the Hostler suddenly pulling back the Top of the Chaise, while we were in it; which caught Mr. Tennent's Head, and pulled him back with such Violence, that he was very much strained and the Blood gushed out of his Nose. Providence, no doubt, has some important Design in these alarming Trials. May they prove seasonable Mortifications before extensive Success, which might otherwise exalt us above Measure!

[206] This marks the end of that portion of the original manuscript in the Library of the Union Theological Seminary. The remainder is located in the Firestone Library, Princeton.

'Tis an Honour to be employed in public Service; and I have Cause of grateful Joy rather than Complaint. But I never engaged in such a Series of wasting Fatigues and Dangers as our present Mission is attended with. And what painful Anxieties about my Wife, Family, Congregation, and the Success of our Applications have disturbed my Breast, this Heart only knows, which has felt them. I have walked in the tedious, crowded Streets of London from Morning to Evening, 'till my Nature has been quite exhausted; and I have been hardly able to move a Limb. It was but seldom that I could release myself in Conversation with a Friend by Reason of incessant Hurries: and when I have had an Opportunity, my Spirits have been so spent that I was but a dull Companion. My Hurries have also denied me the Pleasure of a curious Traveller, in taking a careful View of the numerous Curiosities of Nature and Art in London. But all these Disadvantages have been more than ballanced by the Success we have had, having collected about £1700, notwithstanding the ungenerous Opposition made against us by the pretended Friends of Liberty and Catholicism; which is Matter of the utmost Astonishment to our Friends, as well as ourselves. 'Tis but little that so useless a Creature can do for God during the short Day of Life; but to be instrumental of laying a Foundation of extensive Benefit to Mankind, not only in the present but in future Generations, is a most animating Prospect; and if my Usefullness should thus survive me, I shall live to future Ages in the most valuable Respect.

We passed thro' a great many Villages on our Way to N. Castle; but none very remarkable. This Town is considerably large; and has 6 Dissenting Ministers in it; viz. Messrs Ogilvie,[207] Atkin,[208] Arthur,[209] Murray,[210] Rogerson[211] and Lothian.[212] The two last are Colleagues and have imbibed the Arminian and

[207] George Ogilvie was minister to a congregation in Silver Street and Blackett Street. *FES*, VII, 516.

[208] Edward Aitken was pastor of the Castlegarth Church. *FES*, VII, 516.

[209] William Arthur was minister to the Groat Market Church. *FES*, VII, 516.

[210] Probably James Murray of Earlston, who became minister of the High Bridge Church in 1764. *FES*, VII, 513–514.

[211] Richard Rogerson held the pulpit of the Westgate Church. *FES*, VII, 517.

[212] Samuel Louthian was probably assistant pastor of the Westgate Church. He became full pastor in 1760. *FES*, VII, 517.

Socinian Sentiments. Mr. Lothian is a very smart ingenious young Gent. and I am told a very popular Preacher. The other 4, especially Mr. Ogilvie appear very affectionate, serious and good Men! They were all unanimous to promote the Business of our Mission, and treated us with uncommon Respect.

We are going to the General Assembly with great Discouragement as we expect a powerful Opposition: but the Lord our God is in the Heavens; he doth whatsoever he pleaseth.

Dined last Week at my affectionate Father's Mr. Price, with Mr. Thomas Morgan of Langhorne Carmaerthenshire in South Wales;[213] a very agreeable young Minister, who preaches generally to about 2000 poor People. We agreed to correspond with each other.

⊷§ *Thursd. May 9.* Arrived safe in Edinburgh. Passed by *Preston-Pans,* where Colonel Gardiner[214] was killed. Saw his Seat, and the Field of Battle, which struck me with a melancholy Horror. Passed thro' Berwick upon Tweed, a considerable Town. Scotland makes a better Appearance on the Way that we travelled than I expected; tho' there are a great many of the poorest Huts that ever I saw. My Mind is perplexed about the Success of our Mission here; and all appears gloomy before me. My Spirits are generally low, tho' I feel a Kind of stupid Serenity of Mind.

⊷§ *Fryd. May 10.* Visited the Reverend Mr. Webster,[215] who received us with great Candour and Friendship, and gave us his best Advice about our Design. We find it is likely to be difficult to succeed with the General Assembly, not only by Reason of the Opposition that may be occasioned by Mr. Cross's[216] malignant Letter, but also on Account of the 3 General Collections that have been successively made of late, and the Application expected this Year from Holland.

[213] Thomas Morgan (1720–99) was pastor of the Independent congregation in Henllan Amgoed, Carmarthenshire. John Cecil-Williams, ed., *The Dictionary of Welsh Biography down to 1940* (Oxford, 1959), 653–654.
[214] Colonel James Gardiner had been killed at the battle of Preston in 1745. *DNB,* VII, 854–856.
[215] Alexander Webster (1707–84) was minister to the Tolbooth Church in Edinburgh. He had formerly been chaplain to the Prince of Wales and Moderator of the General Assembly. *DNB,* XX, 1025–26.
[216] Probably Robert Cross, Old Light minister of the First Presbyterian Church in Philadelphia. Weis, *The Colonial Clergy of Maryland, Delaware and Georgia,* p. 74.

We waited on Dr. Cumming, who had received one of Mr. Cross's Letters, and shewed him our Credentials, etc. to remove or anticipate his Objections; and from his professed Benevolence to the Design, after reading them, we had Reason to hope we had succeeded.

Visited Mr. Robertson[217] Professor of the Oriental Languages, who shewed us uncommon Friendship, and seemed to know the Heart of a Stranger. He introduced us to Mr. Hamilton,[218] the Professor of Divinity, a simple candid Gent. who was friendly to our Design.

Took a View of the Royal Infirmary, Harriot's Hospital, etc. which are stately Buildings.

Thursd. May 16. We have visited Professor Hamilton, a very modest, serious Man, Principal Goudie,[219] Mr. Geo. Wishart,[220] the favourite Preacher of the Polite in this City, Mr. James Watson,[221] an affectionate Minister, Mr. Johnston,[222] Minister in the Castle, Mr. Lindsay[223] of Leith, and some Ministers whom we have occasionally seen. They all treat us with great Respect. Last Mond. dined with the Lord Provost,[224] and his Lordship gave us a very friendly Reception, and promised us all the Service in his Power.

Last Sund. heard Mr. Kinlough[225] in the Forenoon, who gave

[217] James Robertson (1714–95) was professor of Hebrew in the University of Edinburgh. He had not yet written his major works. *DNB*, XVI, 1295–96.

[218] Robert Hamilton had just been appointed to the chair of divinity as successor to John Goudie. *FES*, I, 143.

[219] John Goudie was principal of the University of Edinburgh. He had previously served for twenty years as professor of divinity. *FES*, I, 143.

[220] George Wishart was minister to the Tron Kirk in Edinburgh. *FES*, I, 136.

[221] James Watson was pastor of the Canongate Church. *FES*, I, 25.

[222] John Johnston held the pulpit in the Edinburgh Castle Church at this time. *FES*, I, 185.

[223] George Lindsay was personal chaplain to Lord Charles Ker and pastor of the North Leith Parish Church. *FES*, I, 156.

[224] George Drummond (1687–1766) served six terms as Lord Provost (head of the town council) of Edinburgh, where reportedly nothing could be done without his consent between 1715 and 1766. The university was controlled by the council. *DNB*, VI, 25–28.

[225] Robert Kinloch was minister of the High Church in Edinburgh. *Annals of the General Assembly of the Church of Scotland . . .* (Edinburgh, 1838), p. 316.

us an excellent Lecture and Sermon; and Dr. Cumming[226] in the Afternoon, on the Preface to the Lord's Prayer, who preached pretty much in the Strain of fashionable Moderns. Supped with our excellent Friend, Mr. Webster.

Heard Mr. Clog open the Synod of Lothian and Tweedale on Tuesd. on these Words, "Lord, I am thy Servant," etc. His Sermon was simple and honest.

Waited on the Synod, and I was surprized and grieved to see so much Altercation about the Place of Clerk to the Synod, which is here a lucrative Post. In the Heat of the Debate, one Mr. Hume,[227] a young Minister flung out some intolerably severe Reflections on the Presbytery of Dunleith on Account of their prosecuting one Mr. Logan, a Candidate, for false Doctrine. He said that the Presbytery of Dunleith had been upon the Side of Inhumanity and Persecution in their Treatment of as worthy a Youth as ever honoured the Cloth, and he was glad to find them now upon the Side of Humanity, tho' in the mean Time of Injustice. The Presbytery immediately entered a Prosecution against him, and it raised a prodigious Ferment in the Synod. But at length, the Parties withdrew with a Committee, and at length Mr. Hume gave them Satisfaction, and submitted to an open Rebuke from the Moderator. Alas! there appears but little of the Spirit of serious Christianity among the young Clergy. The Patronage-Act is like to be ruinous to the Church of Scotland; for of 980 Parishes in it, about 700 are in the Gift of the King, or of the prime Minister and therefore they are used as Engines of ministerial Power, tempt the Clergy to cringe to the Court, and introduce Mercenaries into the Churches.[228]

[226] Patrick Cumming also held a chair of church history and divinity in the University of Edinburgh. *FES*, I, 143.

[227] Quite possibly John Hume (1722–1808), author of *Douglas*, minister at Athelstaneford, who had been active in previous assemblies. *DNB*, IX, 1129–32.

[228] The Patronage Act of 1712 had reaffirmed the right of individual lay patrons to fill vacancies in the Church of Scotland in the expectation that cultured and educated clergymen would be chosen. The act was designed to encourage the Scottish nobility to return to the Kirk. However, this permitted many Episcopalians to enter the Church and efforts to resolve the problem aroused a great deal of animosity which resulted in two schisms, or "secessions," during the eighteenth century. See George S. Pryde, *Scotland from 1603 to the Present Day* (London, 1962), chap. ix, "The Church Divided," pp. 92–103.

Yesterday preached an Evening Sermon for Mr. Webster on Jer. 31. 18. 19. 20. Sundry Ministers were present.

We have taken a view of the Castle here, which is amazingly fortified by Nature and Art, and has the Command of the whole City, and could soon lay it in Ruins.

We have been busied Yesterday and to-day in writing an Answer to Mr. Cross's Letter; which we find is like to have a bad Effect.

There is one Mr. Logan here who shews us great Respect. He has been a Preacher for many Years; and preaches sometimes still; but has never accepted of a Congregation, and therefore has not been ordained. He seems to be an excellent, holy, humble Man.

  ◦§ *Sund. May 19.* Preached in the Tolbooth Church to a very crowded Auditory on Jer. 31. 33. I had but little tender Sense of the Subject; and yet, to my Surprize, I found afterwards, that many were greatly pleased and edified: only some did not like my using Notes. Preached P.M. for Mr. Wishart in the Trone Church on Rev. 1. 7. with a little more Freedom to a very gay and crowded Auditory. And afterwards supped with him, who treated me very kindly. Yesterday went to Lord Drummore's[229] Country-Seat to wait upon him. I was pleased with his Motto on the Side of his House, as well suited to a rural Seat.

           _____ Seize
  The Plow, and greatly independent live.

Above which was written,

     Deo, Patriæ, Amicis.

Last Night received a Packet from Hanover. The very Sight of which raised my Passions to such a Ferment, that they are not yet subsided. Alas! I find my Dearest has been very ill; but is happily recovered. I am afraid my Friends conceal the worst from me, lest it should make me uneasy. What painful Anxieties I feel about her! alas! I have not received a Line from her own dear Hand.

[229] The courtesy title of Lord Drummore was held by Sir Hew Dalrymple, Judge of the Court of Sessions. *DNB*, V, 407.

92

Last Fryd. visited Mr. Gilbert Elliot,[230] a Lawyer who is also a Member of the Assembly, and has received a Letter to our Prejudice from his Brother in Philadelphia. He promised us that he would review it, and if there were any Objections that required an Answer, he would inform us of them. Waited also on the Reverend Mr. Kay,[231] who was very friendly, tho' he had seen Mr. Cross's Letter.

ᵉᵍ Thursd. May 23. The General Assembly met. The Lord Commissioner went in State from his House to the Church, attended by a great Number of the Nobility, and the Streets were lined with Ranks of Soldiers. The Crowd was very great, both within the Church and without. The Sermon was preached by Mr. Webster, on Ps. 137. 5, 6. and a very masterly, oratorial Discourse it was; delivered with a manly Boldness and Fluency. Professor Hamilton was chosen Moderator, nem. con. and then the King's Commission to the Lord Commissioner was read, which was in Latin: and also the King's Letter to the General Assembly. Then the Commissioner made a Speech; which the Moderator answered in a very handsome Manner. Then followed a long Debate about the Time when they should determine a Debate between Mr. Edmunston[232] and the Reverend Mr. Hindman[233] about the Clerkship. The Earl of Marchmont[234] made a very animated Speech upon the Occasion.

Mr. Tennent being confined by a sprained Foot, I waited Yesterday on the Earl of Marchmont; and in the Evening we both waited on the Lord Commissioner, where we also found the Earl of Findlater.[235] They read our Credentials, etc. and treated us kindly.

[230] Gilbert Elliot, later third Baronet of Minto, was a member of Parliament for Selkirkshire. His brother Andrew was a resident of Philadelphia prior to becoming royal governor of New York. *DNB*, VI, 671–673.

[231] George Kay was pastor of the New Greyfriars congregation in Edinburgh until 11 October 1754 when he was called to Old Greyfriars. *FES*, I, 33.

[232] John Edmondstone was minister to the Parish of Culross and Kilmahew. *FES*, III, 336.

[233] John Hyndman was pastor of the West Kirk in Edinburgh. *Annals of the General Assemby of the Church of Scotland*, p. 336.

[234] Hugh Hume (1708–94), third Earl of Marchmont, was a representative peer and president of the Court of Police in Scotland. *DNB*, X, 226–228.

[235] James Ogilvy, fifth Earl of Findlater, was a representative peer and one of the lords of police for Scotland. *DNB*, XIV, 924–925.

Saw our dear Friends, Messrs McLaurin,[236] Gillies,[237] John Erskine,[238] etc. whose Conversation has been very refreshing to us.

Saturd. May 25. Attended upon the General Assembly, where the Debate about the Clerkship was determined in Favour of Mr. Edmonstone. Sundry long Speeches were made upon the Occasion by Dr. Cumming, Mr. Tremble, Mr. Trail,[239] Mr. Mc-Clagen,[240] Prof. Murryson,[241] Prof. Lumsden,[242] Lord Drummore, the Earl of Breadalbine,[243] the Earl of Marchmont, Mr. Webster, Mr. Gordon,[244] etc. and most of them spoke with surprizing Readiness, Pertinency and Argument.

Yesterd. we waited on the Committee for Bills, where the Petition from the Trustees was read, and it was agreed that it should be transmitted to the General Assembly, with the Opinion of the Committee in its Favour; which is a happy Omen. To-day it was determined that the Matter should be heard on Monday next. We find Mr. Cross's Letter is put into sundry Hands; and sundry are prejudiced against Mr. Tennent on Account of his Notingham-Sermon, which is industriously spread here.

Sund. May 26. Preached A.M. in the Cannon-Gate Church, for Mr. Watson; where a great Number of Ministers were present. My Subject was 1 Joh. 3. 2. and blessed be God, I was not dashed, but had considerable Freedom and Solemnity.

[236] John Maclaurin was pastor of the Ramshorn (or North West) Parish. Because he often spoke in Gaelic he was extremely popular among the Highlanders of Glasgow. *FES*, III, 439.

[237] John Gillies (1712–96) was minister to the College Church in Glasgow. *DNB*, VII, 1246–47.

[238] John Erskine had been minister at Kirkintilloch until February 1753 when he was called to Culross. *FES*, III, 483.

[239] Probably Robert Trail (1720–75), minister at Banff, who became professor of oriental languages at Glasgow in 1761. *FES*, VII, 401.

[240] Probably Alexander Maclagan, minister at Little Dunkeld. *FES*, IV, 159.

[241] Professor James Murison was principal of St. Mary's College, University of St. Andrews. *FES*, VII, 421.

[242] John Lumsden was professor of divinity in King's College, Aberdeen. *FES*, VII, 372.

[243] John Campbell, third Earl of Breadalbane, was a representative peer at this time. *Burke's Peerage*, p. 277.

[244] Probably George Gordon, professor of Hebrew at King's College, Aberdeen. *FES*, VII, 368.

In the Afternoon, heard Mr. Ballantine,[245] who surprized me with a Torrent of strong Sense, poured out extempore, without Interruption from Beginning to End. I think Scotland may boast a greater Number of good Speakers, than any Country I have been in; and I believe their accustoming themselves to speak extempore, has been of great Service to them in it. Drunk Tea at the Reverend Mr. Blair's,[246] in Company with Mr. Shaw,[247] Professor of Divinity in St. Andrews, etc. who conversed with apparent Friendship about the Design of our Mission, and proposed that a Part of the Collection should be applied to the Support of poor pious Youth for the Ministry; which Motion he promised to make in the Assembly.

Supped with the Reverend Mr. Jardine,[248] who intimated that he expected the Assembly would be divided in their Sentiments about our Petition, according as they were Friends or Adversaries to Mr. Whitefield, which gave us very alarming Apprehensions, because his Friends are the Minority.

≈§ *Mond. May 27.* Last Night was so full of Anxieties about the Success of our Application, that I could not sleep. To-day the Petitions from the Trustees and the Synod of New-York, and our Credentials, were read; and Mr. Lumisden, Professor of Divinity at Aberdeen; got up to speak. As I knew not whether he was a Friend or Foe, my Heart palpitated when I saw him rise: But I soon found he was a hearty Friend. He made an ingenious Speech upon—the Importance of a learned Ministry —The Necessity of the College of New-Jersey for that End—The Duty of the General Assembly to promote such Institutions in general—and especially among the Presbyterians in those Colonies, "who (says he) are a Part of ourselves, having adopted the same Standard of Doctrine, Worship and Government with this

[245] Probably Hugh Ballantine of Dirleton, who was then being considered for the Canongate Church. Ronald S. Wright, *The Kirk in the Canongate, a Short History from 1128 to the Present Day* (Edinburgh, 1956), p. 104.

[246] Hugh Blair (1718–1800), a close friend of Lord Leven, was second minister in the Canongate Church. *DNB*, II, 622–623.

[247] Andrew Shaw was professor of sacred theology and biblical criticism in the University of St. Andrews. In 1759, as provost, he made Benjamin Franklin a Doctor of Laws. Franklin, *Papers*, VIII, 280n.

[248] John Jardine (1716–66) had just been called to the Tron Church in Edinburgh. *DNB*, X, 688.

Church." Mr. McLagan got up next, and spoke to the same Purpose. And upon a Motion being made, that the Petitions should be agreed to, there was not one objection thro' the whole House, but it passed without a Vote. This was a matter of pleasing Surprize; and I could not forbear darting up my grateful Praises to Heaven for so remarkable an Interposition of Providence. A great Number of the Nobility and Gentry were present (The Duke of Argyle, the Earl of Breadalbine, Lord Drummore, The Marquis of Lothian, Sir Geo. Preston,[249] Mr. Dundas,[250] etc. etc.) and we knew there were sundry among the Laity and Clergy that were not friendly to our Application; but they did not mutter a Word. The Collection for the German Emigrants in Pennsylvania, I am informed, met with Opposition; and perhaps this was the first Petition of the Kind that ever passed nem. con. Tho' I hardly think there ever was a greater Appearance of Opposition. The Approbation of the General Assembly will be attended with many happy Consequences; particularly, it will recommend our College to the World, and wipe off the Odium from the Synod of New-York, as a Parcel of Schismatics. It must, no doubt, be mortifying to Mr. Cross to find we have succeeded, notwithstanding his ungenerous, clandestine Efforts against us.

Dined with the Marquis of Lothian at Lord Ross's,[251] who treated us with all the Kindness and Freedom of a Friend. Lady Ross appears a serious, good Woman.

Went with the Marquis in his Coach to the Committee, appointed to draw up an Act and Recommendation for a *national Collection;* but they left it to a Sub-Committee, consisting of Dr. Cumming, Mr. Webster, Professor Shaw, Mr. McLagan and Bailie Ingram.[252]

Received a Packet from Virginia; in which was a most tender, ingenious Letter from my Dearest, which I could not but read over and over with the most passionate Emotions. How good is

[249] Sir George Preston, a prominent lay leader in the Church of Scotland, was fourth Baronet of Valleyfield, Perth. Namier and Brooke, *Parliament,* III, 326.

[250] Robert Dundas (1713–87) had been recently elected a member of Parliament from Midlothian. *DNB,* VI, 195.

[251] George Ross, thirteenth Lord Ross of Hawkhead. *DNB,* XVII, 280.

[252] Possibly Archibald Ingram of Glasgow, banker, bookseller, and merchant, with many philanthropic interests. He is listed among Davies' "Correspondents." Plomer, *Dictionary,* p. 321.

God to me in preserving her Life, so important to my Happiness, notwithstanding of threatening Sickness.

There is one Circumstance with Regard to our Application to the General Assembly that seems remarkably providential, viz that Mr. Yair, Minister of Camfire,[253] who intended to present a Petition for the Salsburgers, and which would have interfered with ours, did not arrive till last Saturday, when ours had been presented.

ᴥᔟ *Thirsd. May 30.* Waited on the Society for propagating Xn. Knowledge of which the Marquis of Lothian is President, and at their Request, gave them our best Advice about the best Method of conducting the Mission among the Indians. They also drew up a Letter recommending the College of N. J. to be annext to the Act of the General Assembly.

Dined with his Grace the Lord Commissioner, where we had the most Spended [*sic*] Entertainment I have seen.

ᴥᔟ *Sund. Jun. 2.* Preached A.M. for Mr. Jardine in Lady Easter's, on Luk. 13. 24. and P.M. at South-Leith for Mr. Walker on Heb. 6. 7. 8. I had some Freedom at Leith, but much afraid lest so shocking a Subject should give Offence; and yet I could not get my Mind kept from it. Lodged with Mr. *Walker,*[254] who is a most humble, judicious Man, and I am told, one of the best Preachers in Scotland. He is shortly to be removed to the high-Church in Edinburgh.

ᴥᔟ *Mond. June 10.* Preached Yesterday a.m. for Mr. Kinloch in the High Church before the Lord Provost and the Magistrates, on 2 Cor. 4. 18. But my Head was confused, and my Heart languid. Preached p.m. for Mr. Glen,[255] in the little Kirk on Ps. 97. 1. with much more Vivacity, tho' without a tender Solemnity.

[253] James Yair was pastor to the Scottish congregation in Campvere, Walcheren, Holland. *FES,* VII, 542.

[254] Robert Walker was minister to the South Leith Parish Church in Edinburgh. In October he was called to St. Giles Parish in Edinburgh. *FES,* I, 60, 167.

[255] John Glen was minister of West St. Giles parish in Edinburgh. *FES,* I, 146.

Last Fryday spent a few Hours with Lady Frances Gardiner,[256] who gave me an Account of many of her Trials and Deliverances. She seems to Mind Nothing but Religion, and hardly rises out of her Bed, excepting to go to public Worship.

Last Saturday, Dined with Dr. Cumming; and had sundry Hours of free Conversation with him. Informed him of the Oppression of the Dissenters in Virginia, and solicited his Interest with the Duke of Argyle; which he freely promised me.

Spent an Evening with Mr. Ramsay and Lady Hume,[257] who are a Pattern of Humility and Piety in high Life. Mr. Robertson, Professor of the oriental Languages is a pious, learned Man; and I am often conversant with him.

Last Thirsd. preached in the College-Church on Isai. 66. 1. 2. with Freedom and Solemnity. I find I begin to grow popular here, especially among the Religious.

Spent an Evening at Mr. McLagan's, in a Society of agreeable young Gent. who meet for singing Hymns and instructive Conversation.

&ε Saturd. Jun. 15. 1754. I left Edinburgh the Day before Yesterday in Company with my excellent Friend William Ramsay Esquire. Passed thro' Lithgow, a considerable Town on the Way to Glasgow, where there is a stately old Palace, now going to Ruin. Called at the Reverend Mr. John Adams of Falkirk; who insisted so earnestly upon my staying till Monday, and preaching for him, that I could not refuse. He is a most judicious, pious Minister, a Friend to the Liberty of Mankind in Opposition to the exorbitant Claims of Church-Power which the high-flying Clergy have run into.[258] His Wife, a Great grand Daughter of the

[256] Lady Frances Gardiner was a daughter of the fourth Earl of Buchan. Her husband, Colonel James Gardiner, had been killed by the Scots insurgents at Preston in 1745. *DNB*, VII, 854–856.

[257] Elizabeth Crompton Hume, second wife of Hugh Hume, Earl of Marchmont. *DNB*, X, 228.

[258] In eighteenth-century English usage, a "high flyer" was one who sought to remove power from the congregation and place it in some higher ecclesiastical body and to lodge the power to call clergymen in patrons rather than congregations. Apparently Davies followed this usage rather than the contemporary Scottish in which "high flyer" and "zealot" were terms of opprobrium referring to those opposing the patronage system and supporting the evangelical cause. *Oxford English Dictionary* (12 vols.; Oxford, 1933), V, 281, and J. H. S. Burleigh, *A Church History of Scotland* (London, 1960), p. 291.

famous Mr. David Dickson,[259] is a Gent. of uncommon Sense and Piety. In short, I have hardly been so happy in Conversation since I left Home.

I met with more Xn. Friendship in Edinburgh than any where in Great-Britain. There is too general a Decay of experimental and practical Religion; and yet there is a considerable Number of pious People in the City. I preached twice again in the College-Kirk; and I have had repeated Information, that my languid Ministrations have been remarkably blessed to many.

I have been at Culross visiting Mr. Erskine. He really exceeds the high Character I had heard of him for a hard Student, a growing Genius, and uncommon zeal for the public Good. In short, he promises much Service to the Church of Scotland.

I find a great Number of the Clergy and Laity have of late carried Church-Power to an extravagant Height, deny to Individuals the Right of judging for themselves, and insist upon absolute, universal Obedience to all the Determinations of the General Assembly. I heard sundry Speeches in the House on that Head, which really surprized me. The Nobility and Gentry who are Lay-Elders are generally High-flyers; and have encroached upon the Rights of the People, especially as to their Choice of their own Minister. Violent Settlements are enjoined by the Authority of the General Assembly, and there is no Prospect of a Redress. There is a Piece published under the Title of The Ecclesiastical Characteristics, ascribed to one Mr. Weatherspoon,[260] a young Minister. It is a Burlesque upon the High-flyers under the ironical Name of Moderate Men; and I think the Humour is Nothing inferior to Dean Swift. Mr. Tho. Walker has also written well on the Subject.

Sundry Overtures were bro't into the General Assembly, par-

[259] David Dickson (1583–1663), a prominent tract writer, had been professor of divinity at both Glasgow and Edinburgh. He had lost his position in 1660 for refusing to take the Oath of Supremacy. Robert Chambers, *A Biographical Dictionary of Eminent Scotsmen* (5 vols.; Edinburgh, 1855), II, 78–82.

[260] John Witherspoon (1723–94), minister at Beith and later president of the College of New Jersey, began his rise to prominence with the publication of this pamphlet in 1744, although it was not acknowledged by him until 1763. *DAB*, XX, 435–438. *DNB*, XXI, 742–745. The full title was *Ecclesiastical Characteristics: Or, the Arcana of Church Policy . . . Wherein Is Shewn a . . . Way of Attaining to the Character of a Moderate Man, as at Present in Repute in the Church of Scotland.*

ticularly for examining into the Qualifications of Ruling Elders —for re-examining Ministers licensed or ordained by other Churches before they are admitted into this—altering the Form of Deposition according to the Nature of the Case, and making a Distinction between Deposition from the Office of the Ministry, and Deposition from the Exercise of it in this Church as an Establishment. I found by sundry Speeches on the last Overture, that even Dr. Owen or Dr. Doddridge would have been deposed, had they lived in the Church of Scotland.

Mr. Tennent, set out for Glasgow, and thence to Ireland on the first Instant to attend on the General Synod there: and I am left solitary and sad to take a Tour thro' the principal Towns in England.

I am generally so extremely low-Spirited, and full of Anxieties, that I can hardly live. This disables me from pursuing my Mission with proper Vigour and Alacrity. My dear Wife and Family dwell upon my Heart Night and Day; but I am uneasy about my Congregation, lest they should not be well supplied in my Absence.

 Mond. Jun. 15 [sic]. Was conducted by Mr. Adams on my Way to Glasgow; and I have rarely parted with a Friend with so much Reluctance. Yesterday preached for him to his Congregation, which is very numerous (about 3000) a.m. on Jer. 31. 18, -20. p.m. on Heb. 6. 8. and in the Evening on Josh. 24—"Chuse you this Day whom ye will serve." In the 2 last Sermons I was helped to address myself solemnly and convictively to Impenitents: but I could see no Appearances of any promising Impressions. Mr. Young, Assistant to Mr. Adams, is a Man of great Seriousness and extensive Reading. Passed thro' Kirkintilloch a small Town where Mr. Erskine was formerly settled; but Mr. Stoddard,[261] the present Minister, being abroad, I had not the Happiness of an Interview with him. Passed by Kilsythe, where good Mr. Robe[262] was Minister; and the very Sight of a Place, where the Power and Grace of God was so illustriously displayed, solemnized my Mind.

[261] James Stoddart was minister in Kirkintilloch. *FES*, III, 483.
[262] James Robe (1698–1753) had been preacher in Kilsyth for forty years prior to his death. In 1740 he conducted one of the first revivals of the Scottish Great Awakening. *DNB*, XVI, 1227–28.

⊷§ Fryday July 5. [sic]

Lodged in Glasgow at Mr. Archibald Ingram's, one of the Magistrates of the City, where I was treated with uncommon Hospitality. I staid in Glasgow about 10 Days, and I never was in a Place where I received so many Evidences of public Respect. I spent sundry Evenings in Company with the Lord Provost and the other Magistrates, who met on Purpose to put Honour upon me. They conferred upon me, with the usual Ceremony, the Freedom of the City, and bestowed the same Honour on Mr. Tennent and Mr. Burr.

In Glasgow there is a considerable Number of serious People; and they are very happy in their Ministers. Mr. McLaurin is a most affectionate, public-spirited Gent. of a most facetious Turn in Conversation, and an uncommon Genius, tho' his Modesty denies the World the Advantage of it. He has a surprizing Dexterity of introducing into Prayer all the remarkable Occurrencies of Conversation. Mr. Gillies is a most lively Image of Xn. simplicity, and is uncommonly zealous and laborious in his Ministry. Mr. John Hamilton[263] is a Man of clear Judgment and a graceful Address. I heard him preach an excellent Sermon on the Love of God in sending his Son to be a Propitiation. Mr. Cross is a rational, argumentative Preacher, without much Pathos or Solemnity. Mr. James Stirling[264] is a serious, judicious Man, more fit for the Closet, or the Pulpit than for Conversation. Mr. Cragg,[265] whom I had not Opportunity of seeing, is the Favourite of the Polite. Professor Leuhman[266] is a very modest, bashful Gent. but very accurate and judicious, and his Candour is acknowledged by all; tho' suspected by some of verging towards Arminianism. I spent near a Day in his Company; and he shewed me all the Curiosities of the College. The Library-Room

[263] John Hamilton (1713–80) was pastor of the Cathedral Church in Glasgow. He later became dean of the faculties of the University of Glasgow. W. Innes Addison, comp., *A Roll of the Graduates of the University of Glasgow from 31st December, 1727 to 31st December 1897 with Short Biographical Notes* (Glasgow, 1898), p. 247.

[264] James Stirling was pastor of the East Parish Church in Glasgow. *FES*, III, 463.

[265] William Craig (1709–84) was minister to the Wynd Church and St. Andrews Church of Glasgow. *FES*, III, 433.

[266] William Leechman (1706–85) was professor of divinity in the University of Glasgow. Addison, comp., *A Roll of the Graduates of the University of Glasgow*, p. 327.

is large, but not well filled. The most striking Curiosity that I saw was a Collection of Pictures lately imported from France. One was the Picture of the dead Body of Xt. taken off the Cross and carrying [*sic*] to the Sepulchre. The Prints of the Nails in his Hands and Feet, the Stab of the Spear in his Side, the Effusion of the Blood, etc. were so lively, that they unavoidably excited a sort of popish Devotion in me.

I preached 6 Times, whilst in Glasgow; thrice for Mr. Gillies on Jer. 31. 18,-20, Jer. 31. 32. "I will be your God" etc. and on Luk. 2. "Behold his Child" etc. once for Mr. Hamilton on Isai. 66. 2. Mr. Hill[267] had his Sacrament in the Baronry Ch. There were 2 Sermons within and without on Saturday and Monday; and a great many Sermons in the Tent on Sund. one of which I preached on Rev. 1. 7. on which Text I had also preached on Saturday. There were 23 Tables, two of which I served. The Assembly at the Tent was also very numerous. There appeared a general Attention; but no great Affection or Solemnity. I had an Opportunity once more of communicating; but alas! I felt but little of the Fervour of Devotion: and in all my Ministrations in Glasgow, I perceived more of the Man than the Xn. and I could not see the same Appearances of Success as in Edinburgh. One Thing is remarkably commendable in this City, viz. the Conduct of the Magistrates in general, who very punctually attend on public Worship, not only on Sundays, but Week-Days.

While in Glasgow, I was very much indisposed with a lingering Feaver, and so languid and low-spirited that I was hardly fit for any of the Purposes of active Life. Sometimes I was afraid I should never see my native Country, nor enjoy the Company of my earthly All.

I found, to my agreeable Surprize, that Governor Dinwiddie had kindly recommended me to his Friends particularly to the Provost his Brother[268] and Mr. McCullock[269] his Brother-in-Law. I spent a Night with the former, and he and his Family shewed

[267] Lawrence Hill was minister of the Barony Church in Glasgow. *FES*, III, 393–394.

[268] Probably Laurence Dinwiddie, a Glasgow merchant listed by Davies among his "Correspondents."

[269] William M'Cullock was minister at Cambuslang near Glasgow. He was closely associated with George Whitefield and had begun a revival at Cambuslang in 1742. *FES*, III, 237–238.

me the most friendly Respect. I was also a night with Mr. Mc-Cullock at Cambuslang, the obscure Village so famous for the late extraordinary Revival of Religion. He is a humble, holy Minister of Xt. not formed for Popularity; which is a strong Presumption that the late religious Commotion there was not the Effect of Oratory, but of divine Power. His Wife is an uncommonly judicious, pious Woman; and his only Son a Youth about 14, is very affectionate, and parted with me with Tears. I preached there on "Neither is he that planteth any Thing, etc." and I endeavoured to adapt my Discourse to the Circumstances of the People. I had not much sensible Freedom, and I could not see any uncommon Signs of Approbation or Success among the People; only they heard with Gravity and Attention. The next Day, they sent a Messenger to Glasgow, with a Letter to me, signed by near 30 in the Congregation, thanking me for my Sermon, and requesting a Copy of it to be published, or at lest [sic] for their own Use. The last Part of the Proposal, I consented to.

The repeated Solicitations I have met with in America, in London, Edinburgh, Glasgow, etc. to publish some of my Sermons, have made me think seriously of finishing and publishing a Collection of them, if Providence ever grant me a Return. Perhaps they may be of Service in Places far remote from the Sphere of my usual Labours.

There are 6 Churches in Glasgow. The new Church is a fine Building, but not yet finished. The High Church is an ancient Structure, very large, and contains three distinct Congregations under one Roof.

I had a long Conversation with Mr. McCullock upon the Affairs of the Dissenters in Virginia; particularly their Oppressions from the Government. I have Reason to believe that Governor Dinwiddie would favour them were it not so opposite to his Interest. Mr. McCullock consulted me about a Donation of £200 for propagating the Gospel among the Indians, etc.

Having stayed in Glasgow about 10 Days, I returned thro' Edinburgh; saw sundry of my dear Friends, and preached on Sund. for Mr. Webster a.m. and for Mr. Geo. Lindsay of Leith p.m. in the first Discourse I was fervent and solemn, in the 2nd languid and exhausted.

In Edinburgh, there are sixteen Ministers; and I think all the Churches, but 2 are collegiate. In Leith there are 2 Churches, and 3 Ministers.

I had the Honour of the Earl of Leven and his Family for my Hearers last Sunday.

Mond. July 1. Parted with my Friends in Edinburgh; and as many of them particularly Mr. Hogg[270] and Family, are very dear to me, I have scarcely felt such strong Emotions of Friendship since I left Home. Rode to Haddington, about 12 Miles, in Company with one Mr. Dixon, a serious, devout Man from Edinburgh, who asked my Judgment about the Propriety and Lawfullness of joining in the Sacrament with Mr. Gilles-pie;[271] who was deposed by the General Assembly. My excellent Friend, Professor Robertson conducted me about 6 Miles; He is one of the best Linguists, especially in the oriental Languages, in Great-Britain, has an insatiable Thirst for Knowledge, and has travelled far to gratifie it. His Soul is formed for Friendship. Lodged in Haddington at Provost Dixon's, who treated me with Hospitality. Had an Interview with the Reverend Mr. Stead-man,[272] one of the Ministers of the Town; who, I find, is one of the high-flyers; but he promised me his Friendship in the Business of our Mission.

Tuesd. July 2. Passed thro' a well-improved Country, beautifully variegated with Hills and Vallies and the Sea frequently in Sight: and arrived in Berwick in the Evening.

Wednes. July 3. Waited on Mr. Somervile[273] and Mr. Turner,[274] Ministers in Berwick; and proposed the Business of my Mission. The former has given up his Charge, partly on

---

[270] Davies listed William Hogg, a Glasgow merchant, among his "Correspondents."

[271] In 1752 Thomas Gillespie of Carnock had been removed from his pastorate by the General Assembly. After that date he preached in Dumferline and became an original member of the so-called Relief Presbytery. *DNB,* VII, 1244–45.

[272] Edward Steedman was chaplain to the Earl of Hopetoun and second minister to the Haddington Church. *FES,* I, 372.

[273] John Somerville was minister to the Berwick High Meeting. *FES,* VII, 459.

[274] John Turner was pastor of the Berwick Low Meeting. *FES,* VII, 458.

Account of his Indisposition, and partly on Account of the Divisions in his Congregation, occasioned by one that was formerly his Assistant. The latter has but a small Part of his former Congregation, the rest having chosen his Assistant, Mr. Monteith, for their Minister and rejected him, because he would not receive him for his Copastor. These Reasons discouraged them from soliciting Collections for me. I applied to Mr. Monteith,[275] who gave me some Ground to hope he would raise a public Collection. I went to visit Mr. Thomson,[276] Minister of Spittal, about a Mile from Berwick, but could not see him. However, I waited on Mr. Hatton, the principal Man in his Congregation, and secured his Interest, and wrote to Mr. Thomson, begging he would endeavour to have a Congregational Collection.

Berwick had 2 large Congregations of Dissenters formerly; but they are sadly weakened by their Divisions. The Place is surrounded with high Walls and Mounts, and has sundry Garrisons. The Ruins of the old Castle are very majestic. The Bridge is near as long as that of London, and contains 15 Arches.

⋘ *Thursd. July 4.* Set out for Alnwick. Rode about 10 Miles on the Sea-Shore, which is a very good Road when it is not high-Water. Saw Holy-Island about 3 Miles off, where is a Castle that makes a considerable Appearance at a Distance. Alnwick is a pretty large Town, with sundry very good Houses, a majestic old Castle of great Dimensions, surrounded with a Wall. There are 2 dissenting Ministers in it; Mr. Sayer,[277] and Mr. Waugh. The latter was not at Home, and I had no other Way of communicating my Mission to him, but by leaving a Letter for him against his Return. I waited on Mr. Sayer, who appears a judicious old Gentleman. He proposed to make a public Collection. Wrote to one Mr. Buckham, Minister of Branton, requesting the same Favour.

⋘ *Fryd. July. 5.* As I passed thro' Morpeth, I called upon Mr. Atkinson, the dissenting Minister who seemed willing to

[275] Thomas Monteith was minister to the Berwick Middle Meeting from 1756 to 1771. At this time he was probably a licentiate of the Church of Scotland. *FES*, VII, 506.

[276] John Thomson had been minister in Spittal since 1752. *FES*, VII, 517.

[277] John Sayers (or Sawers) was the first pastor of the Bondgate congregation in Alnwick. *FES*, VII, 504.

make a Collection in his Place. When I came to N. Castle in the Evening, I found a Comedy called the Careless Husband[278] was to be acted: and as I apprehended I should not be known, and consequently could give no Offence, I went to gratifie my Curiosity. But the Entertainment was short of my Expectation.

∽§ *Sat. July. 6.* Waited on Mr. Rogerson, Mr. Louthian, Mr. Atkin, etc. I found they had affected Nothing in Favour of our Mission but they promised to concur with me now.

My Indisposition of Body, the Dissipation of Mind occasioned by constant Company, the Fatigues and Anxieties that attend the Prosecution of my Mission, and my Solicitude about my dear Family and American Friends, have so weakened my Body, and depressed my Spirits, that I am hardly able to walk the Streets, or keep up my Part in Conversation. I am often so mopish, and absent in Mind, that I am heartily ashamed of myself, as making a very ridiculous Figure. What would I now give to spend an Hour in my Study, or in the Endearments of Society with my Chara, my Earthly all! Were I more strongly actuated with the Impulses of a public Spirit, my Labours would be more tolerable; but alas! that languishes, in the present Depression of my Mind. I am also plagued, amid this Languor, with the vigorous Insurrections of Sin. I hardly know a Truth attested by such long, uninterrupted Experience as this, That no Change of Climate, no public Character, no Exercises, no Company, and in a Word, Nothing that ever I have tried, can extirpate the Principle, or suppress the Workings of Sin in this depraved Heart. Spent the Evening with Michael Munzus Esquire a very pious Gent. who was once a Lawyer.

∽§ *Sund. July 7.* Preached A.M. for Mr. Ogilvie, who was out of Town, on Isai. 66. 2. and had some sense of the Subject. In the Afternoon for Mr. Rogerson, on Ps. 97. 1. to a very gay Congregation, with some Freedom: but my Apprehension that the Peculiarities of the Gospel would be disagreeable to their Taste, laid me under a painful Restraint; lest their being offended should prejudice my Mission. Indeed I am puzzled to know what is Duty in this Case.

[278] *The Careless Husband* was a slightly erotic morality play written by Colley Cibber in 1704. Cibber was Poet Laureate from 1730 to 1757. *DNB,* IV, 352–359.

Spent the Evening at Mr. Louthian's, who is a very friendly, ingenius Man; but has unhappily imbibed the Sentiments of Dr. Foster, and Mr. Taylor[279] of Norwich. I had a long Dispute with him upon the Original Sin. I found that the principal Reason of our Difference was, that those secret Tendencies and Workings of the Heart and the Languor in Religion, which I looked upon to be sinful, he tho't entirely innocent; and apprehended, that Men by complaining of these, complained that they were Men, and not Angels; and murmured that they were placed so low in the Scale of Being. And he was of Mr. Pope's Mind.

> In Pride, in reasoning Pride, our Error lies;
> All quit their Sphere, and rush into the Skies.
> Aspiring to be Gods, if Angels fell;
> Aspiring to be Angels, Men rebell.[280]

⋳ *Fryd. July 12.* I have been busy in waiting upon sundry Persons to solicit their Benefactions; and I have got about 30 Guineas in the English Congregation. The Ministers of the Scotch Congregations, which are 5 in No. are very friendly; but their People are poor. They intend to collect what they can, and transmit it after me to London.

Yesterday the Right Honourable Lord Revensworth[281] coming to Town, and hearing of the Design of my Mission, sent for me; and I had a long Conversation with his Lordship about it. He found Fault with our not first applying to the Government etc. etc. and I was afraid from his forming so many Cavils, that he would oppose. But as I took my Leave of his Lordship, he complimented me with 5 Guineas.

⋳ *Sat. July 13.* Went in Company with Mr. Munzus to wait on Jos. Bowes Esquire Member of Parl. for the County of Durham. He is a Gent. of a vast Estate; and he took an ambitious Pleasure like Hezekiah, to shew me all his Glory; and indeed I

[279] John Taylor was co-pastor of the Presbyterian congregation in Norwich and tutor in an academy there. He published several theological works which were strongly opposed by Jonathan Edwards. Bogue and Bennett, *The History of the Dissenters from the Revolution to the Year 1808*, II, 352.

[280] Alexander Pope, *Essay on Man*, epistle i, line 123.

[281] Henry Liddell was the first and only Baron Ravensworth of Ravensworth Castle of the first creation. *Burke's Peerage*, p. 1817.

never have seen so fine a Country-Seat in any Part of Great-Britain. Here a Wilderness exhibits all the rude Beauties of uncultivated Nature. There stately Rows of Trees disposed by Art appear in regular Uniformity. Here artificial Mounts rise, and Vallies descend. There verdant Walks and Porterras open far to the View. Here rises a Pile of Buildings in the antique Form; and there a Obelisk lifts its Head on high. He shewed me his Plate, a Part of which is guilt with Gold; and the Value of the whole is computed to be £17000 Sterl. But alas! he gave me but 5 Guineas. He is of an ancient Family, famous in the Days of Wm. the Conqueror. He advised me to wait upon the Bp. of Durham,[282] which afforded me a great deal of Anxiety, lest I should take a wrong Step.

 ✑ *Sund. July. 14.* Preached a.m. for Mr. Atkin on Jer. 31. 18-20. and p.m. for Mr. Louthian on 2 Cor. 4. 18. and in the Even. for Mr. Ogilvie on Rom. 6. 13. the last to a very crowded Auditory, and with great Freedom, and Appearance of Success. Received a Packet from Hanover, which raised all my friendly Passions into a Ferment. I had a very soft, ingenious Letter from my Chara, and her generous Self-denial in not desiring me to hasten home till I have finished my Mission, gave me an agreeable Surprize, and made me reflect with Shame upon my own Impatience. I find my favourite Friend Mr. Rogers (who still dwells on my Heart) has been universally acceptable, and hopefully successful in Hanover. And that my honest Brother Mr. Wright is extensively serviceable in and about Cumberland. May God take to him his Great Power, and reign!

 ✑ *Mund. July 15.* Rode to Durham, and took a View of the stately Cathedral there. The Art of Painting in Glass, which is lost among the Moderns, discovers its Beauties on the Windows in sundry Pieces of Scripture-Hystory. I am still puzzled whether to wait upon the Bp. or not.

 ✑ *Fryd. July 16.* Determined to wait on the Bp. and his Lordship gave me a condescending Reception. He particularly enquired whether the Church of Eng. had any Share in the

[282] Richard Trevor, seventy-fourth Bishop of Durham, was well known for his interest in philanthropic causes. *DNB*, XIX, 1152–53.

Management of our College—complained of the intolerant Principles of the Dissenters in New-England—asked me if I had waited upon the Abp. of Canterbury, or obtained the Approbation of the Society for propagating the Gospel in foreign Parts; and told me that till I had done so, he could not in a public Character do any Thing in Favour of the Design. But he gave me 5 Guineas as a private Person; which afforded me no small Satisfaction, as it may open the Door for farther Benefactions in the established Church. It is Matter of pleasing Wonder to me, that notwithstanding the present Languor of my Spirits, and my natural Bashfullness, I can with Freedom and Composure, converse with these great Men.

Rode to Darlington, a fine little Town; and came in the Evening to North Allerton, which deserves the same Character. As the Way is tedious without Company, and my Time precious, I read as I ride, and while I am baiting; which is both instructive and amusing. I have read, since I left Berwick, an excellent Piece of Hystory, entitled a short, critical Review of the Life of O. Cromwell.[283] Among other Things new to me, I find that Cromwell had some tho'ts of restoring the King, 'till he found him treacherous. That he had the Offer of the Title of King himself, but tho't it impolitic to accept of it. I am now reading Dr. Watts's excellent Piece on the Happiness of separate Spirits, etc.[284] Wrote a Letter to my Chara.

Wednesd. July. 17. As I heard there is a great Number of rich People that resort to the medicinal Waters at Scarborough this Season of the Year; I determined to go thither, in hopes of some Benefactions. Arrived there in the Evening, having ridden about 50 Miles, thro' a great Number of little Villages, Helmsay, Pickering, Brutton, etc. Supped with a disagreeable Company of young Rakes, and was very low-spirited.

Thursd. July 18. Waited on the dissenting Minister Mr. Whitaker, a serious old Gent. I found his Congregation was

[283] John Banks, *A Short Critical Review of the Political Life of Oliver Cromwell, Lord Protector of the Commonwealth of England, Scotland, and Ireland . . .* (London, 1739).

[284] Probably Isaac Watts, *The World to Come; or a Discourse on the Joys or Sorrows of Departed Souls at Death, and the Glory or Terror of the Resurrection. Whereto is Prefixed, an Essay Toward the Proof of a Separate State of Souls After Death* (London, 1745; Boston, 1748).

very inconsiderable; and that there were but few Strangers come to Town as yet; and therefore that my Journey here will be lost. Scarborough is a fine little Town, situated on the Sea-Shore, where they bathe, and drink the medicinal Waters, which I found purgative. An old Castle, now in Ruins, stands upon an Eminence, something like that in Edinburgh, and is of vast Dimensions.

Fryd. July 19. Rode to Hull, in Company with a friendly Gent. Mr. Ellis,[285] Minister of Cave, one of Dr. Doddridge's Pupils, who like many others of them has embibed the modern Sentiments in Divinity. The very Word Orthodox is a Subject of Ridicule with many here. The Dissenting Ministers here take greater Liberties than I should chuse. They make no Scruple of gaming, attending on Horse-Races, mingling in promiscuous Companies on the Bowling-Green, etc. The Town of Beverly, thro' which we passed, is pretty large, and looks new and flourishing. It has a stately antient Minster, or Cathedral (for I know not the Difference) of a very delicate Structure.

Sund. July 21. I have waited on Messrs Wildboar, Witters, Cuningham[286] and Dawson, Ministers in Hull; and solicited them to raise a public Collection in their Congregations; but they seemed to hesitate about the Propriety of it, which afforded me no small Discouragement: for I can neither take Time, nor do I think it worth while, to make private Applications. I begin to fear that my Expences and Fatigues in travelling to the principal Country Towns will hardly be compensated; and therefore that it will be best for me to return directly to London. But I am quite uncertain what will be most expedient.

Preached a.m. in the Presbyterian Meeting-House for Mr. Witters, and p.m. in the independent Meeting-House for Mr. Wildboar, with some Freedom, especially at the former. But alas! that solemn, affectionate Address which once I was capable of, I seem now to have lost; and I am some times afraid of returning to my own People, lest I should not recover it.

The Presbyterian Congregation here is upon the Decline; and

[285] Davies listed a Thomas Ellis of Cave among his "Correspondents."
[286] The Reverend James Cunningham of Hull was also listed among Davies' "Correspondents."

I am told, an unhappy Difference subsists between the Pastor and Assistant. Here, as well as elsewhere, the Presbyterians have gone off from the good old Doctrines of the Reformation.

Hull (or as it is properly called, Kingston upon Hull) is a large, populous Town, surrounded with a Wall and 3 Trenches. The Buildings are generally good and new. The Harbour very commodious. The River Humber, into which the Hull empties itself, is about 2½ Miles over; about 20 Miles from the Sea. There is an old Castle, where the Invalids of the Army are placed as a Garrison, with sundry Pieces of Cannon.

Had a long Conversation with Mr. Cunningham, Mr. Wildboar's Assistant, a candid friendly Youth, educated in London under Dr. Marryat. He appears a hearty Friend to experimental Religion.

How do I long for Retirement in my Study, and the Company of my Chara!

Mond. July 22. I went to visit sundry Gent. of the established Church; but they were generally from Home; only Ald. Parrat gave me 2 Guineas.

Tuesd. July 23. Received a Letter from my Father and Friend Mr. Tennent, informing me, that the Synod of Ulster, and the Presbytery of Antrim had agreed to make a Collection thro' all their Bounds, and that he was advised to make private Applications in Dublin, which he hardly hoped to finish this Month! How solitary shall I be till the happy Hour of our Meeting!

After repeated Importunities the Ministers in Hull determined to make public Collections; only Mr. Withers complains that he is not able to be active in the Affair, and Mr. Dawson, his Assistant seems very cautious, and apprehensive of Impostures: and upon the whole, I have no raised Expectations. Mr. Cunningham is more and more dear to me, as I converse with him.

Had an Interview with Mr. Harris, Minister of Beverly; but I could not determine whether he purposed to make a Collection in his Congregation.

Thursd. July 25. Having arrived in York last Night, I took a View of the City this Morning in Company with the

Reverend Mr. Root. The City is large, about 4 Miles in Circumference, surrounded with a Wall; along which there is an agreeable Walk. The Cathedral is very magnificent, and the Paintings in the Glass are curious. There are 23 Parishes. The Houses in general have but a mean Appearance and are not so close as in most other Cities. The Goal [sic] is the most stately Building for the Purpose that I have ever seen. Mr. Root, a bold, mercurial Gent. promised to make a Collection among his people. But here I may make a Remark which may be applied to all such Cases. That as I know the natural Negligence of Mankind in the Absence of the Solicitor of such Charities; I have but little Hope that any Thing considerable will be transmitted after me to London.

Fryd. July 26. On waiting on Mr. Whitaker and Mr. Tho. Walker, Ministers in Leeds (where I arrived last Night) I find they have had Collections in their Congregations very lately and are now about another: and consequently that nothing can now be done for my Mission; but they promise to make a Collection some Months hence. Mr. Walker is a solid judicious Man, tho' gone off from the old Divinity. He has the Character of a very popular Preacher.

Sat. July. 27. Went to Wakefield; and proposed the Affair of my Mission to Mr. Auldrid Minister there, who upon consulting Messrs Mills his principal Hearers, gave me Encouragement that they would do Something; tho' they had lately expended a great Sum in building a Meeting-House. Had an Interview with Col. Beverly[287] from Virginia, and my old Pupil Thomas Smith.[288]
Returned to Leeds in the Evening.

Sund. July 28. Tho' I have had a more lively Flow of Spirits since I have been in Leeds than for some Time; yet being engaged to preach for Mr. Whitaker in the Morning, I was so

[287] William Beverly (1698–1756) of Virginia. *DNB*, II, 233.
[288] Thomas Smith had been a student in Davies' home. After graduating from the College of New Jersey in 1758, he held pastorates in Cranbury and Pennsneck, New Jersey, and St. George's, Delaware. Weis, *The Colonial Clergy of Maryland, Delaware and Georgia*, p. 84.

112

much confused in the Prayer before Sermon that I was obliged to break off abruptly, lest I should speak Nonsense, or run into Repititions. I hardly remember that my Understanding was ever so suddenly clouded; and I was really afraid lest the Lord was about to take it away from me. In the Sermon, I a little recovered my Senses, and spoke with unexpected Freedom. Preached p.m. for Mr. Walker, and I hardly ever found my Mind emerge so suddenly out of Darkness and Confusion; or my Body and Mind better disposed to act the Orator.

The dissenting Ministers here have so generally embibed Arminian or Socinian Sentiments, that it is hard to unite Prudence and Faithfullness in Conversation with them. They are many of them Gent. of good Sense, Learning, Candour, and regular in their Morals, entertaining and instructive Companions, and Friends to the Liberty of Mankind. But what shall I say? They deny the proper Divinity and Satisfaction of Jesus Xt. on which my Hopes are founded. They ascribe a Dignity and Goodness to human Nature in its present State, contrary to my daily Sensations: and they are not so dependent upon divine Influences, as I find I must be. Are they or I mistaken? Is the Mistake, in such Circumstances, essential? It is with the utmost Reluctance I would admit the Conclusion; and yet I cannot avoid it. The denyal of the Divinity of Xt. introduces an essential Innovation into the Xn. System: and yet the greatest Number of the Dissenting Ministers under the Presbyterian Name in England, as far as I have observed, have fallen into that Error, and the People love to have it so; and what will be the End of these Things? It is a strong Presumption with me against these new Doctrines, that I have observed, wherever they prevail, there practical, serious Religion, and generally the dissenting Interest too, declines, and People become careless about it. Some of them go off into the Ch. of England, and others fall into Deism. And it is Matter of Complaint, that the Deists generally, if not universally, are of the Whigg-Party, and join the low-Churchmen. Alas! how are the Principles of Liberty abused! In Conversation with the Gent. of the new Scheme, I am generally upon the Reserve about my own Principles, lest it should prejudice them against the Business of my Mission. But when I reflect upon it, I seem to despise myself as a Coward. My Conscience indeed does not generally accuse me of Guilt, in this

Respect; but a Sense of Honour or Pride or I know not what to call it, makes me look mean and sneaking to myself.

⤳ *Tuesd. July 30.* Communicated my Business to Messrs Haines and Wadsworth,[289] Ministers of Sheffield, about 30 Miles from Leeds. They are gone off into the new Scheme; and I apprehended their suspecting me to be of the old-fashioned Faith rendered them more indifferent about my Business. They complained that their People were poor—that they were just about raising a Collection for a neighbouring Minister. However, they faintly promised they would try to do something among their People about Christmas.

Sheffield is a large Town, rich in Cutlery Ware, manufactured in it.

⤳ *Wednesd. July 31.* Waited on Mr. Pye, who was Yesterday out of Town. He is Minister of the Congregation that separated from that where Messrs Haines and Wadsworth now officiate, about 40 Years ago, on Account of their Innovations. Mr. Pye appears a serious Man, deeply concerned about experimental Religion, and I believe will shew himself a hearty Friend to our Mission.

Rode to Chesterfield, a little Town about 12 Miles off; but Mr. Haywood, Minister there, not being at Home, I could only leave my printed Papers for him, and write to him.

⤳ *Thirsd. August 1.* Rode about 27 Miles over the Peaks of Derbyshire, and came to Derby; which is a very agreeable Town, with sundry very good Houses in it. Mr. Rogerson, the Presbyterian Minister, gave me Encouragement that he would collect Some thing among his People.

I was delighted with an Inscription upon a Monument on the Side of the Church, erected by a tender Husband for his Wife, who died in her 6oth. Year.

> "She was————But Words are wanting to say what;
> Think what a *Wife* should be, and she was that."

The longest Epitaph would not have been so striking and significant to me; and it bro't my Chara to my Mind.

[289] Davies listed him among his "Correspondents" but did not use his first name.

114

Tho' I hurry on, as fast as I can; yet I find it takes a long Time to negotiate my Business at so many Places. I often think of Bristol with Anxiety, where, I'm afraid, I shall be long detained. And I am often calculating, with pensive Melancholy, as I ride along, how long it will be before my Return Home; for there my earthly Happiness lies.

I am so diffident of Mankind, that I am afraid these transient Applications will turn to little Account. I suspect they will be forgotten, when I have turned my Back. And this renders my Itinerations more discouraging.

☙ *Fryd. August 2.* Breakfasted with Mr. Rogerson, at Mr. Crompton's, who belongs to his Congregation. He seemed diffident of the Recommendations, because they were in Print; and would do Nothing, 'till he received the Recommendation of Mr. Lawrence[290] etc. from London.

Rode to Notingham, about 26 Miles. It is a large Town, and the Buildings are generally good, and some of them magnificent, tho' I have seen none equal to some in Derby. It is situated on the River Trent, which is navigable for small Vessels.

The Arian and Arminian Controversy has lamentably divided the Dissenters here. Mr. Sloss[291] and his People retain the old fashioned Faith; and Dr. Eaton[292] and his People have embibed the new-fangled Notions. They both received my Mission favourably; and I hope will do something in favour of it. Dr. Eaton is a very grave and contemplative Man, of a reserved, magisterial Behaviour.

I find there are some serious People here, who warmly espouse the Doctrines of Grace. I spent this Evening agreeably in a small Company of them and I met with one Mr. Wells, a pious Youth of the Academy at Plasterer's Hall, who is very friendly; and kindly attends me wherever I go.

Here are the Ruins of an old Castle, with many subterranean

[290] Probably Dr. Samuel Lawrence of Monkwell Street, whom Davies had met in January.

[291] A James Sloss of Nottingham is mentioned in Bogue and Bennett, *The History of the Dissenters from the Revolution to the Year 1808*, II, 407, as a religious disputant of this period. He had engaged in a heated pamphlet controversy with John Taylor of Norwich. *DNB*, XIX, 439.

[292] Samuel Eaton of Nottingham had been awarded a doctorate of divinity by Glasgow in 1738. Addison, comp., *A Roll of the Graduates of the University of Glasgow*, p. 176.

Edifices; and in the Midst, the Duke of New-Castle has a stately Palace. The Castle was demolished by Oliver Cromwell; and I was surprized to observe from what a great Distance he flung his Bombs.

❧ *Sat. August 3.* Visited Mr. Harross, Dr. Eaton's Assistant; and engaged him to make a Representation of the Affairs of my Mission To-morrow, in order to a public Collection. Had an Interview also with Mr. Radford, a good old Minister, who has for some Time declined the Exercise of his Ministry; and with Mr. Williams, who has a large Estate lately fallen to him, and therefore he preaches only occasionally.

❧ *Sund. August 4.* Preached a.m. for Mr. Sloss, with some Degree of Freedom; and p.m. for Dr. Eaton to a very crowded Congregation, with the usual Restraint proceeding from a Fear of prejudicing them against my Mission by a solemn Calvinistic Sermon. After Sermon they collected £21. 15s. which much surpassed my Expectation. Spent the Evening agreeably in a religious Society of a Number of serious Men; who were much pleased and edified by my Sermons!!

❧ *Mund. August 5.* Went in Company with Mr. Sloss and his Deacons to make private Applications to his People; and collected about 30 Guineas in 3 or 4 Hours. Spent an Hour with Mr. Radford who has an uncommon Sense of Religion upon his Spirit, and a peculiar Dexterity in giving the Conversation a religious Turn.

❧ *Tuesd. August 6.* Dined with John Dean Esquire whose Hystory is very extraordinary. He met with a most amazing Deliverance at Sea above 40 Years ago, of which he has published an Account,[293] and which he now annually commemorates by a Sermon. He was about 15 Years in the Service of Peter the Great of Muscovy, and at last banished by him, because he would not join in a War against the English. He was for many Year's his

[293] John Dean, *A Narrative of the Sufferings, Preservation and Deliverance of Capt. John Dean and Company; in the Nottingham-Galley of London, Cast Away on Boon-Island, near New England, December 11, 1710* (London, 1711). There were many editions after the first.

Majesty's Consul at Ostend. Has been at most of the Courts in Europe, and by Conversation with various Nations, has learned 5 or 6 Languages. He is now near 80, and has from Nothing raised such a Fortune, that he has a very handsome Living, and has retired from Business about 15 Years. The Hystory of his Deliverance at Sea is, I think, by far the most extraordinary that I have ever seen.

Spent the Evening in a religious Society.

⋙ *Wednesd. August 7.* Preached for Mr. Sloss to a numerous Auditory on Jer. 31. 18-20; but not with proper Solemnity. I was honoured with the Presence of 3 or 4 Ministers. I afterwards found some of the rigid Calvinists were not pleased with my Sermon; because not explicit upon Original Sin. And I doubt not but another Party were displeased upon a quite different Account. How impossible is it to please Men!

My Success in Nottingham has far exceeded the most sanguine Expectations. I received above £60, which is more than has ever been collected there on such an Occasion.

⋙ *Thirsd. August 8.* Break-fasted with Mrs. Hallows, a Lady belonging to Dr. Eaton's Congregation. She has studied Dr. Clark, and is a dextrous Disputant in the Trinitarian Controversy. I have seldom been so closely attacked upon the proper Divinity of the Son of God; and it cast me, afterwards, in to a pensive melancholy Study upon the Point.

Rode to Loughborough, 13 Miles, and waited on Mr. Statham, the dissenting Minister; but his Congregation is so small, that he could do little for my Mission; tho' very friendly and sociable.

Lodged in Leicester a large Town (11 Miles) but the Minister Mr. Worthington,[294] not being at Home, I could only leave my Papers for him.

⋙ *Fryd. August 9.* Rode to Northampton (32 Miles) thro' Harboro! The Town looked desolate and melancholy to me, when I tho't upon the Removal of the excellent Dr. Doddridge into a better World. The dear Remembrance of him engaged my tender Tho'ts, as I rode along; and threw me into pensive Melan-

---

[294] Hugh Worthington (1712–97) was minister to the Leicester Great Meeting. *DNB*, XXI, 954.

choly. How much has my Mission suffered by his Death! I think I never felt such friendly Sensations towards an entire Stranger. Waited on Mr. Gilbert, his Successor; but found him in Company; so that I had no Time for Conversation.

◄§ *Sat. August 10.* In conversing with Mr. Gilbert, I found there is but little Prospect of Success in this Town; the People being lately put to very great Expence about their own Affairs.

Visited the Reverend Mr. Hervey at Weston Flavel, and spent the most of the Day in endearing Conversation with him. I have observed, that when I have contracted personal Acquaintance with great Authors, they have seldom answered the Idea I had formed of them from their Writings. But Mr. Hervey greatly exceeded it. The Spirit of Devotion animates his Conversation; and the greatest Modesty, and Delicacy of Imagination adorns it. The Scriptures are his favourite Topic, and he charms one with his Remarks upon their Beauties. He also frequently throws out some pertinent Quotation from the Latin and Greek Classics, of which he is an excellent Master. Blessed be God, that there is such a Man on this guilty Globe.

◄§ *Sund. August 11.* Preached a.m. in Dr. Doddridge's Pulpit; and the Sight of his Monument with a very significant Inscription, struck my Mind with uncommon Energy. My Subject was "I will be your God, etc." and I had some Freedom, but little Solemnity. The Congregation is decreased since the Dr's. Death; as they can find none to supply his Place fully. And some of the People have left the Society, pretending that Mr. Gilbert does not preach the Doctrines of Grace. But I hope it is but a Pretence; for I heard him p.m. preach an ingenious, experimental Discourse on "Look unto me, and be ye saved, etc." He also administered the Sacrament and spoke very judiciously and pertinently on the Occasion. And I was not a little pleased to find him a weeping Petitioner to Heaven in Prayer. Drunk Tea with Mrs. Doddridge, for whom I found a greater Friendship than I could decently express. A Number of the People jointly requested me to give them a Sermon in the Evening; with which I complied: and preached on Isai. 66. 2. with considerable Freedom. Many gave me the warmest Expressions of their Satisfaction; and seemed quite revived.

Spent the Evening after Sermon in Conversation with Mr. Gilbert (who is naturally grave and reserved) and his Assistant Mr. Warburton.

◦§ *Mund. August 12.* Went in Company with Mr. Warburton and Mr. Wilkinson to make private Applications among the People, and received about £16 of which Mrs. Doddridge procured me 3 Guineas. Dined with her, and found her Conversation animated with good Sense and Piety. She remembered me as a Correspondent of the Dear Deceased (as she calls the Dr.) and treated me with uncommon Friendship. I was surprized that she could talk of him with so much Composure, notwithstanding her flowing Affections. She told me, she never had a more comfortable Season, than when returning from Lisbon on the boisterous Ocean, after the Dr's. Death.

◦§ *Tuesd. August 13.* Finished my Applications; in which I was much obliged to Mr. Warburton for his Company. Spent an Hour with dear Mrs. Doddridge, and at her Request, parted with Prayer, in which I found my Heart much enlarged. She made a Remark that has often occurred to me since, "That she rejoiced that the dear Deceased was called to the Tribunal of his Master with a Heart full of such generous Schemes for the good of Mankind, which he had zeal to project, tho' not Life to execute." May this be my happy Case! There are such Charms in a public Spirit, that I cannot but wish I could imbibe more of it. And in this View, I rejoice in the Fatigues and Anxieties of my present Mission; tho' I am quite unmanned, when the Tho'ts of my Chara rush upon my Heart; and the Prospect of so long an Absence is hardly supportable.

Rode thro' Newport, a considerable Town, and came to Holbourn in the Evening, on my Way to London. Thither I find the Attraction of Friendship strongly draws me.

◦§ *Wed. August 14.* Called at St. Albans, a large Town, and a prodigious Thoro'fare. Mr. Hirons, the Minister, was not at Home; and therefore I could do nothing there to promote my Mission.

The Country has a delightful Appearance to a Traveller, this Season of the Year. The Turn-Pike Roads are good; and almost surrounded with fine Houses, especially between St. Albans and London. The Fields are covered with all Sorts of Grain, and white [sic] ready for Harvest. It is indeed the Land of Plenty. But oh! it is a sinful Land. I am shocked with the Blasphemy and Profaness [sic] of the Inhabitants, especially of the Vulgar, who are not under the Restraint even of good Manners.

Arrived in London in the Evening, and was revived at the Sight of my Friends.

◄§ *Wed. August 21.* Set out for Yarmouth, and came 29 Miles to Chelmsford. The People in London think we have received enough; and there is little Prospect of farther Benefactions there.

Visited sundry of my Friends, and had great Pleasure in their Company; particularly Dr. Avery, Mr. Ward, Mr. Forfeit, Mr. Thomson, Mr. Samuel Stennet, Mr. Savage, Mr. DeBerdt, etc.

Preached last Sund. for Mr. Hall, on Heb. 12. 14. and saw their Mode of public Baptism. Mr. Hall made a long Discourse, like a Sermon, on the Nature, Design, Subjects, Mode, etc. of the Ordinance; prayed; and without laying any particular Obligations on the Parent, took the Child in his Arms, and baptised it; and then concluded with Prayer.

Waited on Sir Joseph Hankney Knight and Ald. and received £5.5.

Last Tuesd. heard Mr. Bradbury at Pinner's Hall.

◄§ *Thirsd. August 22.* Visited Mr. Heckford, an old Minister and Mr. Philips,[295] his Assistant; who seemed favourable to the Business of my Mission; and promised to do something against my Return that Way.

Proceeded to Colchester (21 Miles) and visited Mr. Cornel, who appears a warm Friend to experimental Religion, tho' I am told, he is, or at least has been of a very peevish, unministerial Temper. He was once Assistant with Mr. Hall in London. He promised to solicit Benefactions for the College.

Colchester is a pretty large Town, I am told, of considerable Trade. The old Wall is almost demolished. Here is also a Church or 2 in Ruins, destroyed by O. Cromwell, because the Place stood out very obstinately against him.

[295] Davies listed Samuel Philips of Chelmsford among his "Correspondents."

120

Here is an Independant, a Presbyterian and a Baptist Congregation. But the Presbyterian is vacant, and the Baptist is supplied only by a Layman; and therefore I tho't it not worth my while to apply to them.

⋙ *Tuesd. August 27.* From last Fryd. till this Morning, I have been in Ipswich, a very considerable Town; and I have hardly spent so many Days so happily, and with such a Flow of Spirits in England. Here lives good Mr. Notcutt,[296] whose pious Sermons I have seen in America. He [is near] his 83 Year and bro't me in Mind of old Simeon. He breathes a Spirit of Devotion, and is waiting for a Dismission from Earth, with patient and yet eager Expectation. His People love their old Prophet, and chearfully afford him a Maintenance, tho' he has been laid aside from public Labour above a Year.

Mr. Gordon[297] is Assistant, and now invited to be Pastor. He kindly invited me to lodge at his House; and I was greatly edified with his free and pious Conversation. He has experimental Religion much at Heart, and preaches it honestly and with some Success, to his People. He is remarkably punctual in private Devotion; and upon the whole, seems to walk with God. I contracted a Friendship with him, which I trust will be immortal; and which I shall endeavour to cultivate by Correspondence, when I return to my native Country. O How delightful is the Conversation of such a Minister, after I have seen so many of a contrary Character.

Preached for him last Sund. a.m. on Jer. 31. 33. and in the Evening on Isai. 66. 1, 2. with some Freedom; and the good People seemed eagerly to drink in the Doctrine, and were much pleased. This gave me hope that they would be generous to the College; and I was not disappointed: for on Monday, Mr. Gordon and his Clark went among the People, and collected £23. 9s. which is very considerable for People in their Circum-

[296] The published *Catalogue of the British Museum* lists a number of theological works by William Notcutt of Ipswich.

[297] William Gordon (1728–1807) had just been made pastor of the Tacket Street Independent congregation in Ipswich. In 1770 he moved to Roxbury, Massachusetts, and may have served under Washington in the siege of Boston. In 1786 he returned to Great Britain to write his well-known *History of the Rise, Progress and Establishment of Independence of the United States of America* (3 vols.; London, 1789). *DNB*, VIII, 235.

stances. It is their Practice, on Mond. Evening to repeat the Sermon of the preceeding Day; with which I complied at their Request.

There is also a Presbyterian Congregation in Ipswich; of which Mr. Tho. Scott[298] is Minister. He is suspected of Arminian and Arian Principles; but if the Suspicion be true, I am sure he differs greatly from the Generality of that Fraternity with whom I have conversed. His Soul seems formed for Friendship; and he loves and speaks well of many Calvinists and Trinitarians. He is a Gent. of extensive Learning, a fine Genius, and a good Poet. He is engaged in a poetical Paraphrase on the Book of Job, with Notes; and I think he has executed his Scheme to excellent Purpose. He also shewed me sundry other poetical Pieces of his, with which he intends to oblige the World. I preached for him last Sund. p.m. on Ps. 97. 1. and he was heartily pleased with my Sermon. I can confide in him, that he will exert himself in soliciting his Benefactions from his People; tho' he did not think it so proper now as hereafter; and his People are few and ungenerous; and therefore he could give me no great Encouragement.

He is Brother to Dr. Scott[299] of London, who was once his Father's Assistant in Norwich, and having imbibed the socinian Sentiments, opposed his own Father; and occasioned a Division in the Congregation. At length he commenced M.D. and laid aside the Ministry.

Rode thro' Woodbridge, Wickam-Market, Saxmundam, etc. and came to Yoxford. As I was riding along, I formed a Resolution, to draw up a Hystory on my Return, of my present Mission, the State of the Dissenters in England, of the Church of Scotland, etc. as far as I had Opportunity of making Observations: and present the M.S. to the College of New-Jersey; as it may be entertaining and instructive to the Students, and perpetuate the Remembrance of the remarkable Providences we have met with in favour of the Institution. But alas! such are

[298] Thomas Scott (1705–75) was a well-known hymnwriter and minister to the Independent congregation at the St. Nicholas Street Chapel in Ipswich. *DNB*, XVII, 1010–11.

[299] Joseph Nicoll Scott (1703–69) apparently practiced medicine in both Norwich and London. His father was the Reverend Thomas Scott of Norwich. *DNB*, XVII, 997.

my Hurries, and the Fickleness of my Mind, that the most of my Schemes of this Kind are unexecuted.

Mond. September 2. Arrived in Yarmouth last Wednesd. where I have continued ever since; and lodged at the Reverend Mr. Frost's;[300] who has treated me with such uncommon Kindness, as I shall never forget. He is an universal Scholar; particularly he understands 7 Languages. He has a public Spirit, and a very devout and good Heart. In Prayer, he has an uncommon Dexterity in descending to particulars; and is almost as doctrinal and hystorical as a Preacher, and as flourishing as a Poet.

Preached for him Yesterday a.m. and in the Evening, with considerable Freedom, and much to his Satisfaction. The People also seemed attentive, and some of them affected. The Congregation here is but small, and poor; and the Friends of my Mission hardly hoped for more than 12 Guin. at the public Collection. But to our agreeable Surprize, I received about £24. This I ascribe to the Blessing of God upon my Sermons, and Mr. Frost's warm Recommendation. And I think it an Evidence of the remarkable Interposition of Providence in favour of the College, that wherever I have staid to make a Collection it has doubled what was ever raised before on the like Occasion.

I waited on the Presbyterian Minister Mr. Milner; but he refused to propose the Matter to his Congregation; under Pretence that he had engaged to use all his Influence to promote a Presbyterian Academy at Lancashire. I strongly suspect that the Institution has been misrepresented to him, perhaps by Dr. Benson, as a Calvinistic Scheme, or as in the Hands of Bigots.

Yarmouth is one of the finest Towns I have seen, in Sight of the Sea, on the River Yarre, with a most spacious, commodious Key. The Buildings generally good, and some of them of Flint, one in particular, of great Antiquity, is of polished Flint.

Sat. Sept. 13. I have been in Norwich about 10 Days; and lodged at Mr. Paul's,[301] an excellent young Gent. who has

[300] Davies listed the Reverend Richard Frost of Yarmouth among his "Correspondents."

[301] Probably the Thomas Paul of Norwich who Davies noted among his "Correspondents" as having asked for a map of Virginia and a copy of his poems.

passed thro' a great many spiritual Trials, and had a series of remarkable Experiences. He was once warmly engaged with the Methodists; but since Mr. Wheatley's[302] brutal Abominations have come to Light, he has left him. This unhappy Man had preached a long Time here with great Warmth and Earnestness; endured with the most Lamblike Patience, the most cruel Treatment from the Mob, which even endangered his Life, and been instrumental to awaken Multitudes to a serious Sense of Religion. But has at last been found guilty of repeated criminal Commerce with sundry Women, tho' his own Wife was then alive. With what a loud Voice does this Event cry to all the Professors of Religion; "Be not high-minded, but fear!" O that none that seek thy Face, o Lord may be ashamed on my Account!

My excellent Friend Mr. Frost attended me to Norwich; and used all his Influence to prepare the Way for me among the People. Mr. John Scott is also remarkably friendly. But Mr. Taylor and his Assistant Mr. Bourne[303] being abroad, and Mr. Wood [304] having retired into the Country for his Health, I found it difficult to introduce the Affair of my Mission; especially as Mr. Fozer, Mr. Wood's Colleague, is not on a good Footing with his People, and is about to remove from them to Exeter; and therefore did not think it prudent to be active in the Business. Preached for him the weekly Lecture last Fryday, on Isai. 66. 2. and also last Sund p.m. on Isai. 45. 22. with considerable Freedom. After which I gave an Account of the Business of my Mission. And I find both the Sermon and the Account were very acceptable to the Hearers. A public Collection was proposed to be made next Sund. but Mr. Scott and some others concluded to make private Applications to the principal People; which he and Mr. Lincoln did Yesterday, and received about £47.

Yesterday the famous Mr. Taylor came home, and I waited on

[302] James Wheatley had been associated with John Wesley until his "criminal Commerce" came to light in 1751. After that time, though no longer officially connected with the Wesleyan movement, he continued to preach at the Tabernacle in Norwich. John Telford, ed., *The Letters of the Rev. John Wesley, A.M. Sometime Fellow of Lincoln College, Oxford* (8 vols.; London, 1931), II, 86; III, 69.

[303] The Reverend Samuel Bourn was associated with John Taylor as pastor of the Presbyterian congregation in Norwich. *DNB*, II, 935–936.

[304] The Reverend Samuel Wood is listed with Davies' "Correspondents,"

him in the Evening. He is a very sociable, friendly Gent. and talks very freely and warmly about Christianity; and seems zealous for its Propagation thro' the World. He gave me the strongest Expressions of Friendship to my Design; but said that as his Congregation was just now at the Expence of about £3000 in building a pompous new Meeting-House, he would not urge it upon them.

Last Mond. on my Way to Halesworth to see Mr. Wood, I passed thro' Beules, a fine little Town; and dined with Mr. Lincoln, a young dissenting Minister there who seems a cordial Calvinist. Spent 2 Nights and a Day with Mr. Wood, and my Soul was charmed with the excellent Spirit of the Man. He is a judicious, solemn, prudent Minister and I think England can boast of but few like him. He is as warmly engaged in the Affair of our Mission as Mr. Tennent, or myself; and notwithstanding his Indisposition, has laboured to promote Collections in the Congregations around. He is generally loved and revered by those of different Sentiments, as well as of his own. He was the favourite Friend of the late Dr. Doddridge, and seems to possess much of his Spirit. His Soul is pregnant with noble Projects for the Good of his whole Species, as far as his Influence extends. His Expressions in Prayer are remarkably striking and solemn.

I intended to have left Norwich to-day, but I find it is so generally desired by my Benefactors, that I should stay another Sab. that I could not but consent.

Norwich is accounted the 3rd City in England, about 1½ Miles in Length, and 1 in Breadth, the Houses very close, and crowded with Inhabitants. It contains about 31 Parishes, a fine Cathedral with a Spire of prodigious Height; 4 dissenting Congregations, besides the Quakers. The old Bridewell Wall of polished Flint, is a remarkable curiosity. The principal Manufacture is weaving Stuffs.

Last Sat. visited Mr. Stearn, a serious illiterate Baptist Preacher, who conversed very freely upon experimental Religion; and promised his Influence for me with his small Congregation.

Sund. Sept. 15. How frail is Life! how uncertain! How thin the Partition betwixt Time and Eternity! how quick the

Transition from the one to the other! Of how great Importance is it, to be always prepared! These Reflections are occasioned by my unexpected, sudden Approach to the eternal World, last Night, I think the nearest that ever I made. My Life hung in a doubtful Scale; and one Grain would have turned it. I spent the Evening at Mr. Lincoln's in Company with him, his Son and Daughter, Mr. Scott and Mr. Paul. At Supper, I was well; but my Appetite was faint. After Supper, I was well while I smoked a Pipe: but when I begun a second, I found my Spirits flagg; and I could not keep up my Part in Conversation. Then I began to sicken; and made a Motion to go home. We walked out of the Parlour; and as I was just taking Leave of the Family, I instanteously [sic] fell down dead on the Floor, and continued, they told me, without any Appearances of Life for near 2 Minutes. Then I begun to struggle, and draw my Breath with great Force and Difficulty, so as to agitate my Breast, and my whole Frame. In about 2 Minutes I suddenly come to myself; and was greatly surprized to find myself fallen on the Floor, and my Friends about me in such a Fright, rubbing my Hands and Temples: for I had lost all Consciousness, and did not in the least perceive my violent Fall. They immediately sent for a Surgeon; but before he came, I begun to recover. I was able to walk home, with one supporting me. And tho' I was greatly enfeebled and exhausted, and my Heart heaved and struggled to throw off the Blood; I had a little refreshing Sleep. This Morning, I found myself very weak, and a Pain at my Heart; occasioned, I suppose, by the Difficulty of the Circulation of Blood. I preached a.m. for Mr. Bourn, Assistant to Mr. Taylor, but had very little Vivacity or Solemnity. Preached p.m. for Mr. Fozer with unexpected Life and Freedom, and to the great Satisfaction of the People. And was surprized to find they collected near £20 at the Doors.

In the Evening, I was so exhausted that I could hardly live; but at Supper, I most remarkably found myself refreshed by my Food.

Mond. September 16. Continued weak, and pained at my Heart; and as the Dr. as well as myself apprehended it was an apoplectic Fit, occasioned by the Stagnation of the Blood, I had Blood drawn this Morning; and I was obliged to defer my Journey.

When I first returned to my Senses after the Fit, I was quite serene and peaceful in Mind. But when I began to reflect upon my Circumstances, as being among Strangers in a strange Land, having a dear, helpless Family so far from me, whose Subsistence depends upon my Life, and being so poorly prepared for the Enjoyments and Employments of Heaven; it gave me no small Alarm; tho' I had much more Firmness and Intrepidity of Mind than I could have expected. Nothing in this World affected me so much, as to foresee the Effect which the News of my sudden Death would have upon my dear Chara. Lord, prepare us both for the parting Stroke.

I can't but reflect upon it as a remarkable Providence—That when I was seized with the Fit, I was at a Friend's House, and among Friends—that I should fall with so much Violence, and yet not be hurt. Had I been riding, my Fall might have killed me. Had I been alone, or among Strangers, I would have none to take proper Care of me. But all Circumstances were happily ordered by divine Providence.

 Tues. Sep. 17. After taking an affectionate Leave of my Norwich-Friends, I set out for Wattesfield (about 30 Miles) and lodged with the Reverend Mr. Harmer,[305] a friendly, sociable, ingenious Gent. His Congregation have formed a Fund for occasional Expences; and instead of a public Collection, he intends to apply to the Deacons to give a Share of that to the College. Wattesfield is a little Country Village; but the dissenting Congregation is pretty numerous; and afford their Minister a handsome Living.

 Wed. September 18. Came to Bury St. Edmund's, where there are 2 dissenting Congregations; but they are few. Mr. Savile is an ancient Minister of great Integrity and Humility, and a Lover of all good Men. He is a warm Friend to experimental Religion, and rejoices in the Conversion of Sinners, by whatever Means it can be accomplished. He has a particular

[305] Thomas Harmer (1714–88) was minister to the Independent congregation in Wattisfield, Suffolk. *DNB*, VIII, 1298–99.

Friendship for the despised Methodists, because one of them, Mr. Skelton, with whom I had some agreeable Conversation, was the Instrument of making religious Impressions upon his Daughter.

Mr. Follet is an ingenious, modest young Gent. a Pupil of Dr. Doddridge's, not so thoro'ly calvinistic as Mr. Savile.

➳ *Thursd. September 19.* Preached Mr. Savile's Lecture p.m. with some Freedom and great Popularity. And I hope the People here will make a handsom Collection, tho' I can't stay to receive it.

Bury is a Town of great Antiquity, but its antient Grandeur is declined. The Ruins of an old Abby, demolished at the Reformation, are very stately; particularly the Gate, which is still entire. The Walls of the Abbey were about 2½ Miles in Circumference.

Here I received the melancholy News of the Death of that excellent Man, my particular Friend, Mr. McLaurin of Glasgow. That City has lost one of its brightest Ornaments, the Church of Scotland one of its most excellent Ministers and the College of New-Jersey one of its best Friends. But Heaven has received a new Inhabitant from this sinful World; May I be prepared to follow.

Sic mihi contingat vivere, sisq; More!

➳ *Fryd. September 20.* Came to Sudbury, and found Mr. Hextal the Minister and Mr. Gainsbourough,[306] one of his People, very friendly to me and my Mission. Lodged with the latter. Mr. Hextal is one of Dr. Doddridge's Pupils, and is possessed of an excellent Spirit. He has not fallen into the theological innovations, but goes on in the good old Way.

Here I was refreshed with an Interview with my kind Friend, the Reverend Mr. Hunt of Hackney.

➳ *Mond. September 23.* Preached Yesterday twice for Mr. Hextal on Jer. 31. 33. and Isai. 45. 22. But alas! with more affected than real Earnestness and Solemnity. I gave an Account

[306] Probably John Gainsborough, father of Thomas Gainsborough, the painter, a prominent leader of the Independent congregation. He was an extremely prosperous woolen manufacturer and smuggler. *DNB*, VII, 801–807.

128

publicly of the Business of my Mission; and they collected about £18.

I find my Lowness of Spirits returned, which makes me affect Solitude, and so impatient of constant Company, that I am quite unsociable. I also feel the Effects of my late Fit, and am sometimes apprehensive of its Return. But alas! Sin is still strong in me, and makes frequent vigorous Insurrections, which I cannot suppress. God be merciful to me, a Sinner. Last Night was much pleased with Mr. Gainsborough's Prayer in his Family.

Mr. Hextal, Mr. Gainsborough and Mr. Fenn went this Morning among the principal People to solicit them to enlarge their Benefactions; and they succeeded so well, that with what they received Yesterday, they made up about £43 besides £5.5 from one Mrs. Rowe of Long Melford. Rode in the Evening to Braintre, in Company with Mr. Davidson.[307] Lodged at Samuel Ruggles' Esquire a Gent. of a vast Estate, and a very serious Disposition. He generously subscribed £30 to the College.

I find the People here are so importunate, that I must stay and preach next Sund. There are few Congregations of Dissenters in England so numerous as this; which consists of about 1200; and they seem in general to be a very serious People.

⋙ *Wed. September 25.* Preached for Mr. Davidson on Isai. 45. 22. and the Lord made the Discourse acceptable to his People.

⋙ *Thursd. September 26.* Went to Coggeshal, the Place where the excellent Dr. Owen was once Minister, and communicated my Business to the Reverend Mr. Petts, a very friendly Man; who promised to lay it before his People. But from what he knew of their Dispositions, he could give me little or no Encouragement. Went thence to Colchester, and spent the Evening with Mr. Cornell; in agreeable Conversation. He had communicated the Affair to his People; but they were not disposed to favour it.

⋙ *Fryd. September 27.* Went to Witham, and waited on the Reverend Mr. Burnet; but his People were not willing to

---

[307] Thomas Davidson of Braintree, Essex, was listed among Davies' "Correspondents."

assist. All the Comfort I can take in this short Tour, is the Reflection that I have taken all the Means in my Power to promote my important Mission.

↜§ *Sat. September 28.* I was at Leisure in the Forenoon; and revived the Remembrance of the many delightful Hours I have spent in my Study at Home in Reading and Contemplation. How do I languish and pine for Retirement! And what painful Anxieties about my Chara distress my Mind!

At the Request of sundry Ministers and others in various Parts of Great Britain, I have determined to give my Sermon on Isai. 62. 1. a second Edition.[308] May God attend it into the World!

The Reading of it was very reviving to Mr. Davidson; who is eminently possessed of the ministerial zeal which it recommends. The more I converse with him, the more my Heart is united to him.

I find Mr. Erskine has published the imperfect Notes of my Sermon on 1 Joh. 2. 2.[309] which he has corrected, in general, to my Taste. His Preface in Favour of the College, has already had happy Effects in Braintre, and excited sundry to double their intended Benefactions.

↜§ *Sund. September 29.* Preached twice for Mr. Davidson with some Freedom; and afterwards joined in the Lord's Supper, with some little Devotion. Gave a public Account of my Mission extempore; and tho' the Collection had been made, I received £6 more. Was entertained with Mr. Ruggles's devout Manner of spending the Evening in his Family, examining his Children, reading a Sermon, Singing and Prayer.

↜§ *Mond. September 30.* As I was parting with Mr. Ruggles, he was pleased to add £20 to the £30 he had promised; and told me, he did not know but he might do yet more. Such

[308] *Supra,* 4 February 1754. There was apparently no second or English edition of this sermon.

[309] Samuel Davies, *The Duties, Difficulties and Rewards of the Faithful Minister. A Sermon Preached at the Installation of the Revd. Mr. John Todd . . . into the Pastoral Charge of the Presbyterian Congregation, in and About the Upper Part of Hanover County in Virginia, Nov. 12, 1752. With an Appendix Containing the Form of Installation, etc.* (Glasgow, 1754).

a remarkable Benefaction could not fail of raising in me a Flow of Gratitude to God, whose favouring Providence has attended me in so uncommon a Manner in this Mission.

Mr. Davidson conducted me about 8 Miles towards Chelmsford. His Soul is formed for Friendship, and I could not part with him without some tender Emotions. He is very happy in his People; who seem to be generally possessed with a very serious Spirit; and are about 1200 in Number.

When I came to Chelmsford, I found the Ministers there, Mr. Heckford and Mr. Philips, had raised £6 in their little Congregation, in my Absence. They importuned me to stay and preach; but my Hurries would not permit.

This day has given me another Occasion to record a providential Deliverance. As I was riding at a Gallop, my Horse fell down, and tumbled almost quite over; and I very narrowly escaped his rolling over me. The People that saw me fall were much alarmed, and apprehended my Life in the greatest Danger. But blessed be God, I did not receive the least Injury. Alas! I am afraid that the Frequency of such Deliverances will render them so familiar, that I shall not take a proper Notice of them; and contract a Kind of Insensibility in Danger.

⇜§ *Tuesd. October 1.* Arrived in London, and found by a Letter from Mr. Tennent, that he has almost finished his Applications in the West; and that he intends to come to London, as soon as possible, to prepare for Embarquing for America. The Prospect of so speedy a Return gave me no small Pleasure. But the Prospect of a Winter-Passage was very shocking; especially as I had such a melancholy Time in my last Voyage. And in the present diffident State of my Mind, I am not a little intimidated at the Dangers of the Seas.

Received a reviving Packet from my dear Mr. Rodgers, Capt. Grant, Mr. Allen etc. which informed me of the happy Situation of Affairs at Home, excepting that the Dissenters are still denyed the Licensure of more Meeting-Houses.

⇜§ *Oct. 20.* My Father and Friend arrived in Town about 15 Days ago; and his Presence and Conversation was very reviving to me. He has had very remarkable Success, and received above £500 in his Tour. We are determined to embarque for

Philadelphia, as soon as possible, with Capt. Hargrave. We shall have but very poor Accommodations; and I am afraid, bad Company.

On settling our Accounts, we are surprized to find our Expences run so high; as we have not been extravagant.

Since I have been in London, I have moved in the same Circle; and nothing new has occured; but that I find by Conversation with Dr. Stennet, there is a Prospect of obtaining Licenses in the Bp. of London's Court, for Meeting-Houses in Virginia.

Since I have been in Town, I have preached for Mr. Gibbons, Mr. Hunt, at Dr. Marryat's Meeting-House, Dr. Gifford,[310] and to-day for Mr. Townsend[311] at Newington, and for Dr. Guyse.

Sund. Oct. 27. Preached for Mr. Hayward a.m. on Heb. 6. 7, 8. with more Solemnity and Freedom than alas! has been usual with me of late; and I tho't I perceived a general Concern among the Hearers, who were numerous by Accessions from other Congregations. I observe a Set of Hearers that generally attend me wherever I preach, particularly the young Students in the Academy. Preached p.m. for Mr. Crookshank on Isai. 66. 1, 2. In the Evening heard Mr. Bulkley[312] at the old Jewry, where the celebrated Dr. Foster[313] was wont to hold his Lecture. His Discourse was finely composed, and delivered with a tolerable Address; but alas! how antievangelical!

Yesterday we waited on Messrs John and Ch. Westley. Notwithstanding all their wild Notions, they appear very benevolent, devout and zealous Men, that are labouring with all their Might to awaken the secure World to a Sense of Religion; and they are honoured with Success. But I am afraid their encouraging so many illiterate Men to preach the Gospel, will have bad Consequences. I heard one of them last Tuesd. Nt. but he ex-

[310] Andrew Gifford (1700–1784) was pastor of the Baptist congregation in Eagle Street and a well-known numismatist and antiquary. *DNB*, VII, 1178–79.

[311] Meredith Townshend had formerly been an assistant to Samuel Price in Bury Street and was now pastor of the Independent congregation in Stoke-Newington. Wilson, *Dissenting Churches*, I, 318–320.

[312] Charles Bulkley (1719–97) was minister to a congregation of Baptists meeting in the Barbican Chapel. *DNB*, III, 234–235.

[313] James Foster (1697–1753) had preceded Bulkley as Baptist preacher in the Barbican Chapel. At his death in 1753 he was pastor of the Independent congregation in Pinner's Hall. *DNB*, VII, 494–495.

plained Nothing at all. His Sermon was a meer Huddle of pathetic Confusion, and I was uneasy, as it might bring a Reproach upon experimental Religion. The despised Methodists, with all their Foibles, seem to me to have more of the Spirit of Religion than any Set of People in this Island.

Mr. Locke's Epitaph written by himself. Hic situs est Johannes Locke. Si qualis fuerit, rogas? Mediocritate sua contentum se vixisse respondet. Literis eo usque tantum profecit, ut Veritati unice litaret: hoc ex scriptis illius disce, quæ quod de eo reliquum est, majore fide tibi exhibebunt, quam Epitaphie suspecta Elogia. Virtutes, si quas Habuit, minores sanè quam quas sibi laudi, tibi in Exemplum proponeret: Vitia una sepeliantur. Morum Examplar si quæras, in Evangelio habes: Vitiorum utinam nusquam: Mortalitatis certè (quod prosit) hic et ubique.

⋙ *Mond. Nov. 18.* We came Yesterday to Gravesend, in the Charming Anne, Capt. Baker;[314] having taken Leave of my Friends, and left London, last Fryd. My Father and Friend Mr. Tennent sailed with Capt. Hargrave for Philadelphia, last Wednesd. The Impossibility of getting the Trustees together, and of my travelling home by Land from Phil. determined me with Mr. Tennent's Consent, to deny myself the Pleasure of his Company, and sail directly for Virginia, that I may sooner see my earthly all at Home. And now, when I am about to encounter the Terrors of a Winter-Passage over the tumultuous Ocean, I would solemnly commend myself to the God of my Life, and the Ruler of Sea and Land: And tho' I am but a very insignificant Creature, yet as I am of no small Importance to my helpless Family, I wish and pray, that if it please God, I may be favoured with a safe Passage.

Since Oct. 27. I have preached for Mr. Hull, Mr. Winter, Dr. Stennet, Mr. Lawson, Dr. Gifford, etc. I cannot but observe that I found unexpected Freedom and Solemnity in preaching a neglected old Sermon, that I tho't not worthy of hearing, from Heb. 11. 1.

I have met with so many Solicitations both in Conversation and by Letters, to publish some of my Sermons, that I continue my purpose of finishing some of them for that Purpose.

[314] Captain Richard Baker commanded the *Charming Anne*. *Virginia Gazette,* 28 February 1755.

Now when I have parted with London, forever, I cannot but think with Affection upon the many Friends I have left behind me; who are entitled to my warmest Gratitude.

I have preached in many of the Pulpits of the 3 Denominations; and from the warm Approbation of a Number, I cannot but hope, I have been of some Service in that Way; tho' alas! nothing to what might be expected or wished.

The Petition from Virginia, being returned, I waited with it on Dr. Avery, Mr. Mauduit, etc. and communicated it also to Dr. Stennet, and begged he would act in Concert with the Committee; which he chearfully promised. And indeed I expect more from his Influence and Zeal, than from the Committee, that seem very slow and dilatory in their Motions. As the Majority of them are of the new Scheme, they cannot look upon the dissenting Interest in Virginia as a religious Interest, because founded upon Principles which they disapprove; and therefore they can only espouse it as the Cause of Liberty: but a Zeal for it in this View, is not so vigorous a Principle, as in the other. The Courtiers are so regardless of Religion, abstracted from Politics, that it will be difficult to carry such a Point with them especially as the whole Weight of the Government in Virginia will lie on the other Side. However, I am in Hopes, the Alternative of taking out Licenses in the Bp's Court, or of presenting the Petition, will succeed; and I have begged the Committee and Dr. Stennet to take one or the other Method, as they think most expedient.

✑ *Fryd. Nov 22.* Came down the River as far as the North-Forland, having been detained by contrary Winds.

We are near 32 Souls on Board; but alas! I am at a Loss for an agreeable Companion. Human Nature appears, among the Sailors, in a very mortifying Light. They are so habituated to Blasphemy, that Oaths and Imprecations flow spontaneous from them: and I am in Pain and Perplexity what Measures I shall take for their Reformation. Considering what sort of Men cross the Seas, it is a Miracle of divine Patience, and an Evidence that is not the State of Retributions, that so many of them are safely conducted thro' the Dangers of the Ocean. Alas! I have my own Share of Sins, and it shocks me to think how unholy I still am.

Thursd. Nov. 28. We came to the Downs last Sunday, and were detained there, waiting for a fair Wind, till this Afternoon, when we set sail.

Thro' the great Goodness of God, I have not as yet felt any Thing of Sea-Sickness, as I expected; and I now hope, I shall escape it.

I spend my Time, as well as I can, in reading, and transcribing my own Sermons for the Press. I have read the Bp. of London's Sermons on the Evidences of Christianity,[315] Dr. Wright on Hardness of Heart, etc.[316]

I have Peace of Mind; but alas! I feel great Languor in Devotion, and but little Zeal to promote the Advantage of those with whom I converse.

Saturd. Nov. 30. The Wind being contrary, we were obliged to put in to Plymouth, a very good Harbour; where there are about 26 Men of War; a Garrison, and 1 or 2 old Castles.

Sund. Decem. 1. I purposed to preach to the Company, but the Hurries of getting fresh Water, and clearing out to Sea again, upon the Wind becoming fair, prevented me. Alas! I live a very unprofitable Life; and long to be restored to my Sphere of Usefullness among my own dear People.

Mond. Dec. 2. Having set Sail Yesterday in the Afternoon Yesterday, we got out into the Channel; but it soon grew calm; and we were tossed up and down all Night with prodigious Swells, which are more disagreeable when there is no Wind. This Morning the Wind shifted, and blew violently; and finding we could not get out to Sea, we put back for Plymouth, and got there in the Evening, after a Day and a Nights useless Labour. I found the Return of Sea-Sickness, which quite depressed my Spirits, and threw my whole Frame into Disorder.

[315] Thomas Sherlock (1678–1761), the crusader for an American episcopate, was the ninety-fourth Bishop of London. A great many of his sermons were published but the *Catalogue of the British Museum* lists none with this specific title. *DNB*, XVIII, 93–95.

[316] Samuel Wright, *A Treatise on the Deceitfulness of Sin, and Its Leading Men to Hardness of Heart; with the Means to Prevent both Its Hardening and Deceiving* (London, 1726).

We have now been about 3 Weeks on Board; but have made but little Way. This Delay is a severe Trial of my Patience. When shall I see my Home? Shall it ever be?

Tho' our Return to Plymouth last Night was disagreeable at first, yet afterwards I could not but look upon it as a happy Providence; for the Wind blew with such prodigious Violence, that had we been in the Channel, we should have been in no small Danger.

Wednesd. December 4. Went to Plymouth, in Hopes to have got Contributions for the College; and waited on Mr. Baron and Mr. Moon, dissenting Ministers there; but they told me, the dissenting Interest there was so low, that I could expect Nothing.

Sund. Decem. 8. The Winds still continue against us; so that we cannot get out of the Harbour of Plymouth. This Delay is the more disagreeable, as the Ships Company, to which I am confined, are a Parcel of the most profligate, audacious Sinners, that I have ever been among. My Ears are grated with the most shocking Imprecations and Blasphemies, that one would think, they could not proceed but from the Mouths of infernal Spirits. Alas! to what a Pitch of Wickedness may human Nature arrive! This Day I had an Opportunity of speaking to them from Heb. 12. 14. and I endeavoured honestly to discharge my Conscience; and found no small Pleasure and Tranquility, after I had unburdened my Heart. What Effect it may have, must be discovered by their future Conduct.

Alas! I languish and fret to be delayed so long from my dearest Creature at Home. How lively and agreeable her Image rises in my Mind! May God give me Patience and Fortitude under the Disappointment!

Wednesd. December 11. We are still delayed in the Harbour of Plymouth; but we have still growing Reason for Thankfullness that we got safe in here: for the Weather has been very uncertain and boisterous; and we have just heard that a Ship was lost last Sund. Night on the Rocks called the Manacles in the Channel, while trying to put in to Falmouth and all the Company perished: and had we been in the Channel, we would

136

probably have shared the same Fate. May I be fortified to meet all the Events before me!

Saturd. December 14. We are still detained at Plymouth; and last Night both the Ship and our Lives were in the greatest Danger. About 6 o'Clock in the Evening, it blew a neer Hurricane, which continued till about 12 o'Clock. The Wind blew so strong, that one could hardly stand upon Deck. It drove a large Dutch Ship from her Anchors, and she ran against a large Rock on Shore. She fired a Gun, as a Signal of Distress; and having got Assistance, she got off. We found she was driving down against our Vessel; and being much larger, she would probably have sunk her, or broke her to Pieces. As we were trying to get out of her Way, our Anchors got loose, and we drove at the Mercy of the Wind and Waves. The Dutch Vessel struck against us once or twice; and afterwards, we ran upon a large Antigua-Ship; and were obliged to lie by her Side for some Time. Another Ship was very near us on the other Side; and we were in Danger of being dashed to Pieces betwixt them. At last, with great Difficulty we anchored in a Place, where we lay safe till Morning; but had not the Wind abated, we should in all Probability have dashed against some of the Ships, or the Rocks, which might have been fatal to us. This Morning we endeavoured to get into a safer Place; but we run aground; and were obliged to stick, till high-Water: and we could not anchor well, till the Evening, tho' the Men had been hard at Work at Day, and most of last Night; and after all, a large Ship came this Evening, within a Yard of us!

I endeavoured to commend myself into the Hands of God, in the Extremity of Danger. But when Death, especially in such Circumstances, appeared near, it filled me with solemn Horror. And when I afterwards reflected upon my Diffidence, it depressed my Spirits not a little, to find I am not fortified against all the Events of this mortal State. Alas! it would not be thus with me, had I lived nearer to God, and under more realizing Impressions of the eternal World. O that I may take the Warning! and may my present Impressions be lasting and efficacious, and not prove a transient Fit of extorted Devotion!

I am sorry to find, that my Discourse last Sund. to the Ship's Company, has had no Effect upon sundry of them. When they vent their Passions, or are in a Hurry, or alarmed with Danger, they cannot speak without Oaths and Curses; which is so shocking, that I dare hardly venture upon Deck, lest I should hear them. Alas! how depraved, how diabolically wicked is human Nature!

～§ *Fryd. Decem. 20.* We have been on Board 5 Weeks, (a longer Time than our whole Voyage from Philadelphia) and this Morning the Wind blowing from the East, and we set sail. I find myself already much disordered with Sea-Sickness; and am like to have a melancholy Passage.

～§ *Saturd. Decem. 28.* For this Week past, we have had the usual Vicissitude of Sailors, sometimes foul, and sometimes fair. We had one Night of very boisterous Weather, and we could not enjoy a Moments rest in any Posture.

Last Sunday I hoped to have spoken once more to the Ship's Company; but I was so disordered with Sea-Sickness, that I was not able. Alas! I lead a most useless Life.

When I am able, I read in Bp. Burnet's Hystory of his own Life and Times,[317] in which is a more full Account of the strange Intrigues of Courts than can be met with in most of Hystories. He is always fond of searching into the Springs and Causes of Actions; and no doubt he often discovers the true ones: but sometimes this Temper betrays him into censorious Conjectures about the Hearts of others, of which he was no Judge. The Spirit of Moderation and Piety that breathes thro' his Writings, is quite charming.

The Reign of K. Ch. 2. appears a Scene of Luxury and Debauchery, Changes in the Ministry, imaginary Plots, and Prostitution to the French Interest.

The short Reign of K. J. 2 was a continued Struggle of Popery and arbitrary Power, against Liberty and the Protestant Religion. But the Steps taken were so hasty and precipitant, that

[317] Gilbert Burnet, Jr., and Thomas Burnet, eds., *Bishop Burnet's History of His Own Time* (London, 1724). The author, Gilbert Burnet (1643–1715), had been successively Bishop of Aberdeen and Archbishop of Glasgow before William III rewarded him with the See of Salisbury for his work in the Revolution of 1688. *DNB*, III, 394–405.

Nothing but an enthusiastic Bigottry could have directed to them or expected Success from them.

The Reign of Wm. and M. would have been one illustrious Day, had it not been so unhappily clouded with Frictions between the Whigs and Tories; and the latter lay as a dead Weight upon all the generous Projects of that Hero for the public Good.

Q. Anne's Reign was nothing but a Contest for Victory between the Whiggs and Tories; and in the last 4 Years of her Reign, the latter unhappily got the Superiority, and concluded the disadvantagious Peace of Utrecht; when the French lay so much at Mercy, that honourable Terms might have easily been obtained.

1755

ᴥᢌ *Thursd. January 9. 1775.* For above a Fortnight, we have had but very little fair Wind. Some Days have been very sually [*sic*], and others quite calm, with very high Swells; which is extremely disagreeable. Two days ago, we had no Wind, and the Seas run very high; and the Ship got between two large Swells, and not obeying her Helm, went almost round, and we were in the greatest Danger of sinking. The Capt. as pale as Death, cryed out to get the Boats loose, that in them we might commit ourselves to the Ocean, and endeavour to get to a Ship in Sight; but it pleased God that the Vessel righted, and we were safe beyond all Expectation. May this providential Deliverance have proper Impressions upon me!

The two last Sundays, I have entertained the Ship's Company with 2 Discourses, one on the Love of God, and the other on striving to enter in at the strait Gate.

I continue much disordered, and so languid and Inactive that I am good for Nothing. When I am able, I spend my Time in reading the Universal Hystory[318] Vol. 5, and 6. but I am not a little mortified to find my Memory so slippery.

ᴥᢌ *Sund. Jan. 12.* Was so much out of Order, that I was not able to entertain the Company with a Sermon: and alas, my

[318] *An Universal History, from the Earliest Account of Time. Compiled from Original Authors; and Illustrated with Maps, Cuts, Notes, &c. With a General Index to the Whole* . . . (65 vols.; London, 1747–68). The first twenty-one volumes had been published by this time.

Spirits were so low, and the Prospect of Success so discouraging, that I had no Heart to attempt it.

◦§ *Saturd. Jan. 18.* This last Week has been the most painful and melancholy that I have seen for many Years. I have had the Tooth-Ake in the most violent Degree; so that I had no Rest Night nor Day; indeed it was sometimes so violent, that it made me almost quite delirious. I have little or no sleep in Bed for these 5 or 6 Nights; but to-day, I have a little Ease; and oh! how sweet is it, after so much Pain.

◦§ *Sund. Jan. 26.* We have some Days of the most calm Weather, that I have seen at Sea: but last Fryd. Night a violent Storm blew up from the N.W. which lasted about 30 Hours. It is impossible for the most lively Imagination, without the Help of Sight, to form an Idea of the Aspect of the Ocean at such a Time; and it is most astonishing the little Vessel we float in, is not dashed to Pieces by the furious Conflicts of the Waves, which toss her about like a Cork, and give her such Shocks, that she trembles in every Joint. It is a very good Subject for a Poem; but alas; all my poetical Powers are dormant.

> Inconstant, boistrous Element! the Type
> Of human Life. Now gentle Calms compose
> The wide-extended Surface; to the Eye
> Opens a level Plain, a Sea of Glass,
> Smooth as the standing Pool, or purling Stream,
> Or only rising gradual and slow
> In vast majestic Swells, not wild, abrupt,
> A watry Precipice; such as these Eyes
> Now see collecting all their Terrors round,
> On every Side. Above, the Clouds replete
> With Winds and angry Fire tremendous lower.
> The Lightening flashes a malignant Glare
> Thro' the thick Gloom, and helps but to descry
> The Horrors of the Dark, and Danger's Frown.
> Now the fierce Flash spreads out in Sheets of Flame
> Round Heaven's wide Canopy, and mean Time the Winds
> Collect their Forces, and discharge their Rage

On the fermenting Deep; ~~The Surges rise,~~
~~And roll in thick Succession far away~~
~~Beyond the Ken of Sight; Or driven adverse,~~
~~sudden~~   ~~in futile sudden~~
~~Together dash in angry furious Conflict dash,~~
[. . .   ]
[. . .] ~~The wild fermenting Foam flies up to~~
    ~~Heaven,~~
~~Or sparkling burns.~~'till watry Hills,
And Mountains rise, and roll along, beyond
The Ken of Sight; or by quick-shifting Winds
Driven adverse, dash in furious Conflict; then
The Mountains break, in a tumultous Roar;
The angry Foam flies up to Heaven, in Showers,
And burns and sparkles in the briny Waves.
Sure 'tis the War of Elements; the Shock
Of Nature in Convulsions; 'tis the Wreck
Of Worlds! What horrid Images can shew
The dreadful Scene! What loud tremendous Sounds,
What wild, tumultuous Verse can represent
The blended Roar of Thunder, Winds and Waves
In Tumult. Now how naturally Distress
Casts up to Heaven the wild imploring Eye,
And eager cries for Help. Now, now we sink!
Strange! we survive that shock! Now fiercer still
The Waves assault our Barque, convulse each Joint,
And spread a Tremor thro' each Rib of Oak.
Now we shall rise no more. Strange! we emerge.
Tossed like a Cork, we float from Wave to Wave.
From the huge, watry Precipice we plunge
The yawning Gulph below; While howling Winds
    ~~surround us~~
And roaring Waves, and Midnight's sullen Glooms
Surround us. O thou Ruler of the Seas,
Send forth thy mighty Mandate, "Peace, be still,"
And calm their Rage. But can even Mercy hear
Such daring Rebels, who in one vile Breath
Blend Prayers and Curses? But alas! My Heart,
Look home; thou art not innocent; My Guilt
May hurl these furious Hurricanes in Air,

And arm each Billow of the Sea against me.
But have not I, a Supplicant at thy Throne,
Indulgent Father have not I bewailed
My Guilt in deep Repentance? has not Faith
Applied the Saviour's Blood?

I have Reason to observe with Pleasure, that my Mind for some Days has been more engaged than usual in calm, and I hope, complacential Surveys of divine Things, especially of the Method of Salvation thro' Xt. I am fully convinced, that is the only Religion for Sinners; and as such I would cordially embrace it. Were it not for this, what insupportable Terrors would Danger and Death wear!

&§ *Fryd. Jan. 31.* The Weather has been very uncertain, and the Winds contrary. The greatest Part of this Day has been a dead Calm; but such violent Seas run as I have never seen; and as the Ship had no Wind to direct her Course, she was tossed about in the most terrible Manner, and it seemed next to a Miracle to me, that she was not dashed to Pieces, or overset. It is 6 Weeks to-day since we sailed from Plymouth; and no less than 11 Weeks since I came on Board. What with Sea-Sickness, what with the Wickedness of the Company, and the Anxieties of Absence from my other Self, it has been a melancholy Time to me. Now when I am out of Business, my Heart is always at Home; and so long a Delay by contrary Winds has been no small Trial to my Patience. What tender Images of domestic Happiness rise before me, whenever I recollect the favourite Idea of my Chara! I have now seen a good deal of the World; and I am more and more convinced that she is the Person fitted to make me happy.

I have had Death frequently before me in this Passage; and it is still quite uncertain whether ever I shall see my Home, tho' we suppose we are now near Soundings. With this solemn Prospect I have been frequently shocked; tho' at Times I seemed supported with more of the Calmness and Fortitude of a Christian, than a Person so unholy could expect.

I am quite discouraged in my Attempts to reform the Ship's Company, particularly the Capt. who has many amiable Qualities blended with his Vices. I have spoken to them repeatedly in the most solemn Manner I could; but after all, they forget themselves so far, that they swear and imprecate in my hearing. Alas! the more I know of human Nature, the more I am convinced of its utter Depravity.

Sund. Feb. 2. It is a remarkable Mercy that I am now alive, and capable to take Memorials of any Thing that happens in the Regions of Mortality. About 10 o'Clock the Night before last, a violent Storm blew up from the N.E. which continued near 36 Hours; and I never was more apprehensive of Danger. The Waves beat with such Violence against the Ship, that one could hardly expect but she would have been dashed to Pieces or overset; and the Capt. and the most veteran Sailors were full of alarming Apprehensions. Alas! how helpless are we, on this boisterous Element all our Dependence upon one feeble Bottom; and no other Way of Safety or Deliverance. I think there is no Phenomenon in Nature so terrible, as a Storm at Sea, especi[ally] in the Night. It requires no small Fortitude to stand upon Deck, and take a View of it.

> What Horrors crowd around! Destruction frowns
> In all its frightful Shapes. The lowering Clouds
> Spread out their solid Glooms, and not a Star
> Emits a Ray of chearing Light. The Winds
> Discharge their whole Artillery; rear vast Piles
> Of Waves on Waves, and watry Pyramids,
> Capt with white Foam, that lash'd to fiery Rage,
> Sparkles and burns, bewixt conflicting Seas,
> Toss'd like a Cork, alas! our feeble Barque,
> Our sole Defence, denies us Hope; the Waves
> In Deluges break o'er her, dash her Sides,
> And threaten to o'erwhelm her. Hark! the Roar
> Of breaking Precipices, and the Howl
> Of furious Winds, that from the Bottom turn
> The wild, fermenting Ocean; while the Night
> Spreads her thick Glooms o'er all the dreadful
>   Scene.

Fryd. Feb. 7. Our Dangers and our Deliverances have again been renewed. After a very calm Morning last Wednesday, when the Sea was as smooth as ever I saw it, it blew up a violent Storm from S. which lasted till this Morning, about 48 Hours.

Its Terrors exceeded all the Appearances in Nature that I had ever seen; and those that had been long accustomed to the Sea, agreed they had hardly ever seen a more dangerous Storm. We were obliged to lie to, as the Sea-Phrase is, near 2 Nights and 2 Days, and drove at the Mercy of the Winds and Waves. I was in a careless, guilty Frame when the Storm came on; and I never felt so deeply the Terrors of being seized by Danger or Death in such a Frame. The Sight of Death frowning upon me on every Side, threw my Mind into a Ferment like that of the Ocean round me. Sometimes indeed I had some Intervals of Serenity and Resignation; but generally my Views were gloomy, my Fears outragious, and my Heart faint. I endeavoured to commend myself to God, and to resign my dear Family to his Care; but alas! I could not do it with Chearfullness.

I never appeared to myself so helpless in all my Life; confined to a little Vessel, in the midst of mountainous Seas, at a dreadful Distance from Land; and no possible Prospect of escaping Death, if any Accident should befall the Ship. I could do Nothing but lie in Bed, hearing the Howl of Winds and Roar of Waves without, and tossed from Side to Side by the Motion of the Vessel; which sometimes rolled so violently, that she lay almost on her Beam-ends, and I was afraid she would not recover. The Waves broke over her, so as to wash the Men from one Side of the Deck to the other; and dashed in thro' the Dead Lights into Cabin. I often fell upon my Face, praying in a Kind of Agony, sometimes for myself, sometimes for the unhappy Ship's Company, and sometimes for my dear, destitute Family, whom the nearest Prospect of Death could not erase from my Heart. To encrease our Calamity, we knew not where we were. By our Log-Book, we should have been on Shore 2 Days ago; but we saw little Signs of Land. It had been cloudy for 4 or 5 Days, so that we had no Observation to discover our Latitude. However, we perceived we had gone too far to the Southward upon the Coasts of Carolina, and were much afraid lest we should run ashore on the dangerous Sands near Cape Hatteras. But hitherto God has preserved us; and if my Life can be endeared to me or my Friends by remarkable Deliverances, it will be of more Importance than ever. To-day has been cloudy and squally, and in the Evening a dead Calm; a sure Presage of a Storm; and now it begins to blow again. May God pity us, and deliver us from this dangerous Element, the Territory of Death.

❧ Wednesd. Feb. 12. Blessed be God, we had the well-come Sight of Land this Morning; and suppose we are on the Coast of N. Carolina, about 20 Leagues S. of Cape Henry. The Wind is contrary; and if a Storm should rise, we might be driven out to Sea again.

Since my last Remarks, we have had strong Gales and violent Storms of Snow, with violent intense Cold. It has been so cloudy; that we have had no good Observation of 9 Days; and our Reckoning for Longitude being out, we knew not where we were. We have been expecting Land, and sounding for Ground, these 14 Days; but were still disappointed 'till this Morning. If the Longitude, which has been so long sought for in vain, could be certainly discovered, it would be vastly to the Advantage of Navigation.

Tho' my Mind has been in such a confusion, during the Passage, that I have not been able to make any useful Remarks to any Advantage; yet the various Phenomena of the Ocean have suggested to me such Hints as might be well improved by a spiritual Meditant. And I shall take short Memorandums of them that if I should happen to be disposed for it hereafter, I may improve upon them.

The majestic Appearance of this vast Collection of Waters, may suggest to us—the Majesty—and Power of God, the Author —and his uncontroulable Government who rules so outragious an Element as he pleases, and stills it with one almighty Mandate, "Peace, be still,"—and the Terror of the Conflagration which shall dry it up.

The alternate Storms and Calms are a picture of the Mutability of human Life on this World—of the various Frames of a Xn.

As Storms and Hurricanes purifie the Sea, and keep it from corrupting; so Afflictions are necessary to purge and sanctifie the People of God, and shall work together for their Good. And so God brings Good out of Evil.

It is calm in some Parts of the Ocean, while it is tempestous [*sic*] in others. So, particular Persons—and Countries, are alternately happy and miserable.

The Sea in the Ferment of a Storm gives us an Image—of a Mind agitated with furious Lusts and Passions—and a riotous Mobb.

The Ship is our only Safety. So is Xt. to the Souls amid the Ruins of Sin.

After a Storm and a gloomy Night, how wellcome and chearing is the Return of a Calm, and the Morning Light! So is the Return of Peace and the Light of God's Countenance to a Soul in Darkness and Distress.

The Want of an Observation to discover the Latitude, in cloudy Weather, leaves the Mariner perplexed about his Course. Thus perplexed is the Xn. when God withdraws the Light of his Countenance, or when the Meaning of the Scripture is uncertain.

It is a great Disadvantage to Navigation, and occasions the Loss of many Ships, that the Longitude is not discovered. Thus would it have been, with the moral [sic?] World, if it had not been favoured with the Light of Revelation; and thus is the heathen Part of Mankind at a Loss about the Way to Heaven.

After a long and dangerous Voyage, how eager are the Seamen looking out for Land; and how rejoiced at the Sight of it! Thus eager are some Xns and thus eager should they all be, to see Immanuel's Land, and arrive there.

It is a striking Evidence of the Degeneracy of human Nature, that those who traverse this Region of Wonders, who see so many Dangers and Deliverances, are generally tho'tless, vicious and impenitent.

Such Remarks as these, decorated with lively Images and good Langue, would be both useful and entertaining.

Arrived in York Feb. 13. 1755. The next Day, called in Williamsburg, waited on the Governour,[319] and rode to Mrs. Holt[320] that Night. Came home next Morning Feb. 15. and found all well. What shall I render to the Lord for all his Goodness!

————————————————————————Expression fails

Come, more expressive Silence, muse his Praise!

A Hymn composed, and frequently repeated or sung by Dr. Doddridge in his last Sickness.

[319] Robert Dinwiddie.
[320] Mrs. William Holt of Williamsburg was Davies' mother-in-law.

Whilst on the Verge of Life I stand,
And view the Scene on either Hand;
My Spirit struggles with its Clay,
And longs to wing its Flight away.

Where Jesus dwells, my Soul would be;
I faint my dearest Lord to see:
Earth! Twine no more about my Heart;
For 'tis far better to depart.

Come ye celestial Envoys, come,
And lead a willing Pilgrim home:
You know the Way to Jesus' Throne,
Source of my Joys, and of your own.

That blessed Interview! how sweet!
To lie transported at His Feet;
Rais'd in His Arms to view his Face,
Thro' the full Beamings of his Grace.

To see Heav'ns shining Courtiers round,
Each with immortal Glories crown'd;
And whilst His Form in each I trace,
Belov'd and loving, each to embrace.

As with a Seraph's Voice to sing,
To fly as on a Cherub's Wing;
Performing with unwearied Hands,
A present Saviour's high Commands.

Yet with this Object full in Sight,
I wait his signal for my Flight:
For 'tis an Heav'n begun, to know,
To love, and praise my Lord below.

ᵉᵍ Correspondents

Edinburgh

Mr. Wm. Hogg Merchant

The Reverend Mr. Alexander Webster

The Reverend Dr. Patrick Cumming, Professor of Divinity and Church History

The Reverend Mr. Robert Walker

Dr. Robert Walker

The Reverend Mr. James Watson

The Reverend Mr. Robertson, Prof. of oriental Languages.

Wm. Ramsay Esquire

Mr. Walter Peter, Book-Seller

Mr. Charles Logan, Preacher

Mr. James Grant Merchant

The Reverend Mr. Robert Hamilton Prof. of Divinity

Falkirk

The Reverend Mr. John Adams

Keallearn
The Reverend Mr. Baine

Cockpen
The Reverend Mr. John Bonnar

Glasgow
The Reverend Mr. Leuhman Prof. of Divinity
John McLaurin
John Gillies
John Hamilton
Mr. Archibald Ingram
James Donald
Geo. Brown }Merchants
Laurence Dinwiddie Esquire

Cambuslang
The Reverend Mr. Wm. McCullock

Culross
The Reverend Mr. John Erskine

Kirkintillock
The Reverend Mr. Stoddard

Berwick upon Tweed
The Reverend Mr. Monteith

Alnwick
The Reverend Mr. John Sayre
Mr. Waugh

Morpeth
The Reverend Mr. John Atchinson

149

New-Castle upon Tine
The Reverend Mr. Saml. Louthian
Richard Rogerson
George Ogilvie
[*blank*] Atkin
Michael Munzus Esquire

Hull
The Reverend Mr. James Cunningham
Tho. Ellis Minister of Cave at Mr. Avison's

York
The Reverend Mr. Root

Leeds
The Reverend Mr. Tho. Walker
[*blank*] Whitaker

Wakefield
The Reverend Mr. Auldrid

Sheffield
The Reverend Mr. Hains
[*blank*] Wadsworth
[*blank*] Pye

Derby
The Reverend Mr. Rogerson

Nottingham
The Reverend Dr. Samuel Eaton
[*blank*] Mr. Sloss

Wilford
John Deane Esquire
    (write to him when I shall embarque.)

Northampton
Mrs. Doddridge
The Reverend Mr. Gilbert
[*blank*] Warburton
[*blank*] Boyce, Kiltering in Northamptonshire.

Weston Favel
The Reverend Mr. James Hervey

Colchester
The Reverend Mr. Cornel

Ipswich
The Reverend Mr. Thomas Scott
Wm. Gordon
Mr. John Flindell[?] Senior
    (write to him against the Fear of Death.)

Great Yarmouth
Mr. Frost, Apoth.
The Reverend Mr. Richard Frost
Mr. John Eldridge, Grocer

Norwich
The Reverend Mr. Saml. Wood
Mr. John Scott
Mr. Thomas Paul
    (send him my Poems and a Map of Virginia.)
The Reverend Mr. John Taylor
[*blank*] Bourne

Wattesfield in Suffolk
The Reverend Mr. Harmer

Bury St. Edmund's
The Reverend Mr. Savile
[*blank*] Follett

Sudbury
The Reverend Mr. Hextal
Mr. John Gainsborough

Braintre in Essex
The Reverend Mr. Thomas Davidson

Bocking in Essex
Saml. Ruggles Esquire

Colchester
The Reverend Mr. Cornell

Chelmsford
The Reverend Mr. Saml. Philips

London
The Reverend Dr.
  David Jennings, Prince's Square Ratcliff high-
    Way
  Joseph Stennet, Charter House Sq.
  John Guyse, near Moorfields
  Dr. Avery, Guy's Hospital
The Reverend Mr.
  Tho. Gibbons, Hoxton's Sq.
  Samuel Pike, Do.
  Richard Winter
  Tho. Towle, Goodman's Fields
  Wm. Prior, Well-Close-Sq.
  Saml. Price, Fenchurch Str.
  Wm. Hunt, Hackney
  Saml. Brewer, Mile-End
  Josiah Thomson
  Wm. Guyse, Artillery Court
  Mr. Wm. Crookshank, Hide Park Corner
  Saml. Morton Savage, Well-Close-Sq.

Saml. Hayward, Burnhill Rowe
Saml. Stennet, Bartholomew Close
Robt. Lawson, near Moorfields
Tho. Oswald
Robt. Cruttenden Esquire near upper Moorfields
Mr. Joseph Forfeit Senior Great Carter Lane
Mr. Benj. Forfeit Leaden Hall Str.
Mr. John Bowles, Cornhill
Mr. John Ward, Do.
Mr. Dennys DeBerdt Artillery Court
Mr. Saml. Savage, Gun Str. Spittal Fields
Edw. Jones Q. Street, Cheapside
Joseph Hurt, Optician, Ludgate Street
Mr. Tho. Holmes, New Gate Str.
Mr. Harriot, Cheapside
Mr. Tho. Cox, Winchester-Street
    (Send Mr. Cox my Poems
Mr. Jasper Mauduit in Lime-Street

Taunton
The Reverend Mr. Richard Pearsal
    —to Mr De Bt's. Care

Amsterdam
The Reverend Mr. David Thomson

Dwelling Houses	⎫	105,000
Inhabitants	⎬ in London	840,000
Fighting-Men		210,000
Ships	⎭	4,000

	⎧ in England	8,000,000
Inhabitants	⎨ in Scotland	1,500,000
	⎩ in Ireland	1,000,000

Inhabitants in Holland	2,000,000

Inhabitants	⎫	13,000,000
Archbishops		18
Bishops		109
Abbeys of Nuns		556
Abbeys of Monks		1,356
Convents of Cordeliers	⎬ in France	700
Priories		12,400
Chapels		15,200
Parishes		36,440
Convents of all Orders		14,077
Religious of all Sorts	⎭	400,000

Inhabitants	⎧ in Spain	5,100,000
	⎨ in Portugal	958,312

ᴥ A Letter to Sir Hans Sloane[321]

Since you, Dear Doctor, saved my Life,
To bless, by Turns, or curse my Wife;
In Conscience I am bound to do
Whatever is enjoined by you:
According then to your Command,
That I should search the Western Land,
And send you all that I could find.
Of curious Things of every Kind.
I've ravaged Air, Earth, Sea and Caverns,
Wine, Women, Children, Tombs and Taverns;
And greater Rarities can shew,
Than Gresham's Children ever knew.
First, I've 3 Drops of the same Show'r
Jove into Danae's lap did pour.
From Carthage bro't, the Sword I'll send

[321] [T. Hearne], *An Epistolary Letter from T. . . . . H. . . . . to Sr. H. . . . .s S. . . . .e, Who Saved His Life, and Desired Him to Send Over All the Rarities He Could Find in His Travels* (London, 1729). Hans Sloane (1660–1753), the prominent physician and scientist, had been president of the Royal Society for fourteen years before his death. *DNB*, XVIII, 379–380.

Which help'd Queen Dido to her End.
A Snake's Skin, which you may believe
The Serpent Cast that tempted Eve:
A Fig-Leaf Apron, 'tis the same
Which Adam wore to hide his Shame;
But now wants darning—I've beside
The Jaw by which good Abel dy'd.
A Whet-Stone worn exceeding small,
Which Time has whet his Scythe withall.
The Pidgeon stuff'd, which Noah sent
To tell the Way the Waters went.
A ring I've got of Sampson Hair,
The same Dalilah used to wear.
St. Dunstan's Tongs, as Story goes,
Which pinched the Devil by the Nose.
The very Shaft, as all may see,
Which Cupid shot at Anthony.
And what beyond the rest I prize,
A Glance of Cleopatra's Eyes.
Some Strains of Eloquence, which hung
In Roman Times on Tully's Tongue;
Which long conceal'd, and lost had lain,
Till Cooper found them out again.
As Moore cures Worms in Stomach bred,
I've Pills cures Maggots in the Head,
With the Receipt, and how to make 'em;
To you I leave the Time to take 'em.
I've got a Ray of Phebus Shine,
Found in the Bottom of a Mine.
A Lawyer's Conscience large and fair,
Fit for a Judge himself to wear.
I've Choice of Nostrums, how to make
An Oath, a Churchman will not take.
In a thumb-Vial you will see
Close cork'd, some Drops of Honesty;
Which after searching Kingdom's round,
At last was in a Cottage found.
I've not collected any Care;
Of that there's Plenty every where.
But after wondrous Labours spent,

I've got some Grains of rich Content.
It is my Wish, it is my Glory,
To furnish your Knick Knackatory.
I only beg, that when you shew 'em,
You'd tell the Friend to whom you owe 'em;
That this may all your Patients teach,
To do as done by yours,

T. H.

Index

Aberdeen, University of, 58n, 95. *See also* King's College

Abney, Elizabeth: Davies visits, 77

Abney, Thomas, 77

Adair, Mr., of London: Davies visits, 67

Adams, John, 100, 148; Davies visits, 98

Aitkin, Edward: characterized, 88; Davies visits, 106; Davies preaches for, 108

Allen, John, 131; signs petition for College of New Jersey, 64; Davies preaches for, 86

Amsterdam Coffee House, 46, 60, 64, 69, 79, 83

Anabaptists: in Philadelphia, 23

Anderson, Adam: and Society for Propagating Christian Knowledge in Scotland, 73; Davies visits, 73

Anne, Queen of England: death, 62; reign characterized, 139

Antinomianism: in Philadelphia, 24; in London, 46

Antrim, Presbytery of: collection for College of New Jersey, 111

Argyll, Archibald Campbell, third Duke of, 97; Davies visits, 70; letter from Jonathan Belcher, 70; attends General Assembly of Church of Scotland, 96

Arthur, William: characterized, 88

Ashurt, Sir Henry, 50

Atkin, Mr., of Newcastle, England, 150

Atkinson, John, 149; Davies visits, 105–106

Auldrid, Mr., of Wakefield, 150; Davies visits, 112

Avery, Benjamin, 65, 152; and dissenters in England, 49; Davies visits, 57, 73, 82, 120, 134

"Bagwell Papers": authors of, 57n

Bailey, Joseph: Davies reads his *God's Wonders in the Great Deep*, 31

Baine, Mr., of Keallearn, 149

Baker, Richard: Captain of *Charming Anne*, 133, 139, 142, 143

Ballantine, Hugh: Davies hears preach, 95

Baltimore, Lord, 42

Banks, John: Davies reads his *Oliver Cromwell*, 109

Baptists, in England, xi, 46; attitude toward education, 65

Barker, John: Davies meets, 64;

159

Brown, John: ordained by Presbytery of Newcastle, 20
Brown, Simon: co-author of "Bagwell Papers," 56n
Buchan, Earl of, 97
Buckham, Mr., of Branton: Davies writes, 105
Buckland, James: Davies meets, 51
Buckston, Charles: Davies visits, 69
Bulkley, Charles: Davies hears preach, 132
Burnet, Gilbert: Davies reads and comments on his *History of His Own Time*, 138–139
Burnet, Mr., of Witham: Davies visits, 129–130
Burr, Aaron: president of College of New Jersey, ix; letter to Davies, 3; marries Esther Edwards, 14n; Davies hears preach, 15; Davies visits, 15
Burroughs, Joseph: Davies visits, 67

Calamy, Edmund: Davies visits, 67
Camp, Philander: and Davies' diary, xii
Campbell, Archibald. *See* Argyll, Duke of
Campbell, John. *See* Breadalbane, Earl of
Canterbury, Thomas Herring, eighty-fourth Archbishop of, 70, 109
Chambers, Mr., of Philadelphia, 24
Chandler, Samuel, 53, 73, 80; Davies hears preach, 45, 46; Davies visits, 47, 57, 58, 59; Gilbert Tennent preaches for, 50; and German schools in Pennsylvania, 58; opposes College of New Jersey, 60; contrib-

utes to College of New Jersey, 62; Davies preaches for, 67
Charles I, King of England: sermon on death of, 21; reign characterized, 138
Charming Anne, 133
Chief, Mr., of Philadelphia, 24
Church of England: and George Whitefield, 66
Church of Scotland, 65, 66, 100; and English Presbyterianism, xi; and Patronage Act, 91
—General Assembly: Davies attends meetings of, xi, 87, 89, 94, 96; petitioned by Synod of New York, 15–16, 94; William Kerr serves as Lord High Commissioner to, 45n; Alexander Webster named Moderator, 89; John Edmundstone named Clerk, 94; approves collection for College of New Jersey, 96
Cibber, Colly: Davies attends his *Careless Husband,* 106
Clark, Dr., 117
Clog, Mr.: opens Synod of Lothian and Tweedale, 91
Colden, Cadwallader: John Ward of London published his *History of the Five Indian Nations,* 52n
College of New Jersey, x, 47, 51, 65, 86, 121; early history, ix–x; supporters, ix–x; Davies chosen president of, xii; Davies diary in library, xii–xiii, xiii; founding, 2; financial situation, 2; criticised by English dissenters, 13; books donated to, 56–57; purpose of, 57; John Witherspoon selected president of, 99n
—Board of Trustees, 59; select Davies for trip to England, 3, 6; petition General Assembly of Church of Scotland, 57, 58, 61, 75, 79, 95
College of Philadelphia: and

Ebenezer Kinnersley, 23n; and
William Smith, 57–58
Collinson, Peter: and Richard
Jackson, 80n
Commissioners for Indian Affairs:
founded, 6
Concannon, Lord, 42
Cornel, Mr., of Colchester, 51,
152; Davies visits, 120, 129
Cornthwaite, Robert: Davies visits,
83
Coward, William: founds King's
Head Society, 63n
Cowell, David, 14n
Clarkson, David, 63
Clarkson, Matthew, 38
Clerkson, David. *See* Clarkson,
David
Cox, Thomas, 153; Davies and
Tennent lodge with, 44
Craig, William: characterized, 101
Crompton, Mr., of Derby: Davies
visits, 115
Cromwell, Oliver, 50, 64, 81, 116,
120
Cromwell, Mr., of London: con-
tributes to College of New Jer-
sey, 81
Cromwell, William: funeral ser-
mon by Thomas Gibbons, 50
Crookshank, William, 152; Davies
visits, 66; Davies preaches for,
67, 132
Crosby, John, 38
Cross, Mr., of Glasgow: charac-
terized, 101
Cross, Robert: letter to Scotland
attacking College of New Jer-
sey, 89, 92, 93, 94
Crutenden, Robert, 153; Davies
visits, 43, 48, 55, 73, 76, 82; and
London dissenters, 43n
Cumberland, William Augustus,
Duke of, 81
Cumming, Alexander, 2–3;
Davies visits, 16, 17
Cumming, Patrick, 96, 148;

Davies visits, 90, 97; Davies
hears preach, 91; and University of Edinburgh, 91n; addresses General Assembly of
Church of Scotland, 94
Cunningham, James, 150; Davies
visits, 110, 111
Cuthbertson, John: errors dis-
cussed by Presbytery of Newcastle, 11

Dalrymple, Hew, Lord Drum-
more: Davies visits, 92; attends
General Assembly of Church of
Scotland, 96
Davidson, Thomas, 131, 152;
Davies preaches for, 129, 130
Davies, George: 36–37; lost at sea,
37n
Davies, Jane Holt: children, 7;
illness, 7–8, mentioned, *passim*
Davies, John Rodgers, 7n, 8
Davies, Margaret, 7n
Davies, Martha, 7n
Davies, Samuel: settles in Hanover, Virginia, x; asked to make
trip to England, x; attends
General Assembly of Church of
Scotland, xi, 87, 89, 94, 96;
elected president of College of
New Jersey, xii; gives reason
for going to England, 1–8; education, 1n; marries Jane Holt,
3; letter from Aaron Burr, 3;
marries Sarah Kirkpatrick, 3n;
quarrels with General Court in
Virginia, 4n, 79; children, 7;
departs from Hanover, 9;
awarded M.A. by College of
New Jersey, 16; serves on committee for Synod of New York,
19n; publishes translation of
"Cleanthes's Hymn to the Creator," 23; ill at sea, 28–31; comments on Gilbert Tennent's
sermon on John III, 5, 34; ar-

Dawson, Mr., of Hull, 111; Davies visits, 110

Dean, John, 150; *Narrative,* 116; Davies meets, 116–117

De Berdt, Dennys, 153; letter to Captain Grant, 12–13; Davies visits, 13n, 43, 48, 53, 120

DeFoe, Daniel: Davies reads his *Roxana,* 39

Denham, John: Davies visits, 66, 68, 71

Dews, Samuel: Davies preaches for, 45

Dicker, Samuel: Davies visits, 72

Dickinson, Jonathan: serves as president of College of New Jersey, ix; Davies reads his *Defense of a Sermon,* 31; Davies reads his *Vindication of Divine Grace,* 32; Davies reads his *Second Vindication,* 32

Dinwiddie, Laurence, 149; Davies visits, 102–103

Dinwiddie, Robert, 102; and Virginia dissenters, 103; Davies visits, 146

Dissenters, in England: criticize College of New Jersey, 13; and Benjamin Avery, 49; activities in Hull, 110; characterized, 113–114, 115

—in London, 43, 48, 74; and Robert Cruttenden, 43n; Committee for the Management of the Civil Affairs of, 45

—in Virginia, 63, 65, 78–79, 85, 97; restraints on, 4, 5, 16–17, 103, 131; and Gilbert Tennent, 6; and Jasper Mauduit, 49; petition for relief of disabilities, 82; and Benjamin Avery, 83; and Joseph Stennet, 83

Dixon, Provost, of Haddington: Davies visits, 104

Doddridge, Mrs. Philip, 151; Davies visits, 118, 119; contrib-

utes to College of New Jersey, 119

Doddridge, Philip, 100, 110, 117, 118, 125, 128; Davies corresponds with, 43n; Davies copies one of his hymns, 146-147

Donald, James, 149

Donald, Mr.: letter to Mr. Mill delivered by Davies, 71

Dorset, Duke of, 37

Drummond, George: Davies meets, 90; and University of Edinburgh, 90n

Drummore, Hew Dalrymple, Lord. *See* Dalrymple, Hew

Dundas, Robert: attends General Assembly of Church of Scotland, 96

Dunk, George Montague, second Earl of Halifax. *See* Halifax, Earl of

Dunleith, Presbytery of, 91

Duplin, Thomas, ninth Earl of Kinnoull and Viscount, 70, 73; and Board of Trade, 70n

Durham, Bishop of. *See* Trevor, Richard

Dushane, Elizabeth: Davies visits, 26

Dushane, Isaac: publishes Finley's *Approved Minister,* 26n

Eads, Mr., of London: Davies visits, 75

Earle, Jabez, 87; Davies meets, 53; co-author of "Bagwell Papers," 57n; Davies hears preach, 64; contributes to College of New Jersey, 73; Davies describes his meetinghouse, 86

Eaton, Samuel, 117, 150; characterized, 115; Davies preaches for, 116

Edinburgh, University of, 90n, 91n, 99

Edmundstone, John: conflict with

John Hyndman for Clerkship of General Assembly, 93

Edwards, Eleazar, 45; Davies visits, 51

Edwards, Esther: marries Aaron Burr, 14n

Edwards, Jerusha: engaged to David Brainerd, 17n

Edwards, Jonathan: and Indian missions, 14n; and John Erskine, 67n; quarrels with John Taylor, 107

Eldridge, John, 151

Eliot, Andrew: opposes College of New Jersey, 93n

Elliot, Gilbert, third Baronet of Minto. *See* Minto, Baronet of

Ellis, Thomas, 150; Davies visits, 110

Elliston, Mr., of London: Davies visits, 45

England: inhabitants in, 154

Erskine, John, 100, 149; Davies visits, 94, 99; and Church of Scotland, 67; and George Whitefield, 67n; and Jonathan Edwards, 67n; publishes Davies' *Faithful Minister*, 130

Evangelical and Literary Magazine: portion of Davies' diary published in, xiii

Evans, John: co-author of "Bagwell Papers," 57n

Fagg's Manor: Davies educated at, 1n

Fenn, Mr., of Sudbury, 129

Field, Mr., of London: Davies visits, 79

Field, Mrs., of London, 50

Fieux, Charles de, Chevalier de Mouhy: writes *La Paysanne Parvenue*, 38n

Findlater, James Ogilvy, fifth Earl of: Davies visits, 93

Finley, Samuel: Davies visits, 9–

12; serves as president of College of New Jersey, 9n; Davies preaches for, 10; serves on Committee of Synod of New York, 19n; his *Approved Minister of God* published by Stewart and Dushane, 26n

Flindell, John, 151

Follet, Mr., of Bury St. Edmund's, 151; characterized, 128

Foote, William Henry: publishes a portion of Davies' diary in *Sketches of Virginia*, xiii

Forfeit, Benjamin, 153; Davies visits, 120

Forfeit, Joseph, 153

Foster, Dr., of London, 107

Foster, James, 67, 132

Foster, Judge, of London: Davies visits, 86

Fozer, Mr., of Norwich: Davies visits, 124; Davies preaches for, 126

France: description of, 154

Franklin, Benjamin: and Ebenezer Kinnersley, 23n; letter to William Strahan, 37n; uses Captain Stephen Mesnard as messenger, 37n; and Richard Jackson, 80n; receives honorary degree from Edinburgh, 95n

Frost, Mr., apothecary in Yarmouth, 151

Frost, Richard, 124, 151; Davies meets and preaches for, 123

Furnace, Philip. *See* Furneaux, Philip

Furneaux, Philip: Davies hears preach, 63; Davies visits, 72

Gainsborough, John, 129, 152; Davies visits, 128

Gainsborough, Thomas, 128n

Gardiner, Frances: Davies visits, 97

Gardiner, James: death at Battle of Preston, 89, 97n

George II, King of England, 79, 85; supports German schools in Pennsylvania, 49, 58; comments on death of Henry Pelham, 84

Gibbons, Thomas, 46, 64, 78, 152; Davies visits, 43, 48, 54, 55, 58; prepares revised edition of Pearsall's *Reliquiæ Sacra*, 44; preaches funeral sermon for William Cromwell, 50; Davies preaches for, 50, 54, 81, 85, 132; publishes biography of Mr. Field, 54; Gilbert Tennent preaches for, 55; contributes to College of New Jersey, 69

Gibson, Mr., of London: Davies meets, 53

Gifford, Andrew: Davies preaches for, 132, 133

Gilbert, Mr., of Northampton, 118, 119, 151

Gill, John: signs petition for College of New Jersey, 65

Gillespie, Thomas: deposed by General Assembly of Church of Scotland, 104

Gillies, John, 149; Davies visits, 94; characterized, 101; Davies preaches for, 102

Glasgow, University of, 94n, 99, 101–102, 115n

Glen, John: Davies preaches for, 96

Godwin, Edward: Davies visits, 47; Davies preaches for, 77

Goldsmith, Oliver, 85n

Gordon, George: addresses General Assembly of Church of Scotland, 94

Gordon, William, 151; Davies meets, 121; publishes *History of the . . . United States*, 121n

Goudie, John, 90

Grant, Captain, of Philadelphia, 22, 131; letter from Dennys De Berdt, 12, 13

Grant, James, 148

Grant, Mr., of Northamptonshire: Davies visits, 83

Grosvenor, Benjamin: Davies visits, 56; author of *Health* and *The Mourner*, 56n, 57; co-author of "Bagwell Papers," 57n; supports College of New Jersey, 63

Grovenor, Captain, of London, 38

Guise, John. *See* Guyse, John

Guyse, John, 65, 78, 84, 152; Davies visits, 48, 54, 61, 67; and King's Head Society, 48n; Davies hears preach, 55; characterized, 61; Davies preaches for, 85, 132

Guyse, William, 78, 152; Davies visits, 67; contributes to College of New Jersey, 74

Guy's Hospital, 54, 57n

Hains, Mr., of Sheffield, 150; Davies visits, 114

Hait, Benjamin: Davies visits, 15, 16

Halford, John: signs petition for College of New Jersey, 65; Davies hears preach, 80

Halifax, George Montague Dunk, second Earl of, 70; and Board of Trade, 51

Hall, Thomas, 24, 45; Davies visits, 43, 62, 66, 117; Gilbert Tennent meets, 48; Davies preaches for, 120

Hamilton, Andrew: and Zenger case, 13n, 17n

Hamilton, James: Davies visits, 13

Hamilton, John, 149; characterized, 101; Davies preaches for, 102

Hamilton, Robert, 148; Davies visits, 90; serves as Moderator of General Assembly of Church of Scotland, 93

Hamlin's Coffee House, 64, 65, 84

Hankey, Sir Joseph: Davies visits, 86; contributes to College of New Jersey, 120

Hardwicke, Philip Yorke, Lord Chancellor and first Earl of; 51

Hargrave, Captain, 132, 133

Harmer, Thomas, 151; Davies visits, 127

Harriot, Thomas, 153

Harris, John: examined by Presbytery of Newcastle, 20–21

Harris, John: Davies reads his *Compleat Collection of Voyages*, 33, 35–36

Harris, Mr., of Beverly: Davies visits, 111

Harross, Mr., of Nottingham: Davies visits, 116

Hatton, Mr., of Spittal: Davies visits, 105

Hay, Thomas. *See* Duplin, Viscount

Hayward, Samuel, 153; signs petition for College of New Jersey, 69; Davies preaches for, 132

Haywood, Eliza: Davies reads her *Fortunate Country Maid*, 38–39

Haywood, Mr., of Chesterfield, 114

Hazard, Samuel, 24; Davies visits, 22

Hearne, Thomas: poem in honor of Sir Hans Sloane, 155–157

Heckford, Mr., of Chelmsford: Davies visits, 120; collects funds for College of New Jersey, 131

Henry, Hugh: appointed to preach in Hanover, 18

Henry, John, 86

Herring, Thomas. *See* Canterbury, Archbishop of

Herver, William: Davies visits, 82, 118

Hervey, James, 151; and John Wesley, 82n; author of *Meditations*, 82n

Heveningham Hall, Baronet of. *See* Van Neck, Joshua

Hextal, Mr., of Sudbury, 129, 152; Davies visits and preaches for, 128

Hickman, Mr., of London, 78

High Flyers, 98n

Hill, Lawrence: Davies preaches for, 102

Hirons, Mr., of St. Albans, 119

Hitchin, Edward, 83; Davies visits, 68

Hoge, John: licensed by Presbytery of Newcastle, 20

Hogg, William, 104, 148

Hoit, Benjamin. *See* Hait, Benjamin

Holland: inhabitants, 154

Hollis, Timothy: Davies visits, 76

Holmes, Thomas, 153; Davies visits, 64

Holt, Jane. *See* Davies, Jane Holt

Holt, Mrs. William: Davies visits, 146

Holt family, 3n

Hopetoun, Earl of, 104n

Horton, Azariah: Davies hears preach, 19

Howe, Mr., of London, 50, 54

Hughes, Obadiah, 67

Hull, Mr., of London: Davies preaches for, 133

Hume, Elizabeth Crompton: Davies visits, 97

Hume, Hugh. *See* Marchmont, Earl of

Hume, John: and Synod of Lothian and Tweedale, 91; author of *Douglas*, 91n

167

Hunt, William, 152; Davies visits, 76, 128; Davies preaches for, 86

Hurt, Joseph, 153

Hutson, William: in England, 55

Hutton, Matthew. *See* York, Archbishop of

Hyndman, John: competes with John Edmundstone for Clerkship of General Assembly of Church of Scotland, 93

Independent Coffee House, 65

Independents: in England, xi; in London, 46, 61, 64

Ingram, Archibald, 96, 149; Davies visits, 101

Ireland: inhabitants, 154

Jackson, Richard: contributes to College of New Jersey, 80; Davies visits, 80; friendship with Benjamin Franklin and Peter Collinson, 80

James II, King of England: reign characterized, 138–139

Jardine, John: Davies visits, 95; Davies preaches for, 96

Jennings, David, 74, 152; Davies meets, 52, 64, 68; Davies visits his school, 72; sermon on Romans VIII, 7–8, 75

Johnston, John: Davies visits, 90

Johnston, Mrs., of Philadelphia: Davies visits, 22

Jones, Edward, 153; Davies meets, 55

Jones, Jenkin, 23

Jones, John: author of *Appeal to Common Reason,* 11n

Kay, George: Davies meets, 93

Keen, Robert: Davies visits, 76

Kennedy, Gilbert: Davies reads his *Great Blessing of Peace,* 34

Ker, Charles: and George Lindsay, 90n

Kerr, William. *See* Lothian, Marquis of

King, William: Davies meets, 64; Davies preaches for, 78

King's College, University of Aberdeen, 94n. *See also* Aberdeen, University of

King's Head Society, 63; and John Guyse, 48n; and Zephaniah Marryat, 66n

Kinloch, Robert: Davies hears preach, 90; Davies preaches for, 96

Kinlough, Robert. *See* Kinloch, Robert

Kinnersley, Ebenezer, 23; relations with Benjamin Franklin and College of Philadelphia, 23n

Kinnoull, Thomas Hay, ninth Earl of. *See* Duplin, Viscount

Kippie, Andrew: Davies visits, 66–67; Davies preaches for, 86

Kirkpatrick, Sarah: Davies marries, 3n

Lamb, Matthew: Davies visits, 76

Lardner, Nathaniel: author of *Credibility of the Gospel History,* 56; Davies visits, 56, 61; co-author of "Bagwell Papers," 57n; contributes to College of New Jersey, 74

Lawrence, Samuel, 115; Davies visits, 61, 63; contributes to College of New Jersey, 62

Lawson, Robert, 83, 153; Davies hears preach, 54; Davies meets, 55; contributes to College of New Jersey, 63–64

Leechman, William, 149; characterized, 101

Lesingham, Samuel: Davies visits, 76

Leven, Alexander Melville, fourth Earl of Melville and fifth Earl of, 95n, 104; Davies visits, 47, 86; serves as Lord High Commissioner to General Assembly of Church of Scotland, 47n; Davies corresponds with, 50

Liddell, Henry, First Baron Ravensworth of Ravensworth Castle of the first creation: Davies visits and secures contribution to College of New Jersey, 107

Lincoln, Mr., of Beules: solicits contributions to College of New Jersey, 124; Davies visits, 125, 126

Lindsay, George: Davies meets, 90; and Charles Ker, 90n; Davies preaches for, 103

Llewellin, Thomas: Davies meets, 58

Lloyd, Samuel: Davies visits, 44, 46; and John Wesley, 44n

Lobb, Theophilus: Davies visits, 81

Locke, John: Davies copies his Latin epitaph, 133

Logan, Charles, 91, 148; characterized, 92

Log College: founding of, 4n

London: Davies boards for England, 27

London: description of, 154

London, Bishop of. *See* Sherlock, Thomas

Lords of Trade and Plantations, 70; and Earl of Halifax, 51n; and James Oswald, 66n

Lothian, William Kerr, third Marquis of: Davies visits, 45, 47, 96; serves as Lord High Commissioner to General Assembly of Church of Scotland, 45n; Davies corresponds with, 50; and Society for Propagating Christian Knowledge in Scotland, 96; attends General Assembly, 96

Lothian and Tweedale, Synod of, 91

Louthian, Samuel, 150; characterized, 88n; Davies visits, 106, 107; Davies preaches for, 108

Lowman, Moses: co-authors "Bagwell Papers," 57n

Lumsden, John: addresses General Assembly of Church of Scotland in favor of College of New Jersey, 94, 95

McAdan, Mr.: examined by Presbytery of Newcastle, 20–21

McCulloch, Captain, of London, 43

McCulloch, William, 149; Davies visits, 102

Macky, Mr., of Philadelphia: Davies visits, 22

Maclagan, Alexander: addresses General Assembly of Church of Scotland, 94; supports College of New Jersey in General Assembly, 96; Davies visits, 97

Maclaurin, John, 67, 149; Davies meets, 94; characterized, 101; death, 128

McMullan, Mr.: deposed by General Assembly of Church of Scotland, 11

McPherson, Captain, of London, 43

Man, Mr., of Philadelphia, 24

Marchmont, Hugh Hume, third Earl of, 97n; addresses General Assembly of Church of Scotland, 93, 94

Marryat, Zephaniah, 111; Davies visits, 66; operates school for King's Head Society, 66; Davies preaches for, 132

Martin's Lombard Street Bank: and Ebenezer Blackwell, 80n

Mary II, Queen of England: reign characterized, 139

Mauduit, Israel: disputes with Gilbert Tennent, 49

Mauduit, Jasper, 78, 153; and Virginia dissenters, 49; Davies visits, 49, 63, 69, 72, 79, 84, 134

May, William: Davies meets, 53

Mayhew, Mathe: sermon on death of Charles II, 21

Melville, Alexander. *See* Leven, Earl of

Melville, Earl of. *See* Leven, Earl of

Mesnard, Captain Stephen, 37; serves as messenger for Benjamin Franklin, 37n

Methodists, 128; and James Wheatley, 124; characterized, 132–133

Mill, Mr., of London, 71

Mills, Mr., of Wakefield, 112

Milner, John: signs petition for College of New Jersey, 69; Davies visits, 85

Milner, Mr., of Yarmouth: Davies visits, 123

Milner, Thomas, 86

Minto, Baronet of. *See* Elliot, Gilbert

Mitchel, Mr., of London: Davies visits, 68; Davies preaches for, 83

Monteith, Thomas, 149; Davies visits, 105

Montesquieu, Charles Louis de Secondat, Baron de: Davies reads his *Spirit of Laws*, 40

Moon, Mr., of Plymouth: Davies visits, 136

Morgan, Thomas: Davies visits, 89

Morris, Samuel, 9

Morris Reading House, 9n

Mouhy, Chevalier de. *See* Fieux, Charles de

Muir, David: Davies visits, 68

Munzus, Michael, 107, 150; Davies visits, 106

Murison, James: addresses General Assembly of Church of Scotland, 94

Murray, James: characterized, 88

Nairn, Mr.: secedes from Church of Scotland, 11

Neate, William: Davies visits, 42

Neave, Richard: Davies meets, 42

Neck, Joshua Van. *See* Van Neck, Joshua

Newcastle, Presbytery of: condemns John Cuthbertson, 12; Davies preaches to, 20; licenses John Hoge, 20; ordains John Brown, 20; examines John Harris, 20–21; examines Mr. McAdan, 20–21

Newcastle-upon-Tyne and Newcastle-under-Lyme, Thomas Pelham-Holles, Duke of, 52, 83; and Archbishop of York, 52n; and Thomas Hay, 70n; description of his palace, 116

New England Coffee House, 53

Newman, Thomas, 64; Davies hears preach, 50; Davies meets, 51, 62

New York, Synod of: and Davies, xi; petition to General Assembly of Church of Scotland, 15–16, 95; minutes of, 60

Notcutt, William: characterized, 121

Ogilvie, George, 150; characterized, 88

Ogilvie, Mr., of Newcastle, England: Davies preaches for, 106

Ogilvy, James. *See* Findlater, Earl of

Oswald, James, 87; Gilbert Tennent meets, 55; Davies visits, 66; and Board of Trade, 66n; Davies preaches for, 77

Oswald, John: Davies meets, 51

Oswald, Thomas: Davies visits, 66
Owen, John, 63, 100, 129

Parrat, Alderman, of Hull: contributes to College of New Jersey, 111
Partridge, Richard: Gilbert Tennent meets, 51; Davies meets, 53
Patrick, John: Davies visits, 66, 81
Patronage Act: effect of Church of Scotland, 91
Paul, Thomas, 151; Davies visits, 123–124, 126
Pearsall, Richard, 153; Davies revises his *Reliquiæ Sacra,* 44
Pelham, Henry, 51; and Archbishop of York, 52n; and Thomas Hay, 70n; death, 80, 82, 84
Pelham-Holles, Thomas. *See* Newcastle, Duke of
Pemberton, Ebenezer, 58; asked to go to England for College of New Jersey, x, 2; visits Davies, 16
Penn, Richard: and Pennsylvania, 52n
Penn, Thomas: Davies probably meets, 52
Peter, Walter, 148
Peter the Great, 116
Peters, Richard: Davies visits, 13; supports George Whitefield, 13n
Petts, Mr., of Coggeshal: Davies meets, 129
Philadelphia, Synod of, xi; animosity for Gilbert Tennent, 60
Philips, Samuel, 152; Davies visits, 120; solicits funds for College of New Jersey, 131
Pike, Samuel, 152; Davies visits, 55, 63; author of *Philosophia Sacra,* 56; author of *Zeal and Charity,* 56; contributes to College of New Jersey, 74
Pitius, Mr., of London, 52

Pope, Alexander: Davies quotes his *Essay on Man,* 107
Portugal: inhabitants, 154
Presbyterian Coffee House, 72
Presbyterianism: expansion of New Light variety, ix
—in England: and Church of Scotland, xi; and evangelicalism, xi; and Unitarianism, xi; and Arminianism, 54; and Socinianism, 54; characterized, 65
—in London, 46, 48, 61; characterized, 65
—in Virginia, x
Preston, George, fourth Baronet of Valleyfield: attends General Assembly of Church of Scotland, 96
Price, Samuel, 132, 152; Davies visits, 46, 61, 63, 89; and Isaac Watts, 46n; and Samuel Morton Savage, 46n; Davies preaches for, 63; signs petition for College of New Jersey, 65
Prince, Thomas: Davies reads his *Natural and Moral Government,* 33
Prior, William, 84, 152; Davies hears preach, 58; Davies preaches for, 58; Davies visits, 58, 61, 68, 86; characterized, 61–62; contributes to College of New Jersey, 68
Privy Council, 79, 85; and Archibald Campbell, 70n
Pye, Mr., of Sheffield, 150; Davies visits, 114

Radford, Mr., of Nottingham: Davies visits, 116
Ramsay, William, 98, 148; Davies visits, 97
Randolph, Peyton: relations with Davies, 59n; presence in London, 79, 82
Ravensworth, Baron. *See* Liddell, Henry

Rawlin, Richard: Davies hears preach, 60, 69; contributes to College of New Jersey, 62, 71; Davies meets, 63

Read, Henry, 82n

Read, James, 82n

Rice, John Holt: publishes portions of Davies' diary in his *Evangelical and Literary Magazine*, xii, xiii

Richards, Aaron, 17

Richardson, John: Davies visits, 66

Roan, John: expelled from Virginia, 11

Robe, James, 100

Robertson, James, 148; Davies visits, 90; characterized, 97, 104

Robinson, William: Davies attends his school, 1n

Rodgers, John, 27, 34, 131; appointed to preach in Hanover, 18; friendship with Davies, 18; serves on committee of Synod of New York, 19; Davies visits, 21, 25; sermon by, 25; Davies writes to, 28; successes in Hanover, 108

Rodgers, Mrs. John: gives birth to daughter, 21–22; Davies visits, 22

Rogerson, Mr., of Derby: Davies visits, 115

Rogerson, Richard, 88, 150; characterized, 88n; Davies preaches for, 106; Davies visits, 106

Root, Mr., of York, 150; characterized, 112

Ross, George: Davies visits, 25

Ross, George, thirteenth Lord Ross of Hawkhead: Davies visits, 96

Ross, Robert: Davies visits, 15

Rothwell, Mr., of Chester, 24

Rowe, Mrs., of Long Melford: contributes to College of New Jersey, 129

Royal College of Physicians, 81n

Royal Society of London, 81n, 155n

Ruggles, Samuel, 130, 152; contributes to College of New Jersey, 129

St. Andrews, University of, 94; awards honorary degree to Benjamin Franklin, 95n. *See also* St. Mary's College

St. Dunstan's Coffee House, 57

St. Mary's College, St. Andrews, 94n

Salway, Mr., of Deptford: Davies visits, 85

Savage, Samuel Morton, 152, 153; Davies visits, 45, 65, 71, 72, 120; and Samuel Price, 46n; and David Jennings, 52n; original hostility to Davies' mission, 65

Savile, Mr., of Bury St. Edmund's, 151; Davies visits and preaches for, 127–128

Sayers, John, 149; Davies visits, 105

Schlatter, Michael: Davies visits in Philadelphia, 13; supports German schools in Pennsylvania, 13n; Davies visits in London, 59

Scotland, Church of. *See* Church of Scotland

Scotland: inhabitants, 154

Scott, John: solicits funds for College of New Jersey, 124; Davies visits, 126

Scott, Joseph Nicoll, 122

Scott, Thomas, 122n, 151

Scott, Thomas, Jr.: characterized, 122

Secondat, Charles Louis de, Baron Montesquieu. *See* Montesquieu

Shaw, Andrew, 96; and Benjamin Franklin, 95; and University of St. Andrews, 95; Davies meets, 95

Sheaf, Samuel, 76

86, 125; asked to undertake mission to England, x, 5, 8; and Virginia dissenters, 6; sermon by, 13, 34, 45, 50, 55, 58; relationship with Davies, 18, 28; and Antinomians in Philadelphia, 24; meets Thomas Hall, 48; meets James Oswald, 55; sermon on *Danger of an Unconverted Ministry*, 59, 60, 75, 94; writes *Irenicum Ecclesiasticum*, 60; co-author of *General Account of the . . . College*, 74; injured, 87, 93; departs for Ireland, 100; writes Davies, 111, 131; returns to London, 131; departs from London for Philadelphia, 133

Tennent, William, x; founds Log College, 4n

Thomson, David, 153

Thomson, John, 105

Thomson, Josiah, 78, 152; Davies visits, 53, 120; signs petition for College of New Jersey, 69; Davies preaches for, 83

Thomson, Mr., Jr., of London: Davies visits, 73

Todd, John, 9, 20; to preach in Hanover during Davies' absence, 6; settles in Virginia, 9n; sermon by, 16; letter to Davies, 86

Towle, Thomas, 69, 152; signs petition for College of New Jersey, 65; Davies visits, 68; contributes to College of New Jersey, 73; Davies preaches for, 86

Townshend, Meredith: Davies preaches for, 132

Trail, Robert: addresses General Assembly of Church of Scotland, 94

Trappe, Mr., of London: Davies copies epitaph composed by, 54

Treat, Richard: opens Synod of New York, 18

Tremble, Mr.: addresses General Assembly of Church of Scotland, 94

Trevor, Richard, seventy-fourth Bishop of Durham: contributes to College of New Jersey, 108; Davies visits, 108–109

Turner, John: Davies visits, 104

Ulster, Synod of: orders collection for College of New Jersey, 111

Union Theological Seminary of Virginia: Davies' manuscript diary in, xii

Universal History: Davies reads in, 139

Valleyfield, Baronet of. *See* Preston, George

Van Horn, David: visits Davies, 16

Van Neck, Joshua, first Baronet of Heveningham Hall: Davies visits, 76

Virginia: Davies quarrels with General Court in, 4n, 59

Virginia Coffee House, 44

Virginia Gazette: publishes Davies' translation of "Cleanthes's Hymn to the Creator," 23

Wadsworth, Mr., of Sheffield, 150; Davies visits, 114

Walker, Dr. Robert, 148

Walker, John: Davies visits, 66, 86

Walker, Robert, 148; Davies visits and preaches for, 96

Walker, Thomas, 99, 150; Davies visits, 112; Davies preaches for, 113

Walpole, Horace: association with Archibald Campbell and Thomas Hay, 70n

174

Warburton, Mr., of Northampton, 151; Davies meets, 119

Ward, John, 153; Davies visits, 52, 53, 60, 120; publishes *Colden's History of the Five Indian Nations,* 52n

Watson, James, 148; Davies visits, 90; Davies preaches for, 94

Watts, Isaac, 16n, 61, 63, 72, 77, 82; and Samuel Price, 46n; Davies reads his *World to Come,* 109

Waugh, James, 149; Davies visits, 79, 105

Webster, Alexander, 96, 148; Davies visits, 89; Davies preaches for, 92, 103; addresses General Assembly of Church of Scotland, 93, 94

Wells, Mr., of Nottingham: Davies visits, 115

Welsh Tract: Davies visits, 26

Wesley, Charles: and Ebenezer Blackwell, 80n; Davies meets, 132

Wesley, John: and Samuel Lloyd, 44n; and Ebenezer Blackwell, 80n; and James Hervey, 82n; and James Wheatley, 124n; Davies meets, 132

Wheatley, James: and John Wesley, 124n

Whitaker, Mr., of Leeds, 150; Davies visits, 109–110, 112; Davies preaches for, 112–113

Whitefield, George, 13n, 43n, 65, 68, 95; Davies hears preach, 47, 51; Davies visits, 55; differences with Thomas Bradbury, 62; relations with Church of England, 66; and John Erskine, 67n; and William M'Cullock, 102n

Whiting, Captain, of Virginia: Davies meets, 40

Wildboar, Mr., of Hull, 111; Davies preaches for, 110

Wilkinson, Mr., of Northampton, 119

William III, King of England: reign characterized, 139

William Augustus. *See* Cumberland, Duke of

Williams, Daniel: Davies receives his *Practical Discourses,* 56

Williams, Mr., of Nottingham: Davies meets, 116

Winter, Richard, 152; Davies preaches for, 45, 133; Davies meets, 51

Wishart, George: Davies visits, 90; Davies preaches for, 92

Witherspoon, John: his *Ecclesiastical Characteristics* compared to Swift's satire, 99

Witters, Mr., of Hull, 111; Davies visits and preaches for, 110

Wood, Samuel, 124, 151; Davies visits, 125

Woodruff, Benjamin: Davies visits, 17

Worthington, Hugh: Davies visits, 117

Wright, John, 18; assigned to preach in Hanover during Davies' absence, 6; arrives in Hanover, 8; reluctance to stay in Hanover, 8; popular criticism of his preaching style, 9; Davies writes from London, 62; preaching success in Cumberland County, Virginia, 108

Wright, Samuel, 50; co-author of "Bagwell Papers," 57n; Davies visits, 74; Davies reads his *Hardness of Heart,* 135

Yair, James, 96

York, Matthew Hutton, seventy-eighth Archbishop of: relation with Henry Pelham and Duke of Newcastle, 52n